EXPLORING
ANCIENT
NATIVE AMERICA

AN ARCHAEOLOGICAL GUIDE

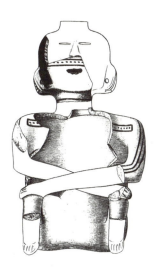

EXPLORING ANCIENT NATIVE AMERICA

△△△

AN ARCHAEOLOGICAL GUIDE

DAVID HURST THOMAS

ROUTLEDGE
New York and London

Published in 1999 by
Routledge
29 West 35th Street
New York, NY 10001

Published in Great Britain by
Routledge
11 New Fetter Lane
London, EC4P 4EE

Originally published in 1994 in hardcover by Macmillan
Copyright © 1994, 1999 by David Hurst Thomas

Printed in the United States of America on acid-free paper

10   9   8   7   6   5   4   3   2   1

Library of Congress Cataloging-in-Publication Data

Thomas, David Hurst
    Exploring ancient native America : an archaeological guide / David Hurst Thomas.
        p.   cm.
    Includes bibliographical references.
    ISBN 0-415-92359-X
    1. Indians of North America—Antiquities.   2. Indians of North America—History.
3. North America—Antiquities.   I. Title.
E77.9.T49 1999   99–14343
970.01—dc21   CIP

This book is dedicated to David Hurst Thomas III,
my son and fellow time-traveler.
He froze his nose at L'Anse aux Meadows.

ACKNOWLEDGMENTS

THIS book evolved as the natural consequence of traveling to and from dozens of archaeological field expeditions, each sponsored by the American Museum of Natural History. I am grateful to generations of Trustees and Administrative staff of this Museum for their foresight and support in overseeing one of the world's great research institutions.

Special thanks are also due to my stellar staff here at the American Museum. Niurka Tyler cheerfully took on the task of corresponding with the archaeological facilities and museums discussed here; she also helped organize the intimidating volume of research and travel background necessary to make this volume current and correct. My research assistant and accomplice, Lorann Pendleton, has visited many of these sites with me, and she deserves thanks for doggedly tracking down numerous addresses, research leads, and details. And as always, Margot Dembo, helped by seeking out difficult-to-find references, streamlining the manuscript, and creating the index with the help of Miranda Pinkert.

As a practicing field archaeologist, I am qualified to tell you about ancient Native America from a scientific perspective. But it is vitally important that you, the reader, likewise understand that American Indian people cannot, and should not, be viewed strictly in either scientific or historical terms. Fortunately for us all, Native American people are still with us, and they are today very active in telling the story of their own past.

Throughout these pages, you will find several sidebars labeled "A Native American Perspective," each designed to augment and amplify the archaeological specifics. I am particularly grateful to several Native American friends and colleagues who agreed to prepare these moving first-hand accounts: Mr. Edward Castillo (Chair, Native American Studies, Sonoma State University), Mr. Roger Echo-Hawk (Graduate student, University of Colorado), Ms. Suzan Shown Harjo (Director, Morningstar Foundation), and Mr. William Tallbull (Elder and Historian, Northern Cheyenne Tribe).

Recognizing the importance of cooperation between the archaeological and Native American communities, partial royalties from this book are being donated to the Native American Scholarship Fund of the Society for American Archaeology. It is imperative that we have more practicing archaeologists who also happen to be American Indians.

This presentation has benefitted greatly from the abundant photographic, archival, and artifactual holdings of the American Museum of Natural History. I have, for instance, used numerous historical photographs to illustrate this manuscript, including several shots taken during nineteenth-century reconnaissance trips to the American Southwest and numerous photographs prepared during the joint Colorado Museum of Natural History–American Museum of Natural History excavations in 1927 at the Folsom site. Several of the site and rock art photographs were taken by archaeologist Nels Nelson during his 1912 traverse of the American Southwest; these early photographs document the condition of these sites before extensive stabilization took place. We have used field excavation photographs taken by Earl Morris during his work in the 1920s at the Aztec ruin and my photographs documenting our own excavations at Hidden Cave, Nevada. I am grateful to the American Museum for permission to reproduce these images and thank the gang in the Special Collections division of the Library— particularly Carmen Collazo, Barbara Mathe, and Joel Sweimler—for their help in rounding up many of the images that appear here, some of which are published for the first time. I also thank Peter Goldberg for preparing numerous black-and-white prints on short notice.

I have also drawn upon dozens of scientific illustrations, prepared over the past century by a host of talented artists in the employ of the American Museum of Natural History: Ms. Ruth B. Howe (who illustrated the Blackfeet artifacts), Mr. Charles R. Knight (for his justly famous historical reconstructions, originally prepared to grace the paleontology halls of the American Museum), Marilyn Weber (who drew the artifacts from Poverty Point), and Nicholas Amorosi, a superb artist with whom I was privileged to work. I also thank the now-unknown artists who left us marvelous illustrations of artifacts from Pueblo Bonito and Aztec Ruin; although your names have disappeared over the ages, we still appreciate the skill and accuracy with which these scientific illustrations were prepared. Finally, I have also drawn upon one-of-a-kind field sketches prepared by ethnologists Herbert Spinden, Clark Wissler, and Gilbert Wilson during their important early twentieth-century fieldwork on the Northern Plains. I thank Belinda

Kaye, Archivist of the Department of Anthropology at the American Museum for making these priceless historical materials available to me.

These historical images have been augmented by numerous illustrations prepared specifically for this book. I thank Ms. Diana M. Salles for her many line drawings of archaeological artifacts and Mr. Dennis O'Brien who prepared most of the maps and other graphics that appear here. I also am grateful to Mr. Anibal Rodriguez, who helped select many of the artifacts for illustration; he also prepared some of the black-and-white photographs that appear here.

Several archaeological colleagues helped out by taking us on guided tours of their sites, suggesting additional sites suitable for visitation, providing background information, maps, photographs, and, in some cases, providing unpublished summaries of their own research.

I am particularly grateful to Dr. Bradley T. Lepper (Curator, Newark Earthworks State Memorials), who supplied original research materials and read part of the rough manuscript. Dr. Robson Bonnichson (Director, Center for the Study of the First Americans, Oregon State University) was particularly generous with his time, providing numerous clues on visitable Paleoindian sites.

I also thank Lynn Anderson (Washington State Historical Society), Merrilee Atos (Public Relations and Marketing, Glenbow Museum); Jon H. Bailey (Head of Visitor Services, Maine State Museum); Jim Barnett (Director, Mississippi Division of Historic Properties); Mark Baumler (Montana Historical Society); Larry N. Beane (Park Ranger, Russell Cave National Monument); Trilby Bittle (Head, Marketing and Public Information, Royal Ontario Museum); Bruce Borque (Maine State Museum); Peter Bostrum (Lithic Casting Laboratory), Dr. Bruce Bradley (Crow Canyon Archaeological Center); M. Diane Brenner (Museum Archivist, Anchorage Museum of History and Art); Jack Brink (Head, Archaeological Survey, Alberta Provincial Museum); Daniel W. Brown (Superintendent, Natchez Trace Parkway); Robert Burgoon (Chief, Information and Resource Management, Hopewell Culture National Historical Park); Chas. Cartwright (Superintendent, Hovenweep National Monument); Dr. Jefferson Chapman (Director, Frank H. McClung Museum); Rebecca Chavez-Houck (Utah Museum of Natural History); Ray L. Claycomb (Assistant Chief, Interpretation and Visitor Services, Natchez Trade Parkway); Susan J. Colclazer (Bryce Canyon National Park); Jack Cooper (Communications Director, The High Desert Museum); Sue Cowdery (Indian Center Museum); Louise Cross (Curator, Frontier Gateway Museum); Gary T. Cummins (Superintendent, Petrified Forest National Park);

LeDonna Curto (Old Mission San Antonio de Padua); Diane L. Davies (Extension Specialist, Rock Eagle 4-H Center); Jill DeChello (Oldest Store Museum, St. Augustine); Anna M. Dooley (Public Information Coordinator, Museum of Science and History of Jacksonville); Julie Droke (Collections Manager, Oklahoma Museum of Natural History); James S. Dunbar (Bureau of Archaeological Research, Florida Department of State); Paula Hale Eliot (Director of Public Relations, Gilcrease Museum); Sally Erickson (Public Services Director, The Burke Museum); Elizabeth Evans (Director of Public Relations, Roanoke Island Historical Society).

Paul Fisher (Marketing and Public Relations, Plimoth Plantation); Deah Folk (Executive Director, Aztec Museum Pioneer Village and Oil Field Museum); Andrea French (Indian Village Curator, Lower Thames Valley Conservation Authority); Dr. George Frison (Department of Anthropology, University of Wyoming); Annette B. Fromm (Project Director, Creek Council House Museum); Peggie L. Gaul (Activities Coordinator, Colonial National Historical Park); Patricia Gladstone (Assistant to the Director, Hartwick College Museums); Dr. Lynn Goldstein (Department of Anthropology, University of Wisconsin), Jim Gormally (Information Assistant, Sandia Ranger District Station); Richard Gould (Curator, Pawnee Indian Village Museum); Dr. Russell Graham (Curator, Illinois State Museum); Michael Gramly (Great Lakes Repository); Dr. Donald K. Grayson (Burke Museum of Anthropology); Gail D. Gregory (Director of Institutional Advancement, Virginia Museum of Natural History); Dawn M. Hagen (Research Assistant, Pipestone County Historical Society); Brian Hatoff (Woodward-Clyde Associates); Elizabeth Haanstad (Membership Coordinator, Utah Museum of Natural History); Dr. Margaret Hanna (Curator of Anthropology, Saskatchewan Museum of Natural History); Emma Hansen (Curator, Buffalo Bill Historical Center); Dr. Donald P. Heldman (Director of Archaeology, Mackinac State Historic Parks); Louise Heric (Administrative Officer; The Friends of Head-Smashed-In Buffalo Jump Society); Inez R. Herrig (The Heritage Museum); Elizabeth Holmes (Associate Registrar, Buffalo Bill Historical Center); David E. Hostler (Curator, Hoopa Tribal Museum); Jerry Howland (Alaska State Museum); James H. Hudnall (Goliad State Park Superintendent); Ken Howell (President, The Smoki Museum); James Hunter (Director/Curator, Huronia Museum); A. B. Isaac (Assistant Director, Peabody Museum of Archaeology and Ethnology, Harvard University); William R. Iseminger (Public Relations, Cahokia Mounds State Historic Site); Dr. Christiana B. Johannsen (Director, The Iroquois Indian Museum).

Dianne Keller (Montana Historical Society); Dr. Henry C. Koerper (Cyprus College); Curtis D. Kraft (Supervising Ranger, Chaw'se Regional Indian Museum); Mary Kwas (Curator of Education, Memphis State University/Chucalissa Museum); Nicky Ladkin (Collections Manager, Lubbock Lake Landmark); Mal Law (Pocono Indian Museum); Dr. Kent Lightfoot (Department of Anthropology, University of California, Berkeley); Dr. Robert C. Mainford, Jr. (Regional Archaeologist, Pinson Mounds State Archaeological Area); Elizabeth West Manning (Curator of Education, Museum of the Great Plains); Brenda Martin (University of Colorado Museum); Linda Martin (Mesa Verde National Park); Dr. Terrance J. Martin (Associate Curator of Anthropology, Illinois State Museum); Duane Mattox (Public Relations Intern, Utah Museum of Natural History); Jeanne McCasland (Office Coordinator, Idaho Museum of Natural History); Douglas C. McChristian (Acting Superintendent, Little Bighorn Battlefield National Monument); Dr. Bonnie G. McEwan (Director of Archaeology, San Luis Archaeological and Historical Site); Nicholas Megalousis (Archaeologist, Mission San Juan Capistrano); Gail Lynn Meyer (Museum Assistant, Indian Temple Mound Museum); Pam Miller (Curator of Archaeology, Prehistoric Museum, College of Eastern Utah); Dr. Joyce L. Morden (Executive Director, Makah Cultural and Research Center); Paul E. Mueller (Administrator, Washington County Land Use and Park Department); Joe Muller (Business Manager, The Mammoth Site of Hot Springs, South Dakota, Inc.); Thomas A. Munson (Superintendent, Effigy Mounds National Monument); Erin Offill (Marketing Director, Fort Worth Museum of Science and History); Kathryne Olson (Curator, Lost City Museum).

E. Breck Parkman (Associate Archaeologist, California Department of Parks and Recreation); The Honorable Reginald T. Pasqual (Governor, Pueblo of Acoma); Donna Pearson (Interpreter, Toltec Mounds Archaeological State Park); Dennis Peterson (Manager, Spiro Mounds Archaeological Park); Becky Phillips (Public Programming, University of Colorado Museum); Joseph R. Phillips (Director, Maine State Museum); Pamela Phillips (Public Relations Specialist, Cranbrook Institute of Science); Brian Preston (Curator, Nova Scotia Museum Complex); Jane Pieplow (Director/Curator, Churchill County Museum and Archive); Heather Pratt (Events Coordinator, University of British Columbia, Museum of Anthropology); Nicole Price (Coordinator, Medicine Wheel Alliance); Todd Prince (Museum Curator, Anasazi State Park); Ruth Rabalais (Manager, Carter's Grove and Bassett Hall, Colonial Williamsburg Foundation); Alan Ray (New York State

Museum); Dr. Charles A. Reher (Department of Anthropology, University of Wyoming); Beth Rhodes (Public Relations Coordinator, Southwest Museum); Barbara Rigutto (Museum Manager, London Museum of Archaeology); Robert Rocco (Assistant Director, Mission Santa Clara); Nicholas Robbins (Park Manager, Yulee Sugar Mill State Historic Site); Richard A. Rojas (Parks Superintendant, La Purísima Mission); Ellen Santasiero (Communications Assistant, The High Desert Museum); Amy Schnurr (Education Co-Coordinator, Crawford Lake Conservation Area); George D. Schrimper (Director, The University of Iowa Museum of Natural History); William T. Schultz (Superintendent of Properties, Ohio Historical Society); Bill Scudder (Park Manager, Old Mission State Park); Joanne L. Serwinski (Public Relations, Field Museum of Natural History); Dave Schwab (Montana State Office of Historic Preservation); Zora Simon (Communications Director, Manitoba Museum of Man and Nature); Nancy Smith (Tourist Assistant, Missouri Department of Natural Resources); Jeffrey Stark (Site Guide, Calico Early Man Site); Peter Stork; Jane Tague (Program Assistant, Oklahoma Museum of Natural History); Sharon Edaburn Taylor (Curator, Churchill County Museum and Archive); Amy Tekansik (Assistant Manager of Public Relations, Denver Museum of Natural History); Dr. Raymond H. Thompson (Director, Arizona State Museum); Caryn Talbot Throop (Curator, The High Desert Museum).

Debbie Ungar (Putnam Museum of History and Natural Science); Jay von Werlhof (Imperial Valley College Museum); Kim W. Watson (Chief Ranger, Flagstaff Area, National Park Service); Sarah Way (Assistant to the Director, Logan Museum of Anthropology); Dr. S. David Webb (Florida Museum of Natural History); Kit W. Wesler (Director, Wickliffe Mounds Research Center); Don Wollenhaupt (Chief of Interpretation and Cultural Resource Management, Effigy Mounds National Monument); Ken Woody (Park Ranger, Knife River Indian Villages); Ronald J. Wyatt (Curator of Anthropology, Garvies Point Museum).

I also thank Deirdre Mullane at Prentice Hall, for instigating this project and painstakingly shepherding it to completion.

—DAVID HURST THOMAS
American Museum of Natural History

CONTENTS

FOREWORD

After five centuries of contact and interrelated history, it can honestly be said that to most non-Indian Americans, Indians are familiar strangers—the first Americans, indeed, but ironically the least known of all members of the American population. Eurocentrism did its job: behind the legends and beyond the myths, few non-Indians yet know the reality.

—ALVIN M. JOSEPHY, JR.
*THE NATIVE AMERICANS:
AN ILLUSTRATED HISTORY*

All too often, early American history is misperceived as little more than a procession of compelling individuals at strategic places during pivotal times: from Christopher Columbus's splashy entrance at San Salvador in 1492 to Jacques Cartier's 1534 penetration of the St. Lawrence River. From Francisco Vásquez de Coronado's futile quest for riches at Quivira in 1540 to the transcontinental trek of Meriwether Lewis and William Clark in 1804–1806, this is how we have been conditioned to think of our own history—the key person, the fateful place, and the turning point in time.

According to Harvard historian, Frederick Jackson Turner, "the fateful place" was the American frontier, where the most distinctive features of American civilization and character were forged. Circumstances peculiar to the frontier—free land, opportunity, and common danger from Indians—molded Americans in specific ways, Turner argued a century ago. They were required to cast off their European legacy and in its place, develop a new set of home-grown, independent beliefs: creativity, curiosity, restlessness, optimism, and individualism. Generations of young New Englanders were able to head out, using the frontier as an "escape valve" for overpopulation and cultural complacency. Escaping to the frontier, Turner suggested, was the means for Americans to break away from their suffocating Puritan roots.

In effect, Turner encouraged white America to rethink its history from the inside out—not as a pale reflection of European events, but as something uniquely American. Good enough.

But in suggesting the frontier comprised the line between "savagery and civilization," Frederick Jackson Turner created a selective history that almost universally ignored America's racial and ethnic minorities. American Indians in particular were written off as irrelevant to mainstream American history.

This tradition unfortunately endures even today. A survey of recent textbooks of American history demonstrates that inaccurate and unjust views of the Indian persist, on a somewhat reduced scale, in even the latest American history textbooks. Textbook Indians are commonly dismissed as either an unprincipled hindrance to Anglo settlement or pathetic chumps and pushovers. When it comes to Indians, the modern American history textbook almost uniformly sets out carping pronouncements about their lack of private property, the illogical nature of Native American governments, and especially the rudimentary or immoral condition of their religion. Today's textbooks are still littered with quaint pejoratives like "war-whooping," "feathered foes," "painted allies," and "tawny-skinned pagan aborigines."

Echoing Hollywood's stereotypes, today's textbook historian misreads Native American culture through a curious blend of racism, sexual imagery, and Victorian sentimentality. Texts still wax poetic about that "vast and lonely North American continent," a "virgin" land that "like all virgins, inspired conflicting feelings in men's hearts." One historian writes that this "vast and virgin continent . . . was so sparsely peopled by Indians that they could be eliminated or shouldered aside. Such a magnificent opportunity for a great democratic experiment may never come again." Against this background, it is hardly a surprise that American Indians have been recently characterized as a "people without history."

Implicit in this Eurocentric conceit is the notion that Americans of European descent brought with them a heritage more progressive and of a higher order than that of Indian people. In matters of background, ethics, faith, lifeways, expertise, and accomplishments, the Euro-American defined a higher plane. It followed that the uncivilized culture of the Indian was irrelevant to mainstream American history.

The truth is rather different. By the time Columbus landed in the "New" World, this was already an ancient world, the scene of countless cultural rises and falls. Five hundred years ago, the Americas were already home to 75 million people. They spoke 2,000 languages. There were incalculable numbers of rich and distinct Native American cultures. Thankfully, many remain with us today.

The handful of Europeans who landed in 1492 brought with them a Judeo-Christian ethical and religious patrimony directly traceable to the classic and well-known civilizations of Dynastic Egypt, Classical Greece, and Rome. But this legacy was unknown and irrelevant to the Indian people who discovered Columbus. Native Americans were totally immersed in their own networks of equally prolonged entitlements, wholly unfamiliar to the European newcomers. We need not burden the fifteenth-century *conquistador* with our own postmodern sense of culpability and penitence. But let us likewise avoid the antiquated brand of cultural and racial narcissism still fostered in the too-common Eurocentric view of American history.

In these pages, I wish to provide something of the flavor of America's abundant and ancient Indian heritage. While this small book will hardly provide a comprehensive history of Native American people, it will sketch both the diversity and the texture of American Indian lifeways. We will see for ourselves what life has been like in America for a thousand generations. The story is told in terms of real places—archaeological sites and museums that can be visited by all. This is an eclectic, personalized journey covering 9 million square miles and 25,000 years. But before we cast off, I'd like you to know who I am and where I want to take you.

The first part is easy. I am a professional archaeologist specializing in Native American studies. For a quarter century, I've directed dozens of archaeological digs, mostly in the western deserts and the Deep South. One year, our archaeological tent city was the third largest "town" in Esmeralda County, Nevada.

Since 1972, I've been employed as a curator at the American Museum of Natural History, located on the west side of New York's Central Park. The American Museum is the largest natural history museum in the world, housing more than 36 million artifacts and scientific specimens. No institution anywhere has more dinosaurs, birds, spiders, fossil mammals, or whale skeletons. Nearly 3 million people visit the forty massive exhibition halls to see things like dinosaur eggs, meteorites, an eight-foot slide made of jade, the breathtaking Star of India.

I curate the North American archaeological collection, more than a million artifacts. When first hired, I was nearly overwhelmed by this vast and important collection. To be an effective museum curator, I would need to learn much beyond my immediate, hands-on archae-ological experience. While working with this monumental collection, I've read thousands of books and professional articles on American archaeology (I've also written a hundred or so of my own). But you can only learn so much from books and scientific journals. To do this collection justice, I needed to get out on the landscape, to see and sense for myself what American archaeology was all about.

As things turned out, it was easy for me to see America. With an office and labs in New York City and ongoing field projects in the western American desert and the Deep South, I found myself living and working on three corners of the North American continent. This posed some logistic problems. Although we were excavating artifacts in Nevada and Georgia, our archaeological lab was in New York City. But because we were reluctant to ship such scientifically important artifacts and field notes, we ended up driving to and from each field expedition: from New York City to Austin (Nevada) in June, then back to New York in August; from New York to St. Catherines Island (Georgia) in October, returning to New York three weeks later. During my first fifteen years at the American Museum, I was "on the road" an average of seven months a year. We've now logged a shade more than 250,000 cross-country miles, hauling archaeological artifacts and scientific equipment to and from our various digs.

In one sense, we were emulating some of the prehistoric foraging people that I study, following a seasonal, seminomadic, semisedentary lifestyle. But unlike ancient Native Americans, I didn't use a travois and burden basket. I got around mostly in a 4 by 4 Ford pickup. Once, it was as simple as packing up my long-suffering dog, Sasha, and heading out. The pilgrimages continue, but today, they are more family ori-ented. My wife, Lori—also an archaeologist here at the American Museum of Natural History—and I are usually accompanied by our son who, by the age of six, had logged five cross-country trips, visiting forty-four states and seven Canadian provinces.

There is no better way of breaking up such long-haul trucking than by stopping to visit exhibits of local history and archaeology. Over the years, I've visited hundreds of roadside displays: museums, on-site exhibits, active mission churches, rock art localities, and assorted "points of historical interest."

In these pages, I want to share with you a bit of what we have seen— the real, hands-on archaeology and history of native North America. America's diverse history is out there for all to see, but you must be willing to look beyond the Monticellos and the Valley Forges to find it. The true American past is also found in places like Mesa Verde National Park, Medicine Wheel National Historical Monument, and Moundville Archaeological Park. But be forewarned: this is not an encyclopedic listing of archaeological sites and museums. Rather, it is a personally guided tour through the first thousand generations of American history.

PRESERVING AMERICA'S ANCIENT PAST

So here's the deal: I agree to guide you through ancient native America. I promise to tell this story strictly in terms of places and artifacts you can see for yourself. The book will only direct you to sites and museums that are available to the traveling public, places that encourage visitation, provide interpretation, and can ensure adequate protection for both the visitor and for the surviving archaeological record. The idea here is both to protect the sites from the public, and the public from the sites. In return, I must ask a favor of you, the reader and traveler. America is, in effect, an immense outdoor museum that chronicles the history of humanity on the continent. But this historical legacy is disappearing at a record clip. Sometimes these losses cannot be avoided, as pieces of the past erode, decay, or wash away.

But far more menacing than these natural agencies is the wanton destruction of the past by thoughtless scavengers and casual collectors. The worst offenders are the so-called pothunters, people who illegally mine archaeological sites for ancient artifacts, which are then sold to the highest bidder. Others simply pick up ancient artifacts from public areas, not realizing the importance of even isolated artifacts to our understanding of America's past. Native American sacred sites are being desecrated at a frightening rate. As we build more roads and bridges, clear more forest land, and take recreational vehicles into desert areas, the ultrafragile archaeological past is being disturbed. Thoughtless looting and inadvertent destruction of America's past is a profound and growing problem.

Throughout these pages, you will hear several horror stories of the inconsiderate and the greedy who have ruined parts of the past that belong to us all. My hope here is to show the larger picture of America's ancient past, and to ask for your help and cooperation in protecting that past for others to enjoy as well. The Bureau of Land Management, one of America's leading protectors of public lands, has a fitting slogan: *The past belongs to the future, but only the present can preserve it.*

As we tour America's remote past, I ask your help in preserving that past for others to follow.

THE GLOBAL PROLOGUE

NATIVE American roots run deep. The very first human, whenever and wherever, carried the American Indian spirit deep inside. To understand the Native American, we must first appreciate how we all came to be.

At a point remote in time, when the Pacific Ocean washed half the globe, the continents were still fused, and dry land was at a premium. Today, this primordial superglob is called Pangaea.

More than 200 million years ago, Pangaea fractured in two, the Laurasian landmass gliding northward, Gondwanaland heading to the south. As more time passed, new oceans splashed between these still-splitting terrestrial fragments—the earth's *plates*—dislocating at constant, yet unrelenting, rates. They still do this today. Sometimes they collide with one another. Sometimes they spread apart. But they keep moving.

Even then, some plates looked like parts of today's continents. Those defining America's western rim, for instance, look basically like today's Pacific shoreline. Elsewhere—from the Alps through the Himalayas, in the Rockies, and throughout America's basin and range province—the plate boundaries created mountain chains that straddle continents.

So it went for millions of years. Life on the separating continental masses diverged and differentiated. Each land raft was evolving its own crew. Dinosaurs roamed freely across the planet's shifting surface until one day, 65 million years ago, they were gone.

Things were changing.

1

GENESIS

The Southern Ape (*Australopithecus*) emerged on the African plain 4 million years ago, unnoticed. Today's best-known fossil remains of Australopithecus come from northern Ethiopia. Named Lucy by her Beatle-loving excavators, she stood nearly four feet tall, walked fully upright, and looked a lot like us—remarkably human.

Through the interplay of extinction and survival, adaptation and evolution, Lucy's descendents would develop into an implement-using, large-brained hominid we now call *Homo habilis* ("handy man"— literally a tool-maker). Handy perhaps, but they still weren't human.

It wasn't until 1.5 million years ago that the first incontestably human form appeared. These so-called *Homo erectus* populations grew throughout the middle Pleistocene (the middle Ice Age) until Africa could no longer contain them. Two million years ago, give or take some, *Homo erectus* took off northward, slowly crossing the connecting lands of the Middle East, then fanning out across Europe and across

Modern humans evolved over a very long time, perhaps 200,000 years ago. These modern human beings may not have migrated out of Africa until much later, until maybe 100,000 years ago. But once expansion began, modern humans populated the globe at a fairly rapid clip, as this map indicates. The occupation of the Americas and the remote islands of the Pacific were among the latest of these major population movements.

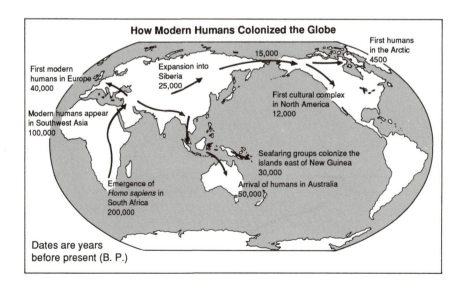

How Modern Humans Colonized the Globe

First humans in the Arctic
4500

First modern humans in Europe
40,000

Expansion into Siberia
25,000

15,000

First cultural complex in North America
12,000

Modern humans appear in Southwest Asia
100,000

Seafaring groups colonize the islands east of New Guinea
30,000

Emergence of *Homo sapiens* in South Africa
200,000

Arrival of humans in Australia
50,000

Dates are years before present (B. P.)

Asia. Flaunting their unrivaled adaptability, people scuttled out—into the tropical rain forests, across the temperate regions, up to the near-arctic. For the first time, humanity asserted itself.

These *Homo erectus* populations remained fairly stable until perhaps 150,000 to 200,000 years ago, when a more evolved human form appeared. The short but tough Neanderthals (*Homo sapiens neanderthalensis*) stood a little over five feet tall, sporting massive brow ridges, burly muscles, and squat bodies.

But they were not like today's cartoon cavemen. Real Neanderthals walked upright and, suitably trained, could compete at tennis or golf. They might even win, but they wouldn't blend in at Wimbledon or the Masters. We stand taller, our foreheads are higher, and our brow ridges are smaller. Although our forearms are longer, our muscles are less well developed.

What happened next is uncertain. Maybe the Neanderthals melded directly into modern humans. Or maybe modern humans evolved only in Africa, where the tropical savannah environment provided an ample food supply. Either way, before too long, the migrating branches of humanity found themselves at opposite ends of the earth.

Recent genetic research suggests a controversial "out of Africa" theory by tracing all living human beings to a single first mother (Eve), who lived about 200,000 years ago in South Africa. Whatever the exact time scale, this Eve theory is supported by some archaeological evidence suggesting that modern humans did not spread out from Africa until rather late in time.

But when they did, our forebears rocked the world. They fit in. They could adapt. They settled new environments. But did they do it deliberately? I doubt it.

The massive Ice Age journeys were probably not planned, deliberate migrations. More likely, our Pleistocene ancestors extended their hunting territories only a few miles each generation. But even as small and scattered clusters, they would still populate the entire globe in tens of thousands of years.

Eventually, these travelers became completely modern people (*Homo sapiens sapiens*). Often called Cro-Magnon—after an important archaeological site in France—they first appeared in Europe roughly 40,000 years ago. They flourished, creating marvelous new devices of stone, bone, and antler—more effective, more artistic than anything the world had ever seen.

Little by little, their skin lightened up, probably to absorb more vitamin D from the limited sunlight in these northerly European

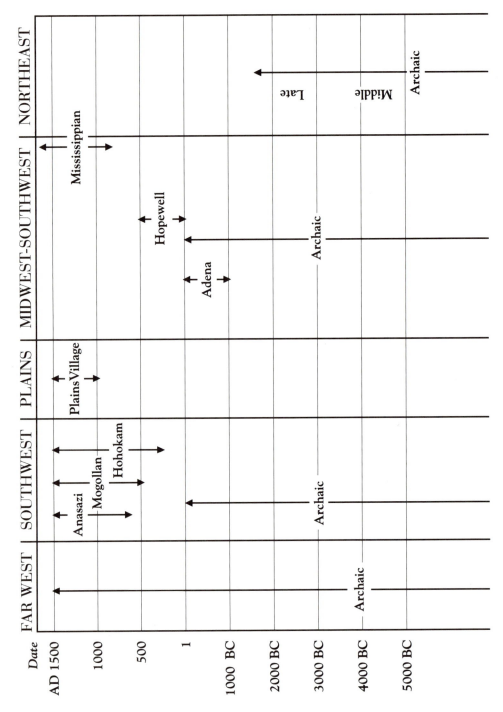

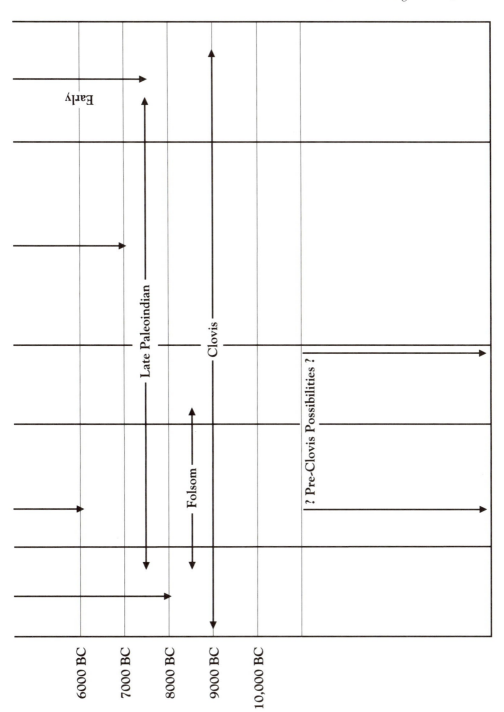

6000 BC

7000 BC

8000 BC

9000 BC

10,000 BC

Early

Late Paleoindian

Clovis

Folsom

? Pre-Clovis Possibilities ?

latitudes. These *Homo sapiens* became the ancestors of the Vikings, the Spanish and Portuguese explorers, and the millions of other Europeans who eventually cruised westward, to explore America.

Much before them, equally intelligent and resourceful people set out eastward across Eurasia. Remarkably, some navigated their way to Australia 50,000 years ago. Sure, their environment helped. The sea levels were considerably lower than today, hooking up many modern islands (including Australia and New Guinea). But still, vast stretches

---

▲▲▲
WHERE WE CAME FROM:
SOME NATIVE AMERICAN PERSPECTIVES

We archaeologists weave a compelling story about how humanity evolved in Africa, nearly 5 million years ago. Then, slowly, our human ancestors spread to the farthest corners of the planet. In the global, scientific sense, this is where and how American Indians came to be.

History may well show that science is correct about the origins and distribution of humankind. But science has yet to find the remains of our first human mother (Eve), or the frozen superhighway that delivered the first Americans across the Bering Straits from Asia. As that Standing Rock Sioux philosopher, Vine Deloria, has cogently pointed out "excavating ancient fireplaces and campsites may be exciting, but there are no well-worn paths which clearly show migratory patterns from Asia to North America, and if there were such paths, there would be no indication anywhere which way the footprints were heading."

Some American Indians believe in the Bering Straits theory; many others do not. Here is a smattering of Native American creation stories:

A Diegueno Case History (California): In the beginning, when Tu-chai-pai, the Maker, made the world, the Earth was the woman and the sky was the man, and the world was a pure lake covered with tules. Sky came down upon the Earth. The Maker and his brother, Yo-ko-mat-is, blew and the heavens rose higher and higher above their heads until it formed a concave arch. The Maker made hills, valleys, little hollows of water, forests, and dug in the ground for mud to make the first people the Indians.

▲▲▲

of open sea separated Australia/New Guinea from the Southeast Asian mainland. The first Australians set out on their incredible voyage in homemade craft, piloting their way across open, uncharted water—far beyond the comforting sight of land. And some made it. Their descendents are still there.

Far to the north, other mammoth-hunting pioneers pressed on across the Siberian tundra. Their specialized tools of bone and antler equipped them to survive in the most elemental way. Our high latitude

———————————————— △△△ ————————————————

A Pawnee Case History (Oklahoma and Nebraska): In the beginning, the Power needed help, so stars, sun, moon, clouds, winds, lightning, and thunder were created. The Power told the Evening Star to order her priests to sing and shake their rattles. A great storm came up and rolled across the formless world and passed the Power, who dropped a pebble into the clouds. After the storm, the world was water. The Power sent out Black, Yellow, White, and Red stars each carrying a cedar war club. Each struck the water with the club and the waters parted and Earth appeared. Again, Power told the Evening Star to order her priests to rattle and sing. Again a storm ensued. The thunders shook Earth, and hills and valleys, mountains and plains were formed. Then Power created life on Earth.

A Tohono O'odham Case History (Arizona): In the beginning, Earthmaker made the whole Earth out of a little ball of dirt. He danced on the ball and pushed it until it expanded. There was a great noise and I'itoi jumped out of the Earth to help Earthmaker give the world its shape. Coyote, who was with Earthmaker from the beginning, followed Earthmaker and I'itoi everywhere while they made and shaped people of the Earth.

In the next chapter, Roger Echo Hawk (Pawnee) offers his own case history, pointing up some of the commonalities between archaeological and Native American creation stories, suggesting that perhaps the chasm separating science and theology may be narrower than most think.

———————————————— △△△ ————————————————

ancestors used everything at their disposal to survive—even discarded mammoth bones, which were burnt as fuel and propped up to support the roofs of their impressive pit houses.

Not everybody left Africa, of course. Those who remained on the steppes hunted elephants, buffaloes, rhinoceroses, and antelopes. Twenty thousand years ago, these African people introduced the bow and arrow to the world. Through time, their skin would slowly darken as a genetic sunscreen against potentially lethal doses of ultraviolet radiation. Some of those remaining in Africa would, beginning in the sixteenth century, reluctantly immigrate to America in chains.

The earth matured. People and continents drifted apart. Only in the Americas would these diverse strains of humanity reunite. The European colonist and the African hostage would eventually arrive in the same ships. They would be greeted by other descendents of Eve. But the indigenous, Native Americans had taken a very different journey to their New World homeland.

This is the story of how American Indians got there. And the remarkable things they did once they arrived.

THE FIRST AMERICANS

A CENTURY ago, the American archaeological scene was dominated by a single key question: *When did Indians first arrive in America?*

During the nineteenth century, certain well-publicized finds suggested that Ice Age people may have arrived in America sometime during the Pleistocene, a geological epoch that began 2 million years ago, during which giant mammals moved across a landscape characterized by massive ice sheets. But the evidence for Pleistocene people in America was not entirely convincing, and two distinct schools of thought emerged. One group accepted the evidence at face value, arguing boisterously that Ice Age Americans must have hunted the giant game animals that once lived here. With few exceptions, the "early man" advocates were amateur relic hunters or fossil collectors—impassioned and committed, but poorly versed in the scientific methods and theories of the day.

These crusaders for the Ice Age were countered at every turn by the big guns of American archaeology, establishment men brandishing advanced degrees, mostly curators and professors at places like the Smithsonian Institution, the Universities of Chicago and California, and, yes, the American Museum of Natural History in New York. These learneds contended that American Indians were relative newcomers in America—probably arriving no earlier than the Moundbuilders, Pueblo Indians, and the Classic Maya—all of whom left easy-to-recognize archaeological traces dating from the last couple thousands of years.

These battle lines were firmly drawn in the early twentieth century. It was obvious to all that—if the truth were to be known—better sites must be found: the bones of late Pleistocene animals had to be scientifically investigated by trained observers. If any solid evidence could be found—that is, undisturbed associations of artifacts with extinct animal bones, still in place in sediments of the Pleistocene age—these associations must be presented to a range of scientific witnesses for verification.

EVIDENCE AT FOLSOM

This is exactly what happened at Wild Horse Gulch, about eight miles west of Folsom, New Mexico. In 1926, paleontologists from the Colorado Museum of Natural History in Denver were excavating ancient

---

△△△

WHO ARE THE PALEOINDIANS

The Paleoindians are the oldest-known cultural tradition in native North America. Paleoindians lived here between about 11,000 B.C. and 6,000 B.C., and their archeological remains have been found from the Pacific to Atlantic shores, from Alaska to the southern margin of south America.

Archeologists recognize three major cultures within the overall Paleoindian tradition:

Clovis culture	9500–8500 B.C.
Folsom culture	9000–8200 B.C.
Late Paleoindian (or Plano) culture	8000–6000 B.C.

Paleoindians survived, at least in part, by hunting large, now extinct mammals: the Columbian mammoth (during Clovis times only), extinct forms of bison, American horse, and camel. They probably also ate a wide variety of other foods, but evidence for broader diets is difficult to find. As archeologist Donald Grayson has put it, if Paleoindians "spent most of their time hunting mice and gathering mice, we probably would not know it."

Although the Paleoindian tradition ceased about 6,000 years ago, the Paleoindian people are without question the biological ancestors of many modern Native Americans.

△△△

---

bison bones buried beneath a layer of clay and gravel several feet thick. Because this kind of bison was known to have been extinct for thousands of years, these paleontologists were shocked to find two pieces of chipped flint, clearly artifacts of human manufacture, lying loose in their spoil dirt. Once alerted, they soon found another artifact, this one still in its original position, imbedded in the clay surrounding a bison rib. They carefully removed the entire block of matrix, containing both bone and flint.

Excited by the evidence of human artifacts associated with extinct Pleistocene animals, J. D. Figgins, the museum's director, couldn't wait

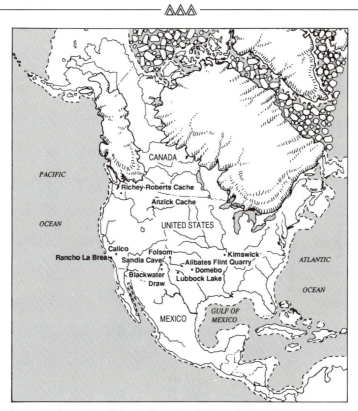

Some of the major Paleoindian sites in North America that can be visited or for which artifact collections can be viewed in a museum. The dotted line represents the Pleistocene shoreline during the peak of Ice Age glaciation. Note that during this period Alaska was directly connected via dry land to northeastern Asia.

to share his news with colleagues: people had been in the New World far longer than responsible scientists believed possible. But Figgins was soon confronted by a solid wall of doubt and disbelief. Most of his colleagues dismissed his evidence. Maybe the strata were jumbled in the geological past. Maybe the excavators inadvertently mixed ancient strata themselves. Maybe the flaked stones dated from much later than the bones, having fallen into the excavation, undetected, from above. Maybe, maybe, maybe.

Still believing in his Folsom finds, Figgins vowed to find better evidence the following year. The 1927 expedition to Folsom was jointly sponsored by the Colorado Museum of Natural History and the American Museum of Natural History. Before long, the excavators came across additional ancient artifacts—wonderfully crafted spear points still embedded against the ribs of extinct bison. Having learned from

The original excavations at the "Folsom Bison Quarry" (as it was then called in 1927). Mr. Carl Schwachheim (left) is pointing to the fifth spear point found in position between two bison ribs; on the right is paleontologist Barnum Brown. (Courtesy of the American Museum of Natural History.)

previous disappointments, Figgins and the others left everything in the ground, exactly as found.

Telegrams went out, announcing the discoveries to the leaders of American archaeology. In a matter of days, scientists began flocking to Folsom, to see firsthand the revolutionary finds. This time, the scientific evidence was conclusive.

So it was that virtually overnight, a bitter forty-year-old controversy evaporated. Those sparsely trained, obstreperous amateurs were right after all. The elite of American archaeology, the former critics, had changed their minds. Only a month after his visit to Folsom, one highly influential archaeologist could confidently crow to the world: the first American must have arrived "at least fifteen or twenty thousand years ago."

CLOVIS: THE ORIGINAL AMERICANS?

With the Folsom discovery, science suddenly had unimpeachable evidence that humans had been in the New World since the late Pleistocene. In effect, the Folsom discovery changed the rules of American archaeology. Now that archaeologists knew what to look for, evidence of ancient Americans proliferated. In 1932, just down the road 150 miles or so south of Folsom, came another startling disclosure. Not far from Clovis, New Mexico, a road construction company, digging a gravel pit into an isolated place called **Blackwater Draw**, plowed up a large, extremely thin stone tool and a huge animal tooth.

Fortunately, scientists were quickly notified. Recognizing the importance of the initial find, archaeologists from the Academy of Natural Sciences of Philadelphia and the University of Pennsylvania Museum began serious work at Blackwater Draw. The next year, they found stone tools, quite like those from Folsom, also associated with extinct bison bones.

Then came the breakthrough. In 1936–1937, archaeologists excavating *below* the Folsom strata found unquestionable associations between even more ancient human artifacts and the remains of mammoths—the American elephant. Today, archaeologists around the world know this earlier complex as *Clovis*—the oldest clearly defined Native American culture.

Without established cultural antecedents, Clovis sites consistently date between about 9500 B.C. to 8500 B.C. Isolated Clovis points, thought to be approximately this age or slightly later, are widespread across North America. In all, such sites contain thousands of artifacts

△△△

WHAT'S IN A NAME?
A NATIVE AMERICAN PERSPECTIVE

Suzan Shown Harjo (Cheyenne/Hodulgee Muscogee)

The question we are asked most often by non-Indians is about what term to use when referring to our collective race of people who are indigenous to the Western Hemisphere. The first thing to know about traveling in Indian Country is that words and proto-col are important, but that many terms, especially those rising out of European Manifest Destiny notions and colonization, are inac-curate though not necessarily inappropriate. Other names, how-ever, are best left to history.

The name *Indian* is the legacy of the lost European sailors in 1492, who thought this quarter of Mother Earth was another continent to the west, the one with India. *American* is derived from the first name of another European. Native Peoples here could have been called *Vespuccinders* as easily as *American Indians* or *Native Americans*, the most commonly used misnomers these days. With North American–born descendants of immigrants referring to themselves as *Natives*, the issue becomes further clouded.

Indian is the term of art that has made its way into U.S. and Canadian treaties, statutes, case law, governance documents, and modern English and French parlance. *Indian* replaced far less desirable names in popular North American culture, such as *Savage, Redskin,* or *L'Indian Rouge,* which are still considered fighting words. Compared to these, *American Indian, Canadian Native, Native American, Indian,* and *Native* seem mild, and are currently viewed as inexact and silly, rather than offensive.

Most Native Peoples in North America use these imprecise and awkward terms interchangeably when referring to the race as a whole. With some 600 different Indian Nations in the United States and Canada, having nearly as many separate languages, histories, territories, religions, and cultures, more emphasis is placed on the tribal names than on the collective. The most notable exceptions to this involve: 1) intertribal coalitions to stop

△△△

name-calling and discrimination against the race as a whole, and 2) dealings with Canadian or U.S. laws affecting Natives nation-wide.

A greater Native priority now is on Indian national and personal names, and on substituting traditional tribal names for those imposed through the missionizing and colonizing processes. The Diné, for example, in the early 1990s, issued a formal call for all to use their traditional name, which means "People," rather than the name by which they are widely known, Navajo. With the success of the movie *Dances with Wolves*, the general public is now more aware of the original and preferred names *Lakota* and *Dakota* over the imposed name *Sioux*, a French variation of an Anishinabe (Ojibwe or Chippewa) word meaning "enemy."

Throughout world history, when one group has exerted control over another, it has first stripped that group of its basic identity by using pet names, misnomers, or pejorative terms. The dominant group has then forced others to use the foreign names. This is evident in North American history with slave-owners imposing their names on slaves, European churches placing "Christian names" on those to be converted, and assimilationists at Ellis Island "Americanizing" the given names of refugees.

Both U.S. and Canadian churches and states zealously pursued this practice, imposing French, English, and Spanish names or poor or insulting translations of Native names on Indian people, families, clans, tribes, and nations. Often, the Indians were made to use national names of places or objects, as with the British-imposed *Creek* for the Muscogee Nation, because the English saw that the Muscogees lived near running waters. As the Tohono O'Odham leaders told U.S. Bureau of Indian Affairs (BIA) officials in the early 1980s, they wanted their name changed back to the original in all the agency's subsequent records, not solely because *Papago* means "bean-eater," but because it is not their name for themselves in their own language.

This matter was addressed poetically by Pulitzer Prize–winning author N. Scott Momaday, a Kiowa, in his 1976 memoir *The Names*. Written "in devotion to those whose names I bear and to those who bear my names," its opening words are: "My name is

△△△

Tsoai-talee. I am, therefore, Tsoai-talee, therefore I am. The storyteller Pohd-lohk gave me the name Tsoai-talee. He believed that a man's life proceeds from his name, in the way that a river proceeds from its source."

The reader and visitor should not be discouraged about what is or is not correct, only mindful of what is or is not respectful. The basic rule, as it applies to all human relations, is to simply ask Indians how they would like to be addressed and referred to, and to respect their responses.

△△△

manufactured in the Paleoindian tradition—not only the signature "Clovis" fluted points (more about those later), but also tools for chopping and cutting, slicing and dicing, mashing and squashing various extinct animal parts.

As important as these sites are, there is hardly any place in America where you can visit an actual Clovis or Folsom site today. Archaeologists have plenty of trouble finding such evidence in the first place, and almost no bona fide Paleoindian sites have been adequately protected and interpreted to allow public visitation.

We can all go to Blackwater Draw, however, the place where archaeologists first recognized the Clovis culture. The Clovis bands arrived here about 11,300 years ago, leaving the remains of their Clovis-style picnic spread about. Today, much of that Paleotrash is still there, on display for all of us to see. Blackwater Draw is America's premier Paleoindian showcase.

Anyone visiting Blackwater Draw is intensely aware of the surrounding *Llano Estacado*, the almost featureless high plain surrounding Blackwater Draw and everything else you can see in any direction. Nobody seems too sure how the Llano Estacado, Spanish for the "staked plain," got its name. Some think that early inhabitants drove stakes into the ground to mark a route across the featureless landscape. Others think the name might refer to the spear-like stalks that shoot upwards from the countless yuccas that grow across the Llano Estacado. But however it was named, the Llano Estacado remains the largest, flattest, most level, plainest place in North America, maybe anywhere.

The Llano Estacado did not always look like this. During the late Pleistocene, water streamed through Blackwater Draw, a drainage

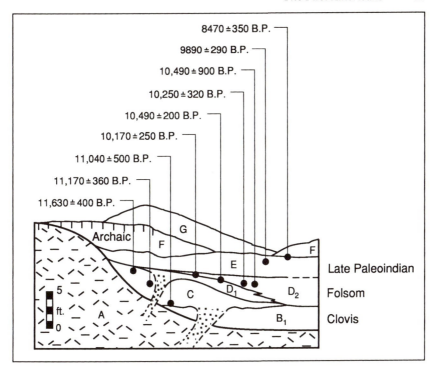

8470 ± 350 B.P.

9890 ± 290 B.P.

10,490 ± 900 B.P.

10,250 ± 320 B.P.

10,490 ± 200 B.P.

10,170 ± 250 B.P.

11,040 ± 500 B.P.

11,170 ± 360 B.P.

11,630 ± 400 B.P.

Archaic

G

F

F

E

Late Paleoindian

5

C

D₁

D₂

Folsom

ft.

A

B₁

Clovis

0

This generalized stratigraphic diagram of Blackwater Draw, New Mexico, shows the position of radiocarbon dated samples with respect to the lettered geological strata and the cultural affiliations. This stratigraphic section is important because it represents one of the very few unequivocal cases of Folsom culture artifacts superimposed over (and therefore "later") than artifacts of the Clovis culture (after an original drawing by C. Vance Haynes, From Kostenki to Clovis).

channel flowing across the western edge of the Llano Estacado. By the time Clovis people arrived, the climate was already changing, drying the stream in Blackwater Draw into several shallow, seasonal ponds that filled only during periods of runoff.

Large mammals—the mammoths, the extinct forms of bison, and the others—were naturally attracted to these ponds. And so were the human hunters. Maybe they ambushed prey at the waterholes. Or sometimes, they may have shot the animals elsewhere, then followed their crippled quarry to water.

Once dispatched, a single mammoth would provide tons of meat for the coming winter, and everyone probably helped out preparing the carcass. Almost everything was used in one way or another: meat, hide, sinew, tusks, and even the bones, which were fashioned into weapons

◭◭◭

OTHER TRACES OF THE FIRST AMERICANS?

Archaeology continues to be the best single source of information about the first Americans. But three independent lines of evidence have recently been brought to bear on the subject, and all three support an Asian homeland for America's Indians. Geneticists have analyzed the DNA contained within human mitochondria, small energy-producing bodies found in each cell. Comparisons of genetic similarities and differences in widely separated contemporary American Indian groups strongly suggest that these people share a common genetic ancestor, with estimates varying from about 15,000 to 30,000 years ago. Some microbiologists even believe that more than 95 percent of all Native Americans are descended from a single pioneering founder population—perhaps a few families that crossed the Bering Strait together in the late Ice Age. The same genetic evidence suggests that the Eskimo (Inuit)-Aleut and Nadene people—today confined mostly to the northern rim of North America—may derive from later migrations out of Asia, perhaps 7,500 years ago.

Christy Turner, a physical anthropologist from Arizona State University, tells a similar story based on his extensive studies of variability in human teeth. Focusing on the crown and root areas, Turner discovered that modern and precontact American Indian teeth are most similar to those of northern Asians. Turner, too, postulates an initial migration out of northeast Asia at the end of the Ice Age, followed by two later migrations.

Other controversial evidence comes from linguist Joseph Greenberg of Stanford University, who has recently reanalyzed the available data from every known American Indian language—a gargantuan task. He agrees that Native Americans arrived in the New World in three basic waves of migrants, with the Eskimo (Inuit)-Aleut and Nadene populations arriving in relatively recent times. And like the mitochondrial DNA assessment, his linguistic reconstruction suggests that the earliest wave of immigrants—the large "Amerind" language family—must have arrived about 12,000 years ago. These ancestral American Indians spread throughout most of North, Central, and South America. According to Greenberg, virtually all of the indigenous

◭◭◭

The large map presents the generally accepted distribution of the major Native American language stocks at the time of European contact. The inset arrays the controversial linguistic synthesis by Joseph Greenberg (Stanford University), suggesting that most language stocks in North America belong to an "Amerind" language family, presumably representing the earliest wave of immigrants. The restricted Na-Dene and Eskimo (Inuit)-Aleut languages are spoken by populations arriving in later times.

languages spoken throughout the Americas derived from this single ancestral language.

Numerous skeptics question the relevance of the linguistic, dental, and genetic testimony in tracing the first Americans. Nevertheless, both biology and language point to an Asian homeland, a possibility strongly confirmed by today's archaeological evidence.

and tools. The brains were used to tan the hide, and the rib bones may have become the rafters for hut-like shelters.

Clovis were the first people to visit Blackwater Draw, but they were hardly the last; several cultural occupations are stacked up on top of the lowest, or Clovis, level, creating a multicultural layer cake. In all, there are seven stratified layers of sediment, four of which contain associations between ancient artifacts and animal bones.

Artifacts aside, Blackwater Draw is also a major paleontological site. Thousands of extinct animal bones have been found here: woolly mammoth, camel, horse, bison, mastodon, turtle, saber-tooth tiger, peccary, four-prong antelope, short-faced bear, ground sloth, and dire wolf.

Above the Clovis level is a later stratum, containing distinctive Folsom points, smaller and more finely flaked than their Clovis counterparts. With only one possible exception, Folsom culture diagnostics have never been found with mammoth, horse, or camel bones. *Bison*

The Great Woolly Mammoth, *by Charles R. Knight (1909), depicts an arctic cousin to the Columbian mammoth about to encounter an unseen enemy in its high latitude Pleistocene environment. Although mammoths became extinct about 9000* B.C.—*shortly after the arrival of the Clovis hunters—there is no compelling evidence to indict the first Americans as the culprit in this massive extinction episode.* (Courtesy of the American Museum of Natural History.)

antiquus predominates at Folsom sites, and may have been the only species hunted. Folsom sites date between about 9000 B.C. and 8200 B.C. Late Paleoindians showed up after that.

Then the Blackwater Draw ponds dried up, filling with windblown sand, which also accumulated in dunes around the old lakeshore. But even with this progressive desiccation, water was still to be found at Blackwater Draw. Post-Paleoindian foragers were to arrive sometime after 5000 B.C.

Blackwater Draw, Locality 1 (Clovis, NM; 5 mi. from south gate of Cannon Air Force Base, on SR 467) has become a living laboratory for those who would better understand the Paleoindians who once lived there. In 1990, the Blackwater Draw site was officially opened to the public, and guided tours are available daily. Archaeological investigations also continue during the summer, fall, and spring semesters. Phone (505) 356-5235.

Blackwater Draw Museum (Clovis, New Mexico; 12 mi. S. on SR 70) is the best facility dedicated strictly to Paleoindian archaeology and paleontology in native North America. It has numerous displays of extinct animals and the ancient weaponry suited to hunt them. Phone (505) 562-2202.

CLOVIS QUARRIES AND CLOVIS CACHES

Today, the characteristic Clovis spear points, found at Blackwater Draw and elsewhere, are considered to be superb works of art. Using the simplest of tools—mostly stream cobbles and hammers made of antler—Clovis craftsmen were masters of flaking stone into wonderfully practical implements. Even in today's high-tech world, only a handful of skilled flintknappers can match what the Clovis artisans once routinely produced. Most of the disparity is cultural: Clovis stoneworkers developed specialized motor skills. Then as now, it took years to master these techniques.

But these handsome Clovis points could not be simply whacked out of just any old stone. Clovis stoneworkers deliberately sought out raw materials with exceptional flaking qualities. These Clovis artisans were probably the first people to exploit the vast geological resources of the American continent. Nothing had been picked over: everything America had to offer, geologically speaking, was lying there, ready for the taking. But the longer the Clovis flintknappers stayed in one place, the sooner they used up the easier-to-get raw materials. As they spread across America, Paleoindians inevitably found it necessary to begin actual quarrying operations to extract the right kind of quality raw material.

At the **Alibates Flint Quarries** (in the Texas Panhandle), you can see firsthand evidence of such Paleoindian quarries. Some of the very finest Clovis points are made of the distinctive Alibates flint (actually, a fine-grained, mottled or banded agate, ranging in color from rich red through blues and purple). From earliest Paleoindian times through the historic period, artifacts made from this readily recognizable stone were exchanged throughout the Southwest and Great Plains.

This remarkable outcrop of horizontal flint beds forms a slight arc across the canyon country along Alibates Creek. The quarry itself is about three-quarters of a mile long, averaging 50 to 300 feet across. The byproducts of prehistoric stone quarrying and toolmaking are everywhere. Waste flakes, broken cores, rejected and incomplete stone points and other tool fragments litter the ground, piling up in strata several feet thick. Occasionally, one finds discarded hammerstones—natural stream cobbles once used for battering and shaping the raw toolstone. There is evidence that people dug pits downward, trying to get at higher quality seams. As one early observer put it, "some of these hillsides look from a distance as if they had been peppered with artillery concentrations."

Archaeologists first learned about the Alibates quarry in the mid–1920s. For years after, professional archaeologists, rock hounds, and artifact collectors roamed these hills, picking over the tons of prehistoric waste. Tremendous damage was done by thoughtless collectors and vandals; fortunately, the site is better protected today. Although quarry sites have a certain rough-and-ready character to them, the

Alibates Flint Quarries National Monument (Amarillo, TX; 34 mi. NE of Amarillo off SR 136) preserves a series of extensive quarry excavations exploited from Paleoindian times through the protohistoric period. To protect this vulnerable site, these ancient quarries can be visited only by a 1-mi. ranger-guided walking tour, which includes a flintknapping demonstration. Phone (806) 857-3151.

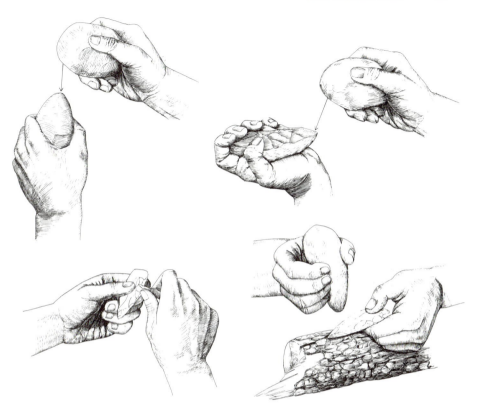

Various methods of flintknapping, hand-held techniques for stone-on-stone percussion, probably like those used to craft Clovis spear points. At the lower right, an anvil is employed to steady the working surface for added control in flake removal. At the lower left, a bone (or antler) tool is used to remove flakes by direct pressure; this technique produced the outstanding flaking seen on Folsom spear points.

truth is they are tremendously fragile resources and we must protect them.

Some of the Clovis points made of prized Alibates agate were carried into present-day northeastern Colorado, where they were deliberately hidden (or *cached*) underground, along with some mammoth ivory. For years, archaeologists puzzled over this curious Clovis cache: Why would anybody go to all the trouble of quarrying tool stone in Texas, knapping it into high quality Clovis spear points, transporting these tools for hundreds of miles, then burying them in a pit and walking away? And what's the mammoth ivory doing in there?

Then, in 1988, another similar find turned up near Wenachee, Washington. While trenching through an orchard, an earthmover dug up several bone cylinders, some Paleoindian cutting tools, and—most surprising of all—several whopping Clovis points made to gargantuan proportions.

At the so-called Anzick Site cache, accidentally discovered by another construction worker operating an end loader near Wilsal (southeastern Montana), a small collapsed rock-shelter contained, among other things, a small amount of human remains—all that survived of two Clovis youngsters, whose bones were covered with red pigment.

The **Anzick Site** is the only Clovis burial ever found. Buried with the bones were more than 100 artifacts of stone and bone: Clovis spear points, chopping and cutting implements, and several bone tools (apparently once used for fastening Clovis points on the tips of thrusting spears). Although exact identification of the bone foreshafts is difficult,

Two reconstructions showing how Clovis spear points might have been hafted onto bone foreshafts, based on artifacts recovered in the Anzick cache. On the left, the spear point is lashed to one of the single beveled bone foreshafts. The middle and right-hand drawings show how both beveled and bibeveled bone artifacts might have been used for wedging a Clovis point into its binding (after reconstructions by Larry Lahren and Robson Bonnichsen in Science).

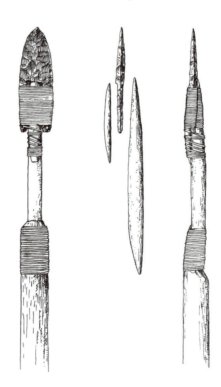

─── ⩗⩗⩗ ───
WHAT IS RADIOCARBON DATING?

In 1949, a physical chemist named Willard F. Libby announced to the world that he had discovered a revolutionary new radiocarbon (C-14) dating technique. The world apparently agreed and handed Libby the Nobel Prize in chemistry for his breakthrough.

Like many great thoughts, the basic principle behind radiocarbon dating is deceptively straightforward. Cosmic radiation produces neutrons, which enter the earth's atmosphere and react with nitrogen to produce the "heavy" carbon isotope carbon-14.

$$N^{14} + neutron = C^{14} + H$$

Carbon-14 is "heavy" because its nucleus contains fourteen neutrons, rather than the more common load of twelve. The extra neutrons make the nucleus unstable and subject to gradual (radioactive) decay.

Libby calculated that after 5,568 years, half of the C-14 available in a sample will have decayed; this is termed the *half-life* of C-14. Whenever a neutron leaves a C-14 nucleus, a radioactive (beta) particle is emitted, and the amount of radioactivity remaining can be measured by counting the number of beta emissions per gram of carbon.

$$C^{14} = B- + N^{14} +$$

These fundamentals established, Libby proceeded to convert the fact of radiocarbon decay into a chronometric tool.

Plants and animals are known to ingest atmospheric carbon in the form of carbon dioxide throughout their lives. When an organism dies, no more carbon enters its system, and that which is already present starts its radioactive decay. By measuring the beta emissions from the dead organism, you can compute roughly how long ago that organism died.

Radiocarbon decay is, strictly speaking, a random process, as nobody can ever predict exactly which C-14 molecule will decay. It is an actuarial matter, like a life insurance table (nobody knows who will die this year, but it's a dead certainty that a certain number will).

─── ⩗⩗⩗ ───

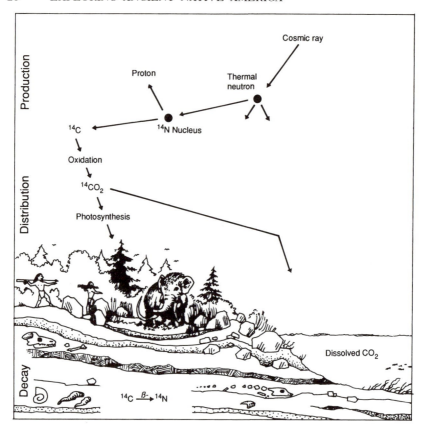

This reconstruction shows the theoretical basis of the radiocarbon dating method. The natural production of ^{14}C is a secondary effect of cosmic-ray bombardment in the earth's upper atmosphere. Most of the ^{14}C is then absorbed into the oceans, but a small percentage becomes part of the terrestrial biosphere. Normal metabolic processes maintain an equilibrium of ^{14}C content in living organisms. But once the plant or animal dies, metabolism ceases, and the proportion of ^{14}C begins to decrease. Measuring the progress of such random decay provides the basis for modern radiocarbon dating (after a drawing by R. E. Taylor, Radiocarbon Dating: An Archaeological Perspective*).*

△△△

The radiocarbon lab reports a date using notation like this:

UCLA-1926A 5200 ± 120 radiocarbon years B.P.

This is an actual date, from charcoal found in Hearth A on Horizon 12 at Gatecliff Shelter (Nevada). The first designation records the laboratory and sample number: University of California (Los Angeles) Radiocarbon Laboratory sample number 1926A. The second part—5200—estimates the age of the sample in radiocarbon years B.P., the latter an abbreviation for "before present" (arbitrarily defined as the year A.D. 1950).

The "± 120", or *standard deviation*, estimates the consistency (or lack of it) between the various "counting runs" performed at the laboratory. This statistical appendage, read as "plus or minus," is the standard deviation (or "sigma"), or projection of the error in the estimate, and expresses the range within which the true date probably falls.

We know from statistical theory that there is a two-in-three (67 percent) chance that the true date falls within one "sigma." Specifically, by both adding and subtracting 120 from the age estimate, we will find the probability to be 67 percent that the true age of UCLA-1926A falls between 5080 (*minus* 120) and 5320 (*plus* 120) radiocarbon years B.P.

The recent development of the *accelerator mass spectrometric (AMS) technique* for radiocarbon dating drastically reduces the quantity of datable material required. When a Geiger counter was used to monitor the beta-ray emissions, several grams of organics were required. But because the new accelerator technology counts the proportion of carbon isotopes directly, the sample required is only a few milligrams.

The earliest radiocarbon dates worked on organic materials younger than about 30,000 years. But more recently, technical refinements have extended the effective range of the C-14 method to over 75,000 years. But beyond that point, the amount of undecayed C-14 is minuscule and the degree of radiocarbon decay is unmeasurable.

△△△

Scaffold burials such as these might have been used by Clovis people; after the body decayed, the bones were collected and interred in the famous Clovis burial caches, such as that at Anzick. These reconstructions are based on nineteenth-century examples constructed by Australian aborigines (top) and Plains Indian tribes.

they seem to have been made from mammoth bone. The three radiocarbon dates available for the Anzick site average about 8870 B.C.

Although early Paleoindian caches like Anzick are still uncommon, they are providing archaeologists with rare insights into Clovis lifeways. It may be that the Anzick cache is the final product of a Clovis-period platform burial, a common Native American mortuary practice in which the deceased was laid out and exposed for a considerable time before final burial. If such burial rites were as commonplace in Clovis times as they were among the Plains Indian tribes of historic times, this might be why archaeologists have so rarely come across the human remains of Paleoindians.

The Anzick Site is one of the earliest and most important archaeological sites in native North America. There is nothing to visit today because it was inadvertently destroyed by gravel operations—an accident, but an irrevocable loss just the same.

Fortunately, the outstanding collection of artifacts recovered from the Anzick cache—the Clovis points, the large flint bifacial tools, and the bone foreshafts—are today displayed at the *Montana Historical Society Museum* (Helena, MT; 225 N. Roberts St.) as part of their "First People" exhibit. Phone (406) 444-2694.

HUNTING MAMMOTH

The Clovis projectile point is the first piece of flaked stone weaponry in the world that was well-enough designed to allow a single hunter a dependable and predictable means of pursuing and killing a large mammal such as a mammoth or bison on a one-to-one basis.

— GEORGE FRISON, NORTH AMERICAN HIGH
PLAINS PALEO-INDIAN HUNTING
STRATEGIES AND WEAPONS

Since the early days at Blackwater Draw, about twenty Clovis sites have been found with solid stratigraphic associations. The most common faunal association is mammoth, with bison remains running a distant second. Camels and native American horses may also have been hunted. Even bears and rabbits have turned up in Clovis contexts.

So it seems quite unlikely that the Clovis people were totally dependent on elephant hunting for their survival. Few nonagricultural people focus exclusively on a single food source—particularly one so difficult to hunt as an elephant. Perhaps, as one archaeological wag put it, the average Clovis hunter found a mammoth once in his life, and never stopped talking about it—like some archaeologists.

Be that as it may, the fact is that mammoth kills remain the most visible evidence we have of the first Americans. Because they are all we have, archaeologists are always going to dig at places like Blackwater Draw, and they are going to continue studying mammoth bone artifacts like those in the Anzick cache.

But these same archaeologists are increasingly hoisting themselves out of the trenches and pushing back from the lab tables, looking for suitable analogies to "see" such ancient behavior patterns firsthand. Looking at analogies is nothing new in science. Geologists studying glacial processes will, with any luck, never analyze firsthand the massive continental glaciers that once draped the North American continent. But they often study the smaller mountain glaciers that can still be found at the highest altitudes and the higher latitudes.

Archaeologists are now doing the same thing, closely studying the plausible analogies in order to understand ancient behavior patterns. Sometimes, they try to replicate artifacts, to reconstruct Paleoindian conditions experimentally (see **Can You Make a Folsom Point?**).

But what about studying Clovis hunting practices? Nobody today hunts mammoths, which have been extinct since shortly after Clovis times. So how can science stage a confrontation between a modern hunter and a mammoth standing fourteen feet tall at the shoulder?

One archaeologist seems to have found the way. Although a professor and practicing archaeologist at the University of Wyoming, George Frison is also an experienced hunter, and a lifelong student of primitive hunting practices. Figuring that the best analogy to a mammoth must be the modern African elephant, Frison took off for Zimbabwe, where he conducted extensive experiments on endangered African elephant populations.

Such "experimentation" was possible only because these elephants have multiplied far beyond the carrying capacity of the National Parks, forcing game officials to cull the herds. The Zimbabwe Division of Wildlife agreed to carefully supervised experimentation with Paleoindian weaponry—provided only dead or dying animals were targeted. So there was Frison, Clovis-style replicas in hand, trying to learn what Clovis hunters knew 12,000 years ago. He came away from the experience understanding several things not evident from simply studying archaeological remains.

For one thing, Frison was impressed with the physical strength required to down an elephant with a spear. Frison concluded that hunting elephants is not only dangerous, it's hard work! He knew from looking at frozen Siberian mammoth hides that Ice Age elephants were protected across the vital rib cage area by a one-half-inch-thick covering. African elephants are built about the same, and it takes an extraordinarily well-designed weapon to penetrate such natural protection.

It turns out that Clovis points are not only gorgeous, but they were deliberately made to maximize penetration and minimize breakage. The lateral indentations—the distinctive "flutes"—allowed them to be smoothly and efficiently tied to foreshafts (like those buried at Anzick). The point bases were ground smooth to keep them from cutting the shaft bindings.

The Clovis point was the business end of a thrusting spear or dart. Paleoindian weaponry probably included a throwing stick (atlatl), which Frison found gave him a good combination of leverage and distance. The Clovis point was tied with sinew to a bone or wooden foreshaft which, in turn, fit into a long, heavy main shaft, probably with a carefully designed hole so the foreshaft would fit snugly.

This composite shaft-foreshaft-point construction provided Clovis hunters with a detachable lance head—a sophisticated piece of hunting equipment well suited for killing at close range. When ambushing, tracking, or holding quarry at bay, hunters could make numerous accurate shots at vital nerve centers. Retrieving the lance and inserting another shaft with a stone point could be done in seconds—a much safer and more effective technology than trying to carry and manipulate several lances in such a dangerous situation.

This Clovis firepower was most effective when aimed at the elephant's lung cavity, between the bottom of the rib cage and the top of the back (where the skin is a little thinner). The ribs around here are also rounded, allowing easier penetration of stone-tipped spears. Aim too high, you hit thicker hide; shoot too low, and the wider, flatter ribs tend to protect the heart area.

Weapons, Frison discovered, become a subtle extension of the hunter's own body. He thinks that Clovis hunters must have spent considerable time making and maintaining the weapons. If the shaft is not perfectly straight, the spear may not transmit the necessary force to the stone point. And even invisible flaws in the stone point can cause a Clovis point to fail at the critical moment—allowing a prey to escape or exposing the now-unarmed hunter to sudden danger. Clovis hunters must have continually tested and retested their equipment before setting off on a large-scale kill.

His Zimbabwe experience made Frison skeptical of earlier reconstructions of Clovis hunting. Traditionally, artists have drawn Clovis hunters armed with spears, darts, and rocks incapacitating a mammoth trapped in a bog or pit. Barking dogs, women, and children are often pictured in the background, creating a general picture of mayhem and commotion.

Frison thinks this scenario goes against smart hunting know-how. First, if a healthy mammoth were mired in mud and unable to escape, no band of human hunters would be able to drag it out either. The mammoth would be unbutcherable. The smart hunter would remain on solid ground, away from crowds, relying on individual prowess and a carefully prepared set of weapons.

THE PALEOINDIAN BUTCHER SHOP AT LUBBOCK LAKE

Few incontrovertible Paleoindian sites can be visited today. Fortunately, **Lubbock Lake State and National Landmark** is another of the rare places containing clues about the various American Indian communities who hunted and camped here over the past 12,000 years. Like Blackwater Draw, Lubbock Lake has textbook stratigraphy. Both are rarities, two of the very few sites in North America that contain a complete cultural sequence, from Clovis times to the present.

Archaeological interest in Lubbock Lake also dates back to the 1930s, when a WPA crew was dredging an old meander of Yellowhouse Draw, just north of Lubbock, Texas. They renovated one of the ancient springs known to exist here, and once released, the water flow was dammed for use by the Lubbock Fire Department. During the dredging, the bones of several extinct animals were brought to the surface, along with a Folsom spear point. Fortunately, the artifact was retrieved and shown to W. Curry Holden of nearby Texas Tech University. Holden recognized the importance of the find and took immediate steps to protect the site. Since then, Lubbock Lake has been intensively studied by teams of archaeologists, geologists, zoologists, botanists, and soil scientists. We now recognize Lubbock Lake as one of the largest non-agricultural complexes in the New World.

The earliest Paleoindian occupation at Lubbock Lake contains Clovis materials, dating about 9500 to 9000 B.C. During Clovis times, a flowing stream cut through the site, and nearby were buried the bones of mammoth, two kinds of extinct horses, extinct camel, extinct bison, and a giant armadillo. Also discovered here were bones of an extinct short-faced bear—three times the size of the modern grizzly.

Lubbock Lake at this point became, among other things, a Paleoindian butcher shop where at least three elephants were carved up in an 11,000-year-old assembly line. We know from archaeological experiments that slaughtering elephant is not exactly a fast food operation.

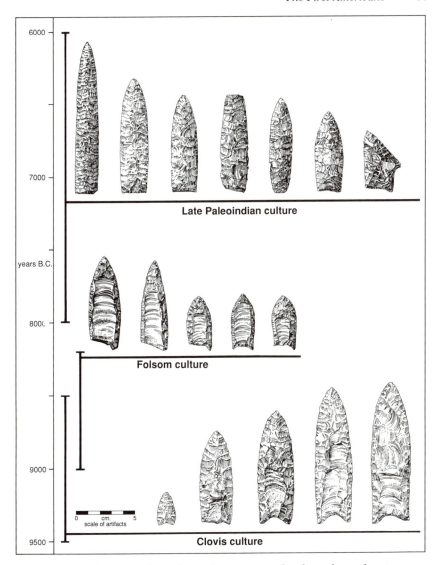

6000

7000

Late Paleoindian culture

years B.C.

8000

Folsom culture

9000

0   cm.   5
scale of artifacts

9500

Clovis culture

This hypothetical stratigraphic column demonstrates the chronology of various projectile point styles spanning the Paleoindian period.

Huge slabs of meat were laboriously sliced and hacked. The same ingenious Clovis points that killed the elephants could be readily detached from their spear shafts, an instantaneous conversion from guided missile to bowie knife.

Curiously, not a single Clovis point was scientifically excavated at Lubbock Lake. In fact, all that was left at this 11,000-year-old butcher

Lubbock Lake Landmark State Historical Park (Lubbock, TX; access is via a special ramp near Intersection of Loop 289 and US 84) is an ongoing archaeological research station, with archaeological excavations spanning the last five decades. The on-site interpretive center displays finds from this important Paleoindian locality, and public trails lead visitors to key areas of the site. Phone (806) 741-0306.

Museum of Texas Tech University (Lubbock, TX; 4th St. and Indiana Ave.) displays background materials on ancient environments, history, and cultures of this area, with emphasis on the Paleoindian excavations at nearby Lubbock Lake and elsewhere in Texas. Phone (806) 742-2490.

shop were slightly modified smashing tools, mostly pounding stones and boulders. And lots of bones. The most notable was the battered, disarticulated skull of a two-year-old mammoth. These Clovis butchers tried to use everything at hand. As the mammoth steaks sizzled on the Paleoindian barbecue, everyone set upon the rest of the carcass. Bones the size of coffee tables were smashed to get at the nutritious marrow contained inside. These same mammoth bones were also turned into ad hoc artifacts, things like hammers, chisels, and cleavers. The regal mammoth was battered into edible bits with its own bones. In the ultimate indignity, the axed became the axe.

As informative as this Clovis butcher shop may be, Lubbock Lake is better known for its later Folsom finds. In all, nine Folsom points were recovered here, five of them directly associated with remains of extinct bison (*Bison antiquus*). One of the Folsom cutting tools was made of Alibates agate, as were several other Paleoindian artifacts recovered at Lubbock Lake.

After killing a half-dozen bison along the marshy pond edges, the Folsom people completely processed the carcasses, removed some marrow, and made a number of bone tools, once again probably to expedite the butchering process. The discarded bison bones were stacked into distinct piles.

Paleoindian bison hunters, like those at Lubbock Lake, developed the best weapons known anywhere in the world at that time. They organized communal buffalo hunts, and some Paleoindian sites show

CAN YOU MAKE A FOLSOM POINT?

Over the past couple of decades, a school of highly dedicated experimentalists have been rediscovering the technology necessary to fabricate stone tools. The late, great Don Crabtree (affiliated with the Idaho State University Museum) began this research by undertaking a series of carefully documented studies to uncover the nature of prehistoric stoneworking.

Accomplished flintknapper Bruce Bradley uses a bone flaker to remove pressure flakes from a large corner-notched projectile point. Although he attempts to protect himself with a leather shield, flintknapping is a bloody business and Dr. Bradley sports numerous scars from his years of experimental flintknapping. (Courtesy of Bruce Bradley and the Crow Canyon Archaeological Center.)

One of Crabtree's many projects was to rediscover the techniques necessary to create the Folsom point, one of the world's most exquisite stone artifacts. Although Folsom points are typically only about two inches long, Crabtree counted over 150 minute sharpening flakes removed from their surface.

The distinctive property of Folsom artifacts is the *flute* (or channel flake) removed from each surface. Nobody is really sure why these artifacts were fluted in this distinctive fashion, but everybody agrees that fluting is an extraordinary feat of flintknapping. The technical quality and intrinsic beauty of the Folsom point intrigued Crabtree.

⟁⟁⟁

Most projectile points can be fashioned in a few minutes. But making a Folsom must have taken hours—assuming an understanding of how to do it in the first place. And in the mid-twentieth century, nobody had that.

Many archaeologists thought that the channel flakes must have been driven off by indirect percussion, or pressure, with a bone or antler punch serving as an intermediary to transfer the blow to the artifact. Interested in flintknapping for most of his life, Crabtree thought about this, tried it out himself, and concluded that it doesn't work.

So began an experimental period that lasted over forty years. Crabtree tried every way he could think of to manufacture Folsom replicas. At one point, he described the eleven different methods he had tried to remove fluting flakes. Most techniques simply failed: either the method was impossible with primitive tools or the flute was different from those on the Folsoms. One method succeeded only in driving a copper punch through Crabtree's left hand.

Crabtree eventually concluded that fluting flakes could be removed in only two ways. In one experiment, he placed an antler shaft on the bottom of the unfinished artifact and then struck the punch with a sharp upward blow. But because placement of the antler punch was critical, this technique requires two workers—not a very satisfactory solution.

Crabtree then came across a documentary source describing some long-lost flintknapping techniques once practiced by Native Americans. Particularly interesting were the observations of a Spanish Franciscan friar, Juan de Torquemada, who had traveled through the Central American jungles in 1615:

They take a stick with both hands, and set well home against the edge of the front of the stone, which also is cut smooth in the front of the stone, which also is cut smooth in that part; and they press it against their breast, and with the force of the pressure there flies off a knife. . . . Then they sharpen it on a stone using a hone to give it a very fine edge; and in a very short time these workmen will make more than twenty knives in the aforesaid manner.

⟁⟁⟁

Although Torquemada was describing an advanced, Aztec technique, Crabtree wondered whether the method might work to produce meaningful results on his Folsom replicas. Manufacturing a chest crutch following Torquemada's descriptions—padding one end and equipping the other with a sharp antler flaker—he tied an unfinished, unfluted Folsom point into a wood-and-thong vise, which he gripped between his feet. Bracing the crutch against his chest, he successfully detached perfect fluting flakes, time after time. The resulting artifacts were almost identical to prehistoric Folsom points.

Crabtree's pioneering research unleashed an avalanche of interest in the fluting problem. One archaeologist was able to detach fluting flakes with direct percussion, using wood or stone as a backstop. George Frison and Bruce Bradley once dug up a portion of elk antler amidst Folsom point-manufacturing debris at the Agate Basin site in Wyoming; after extensive experimentation, they concluded that channel flakes could be successfully removed with a wood-and-antler lever/fulcrum device. Somebody else used indirect percussion with a grooved anvil-and-backstop arrangement, and yet another experimenter was able to detach channel flakes with a simple, hand-generated pressure technique.

Which method was actually used in Folsom times? Who knows? I find it fascinating that all these scientists are spending so much time knocking rocks and bloodying their fingers to figure out what was common knowledge 10,500 years ago. Makes you think about how much has been forgotten over the years.

Bruce Bradley has recently injected a spiritual tone into the fluting question. Speaking as one of the world's experts on prehistoric lithic technology, Bradley wonders why anybody would bother to do something so tricky in the first place.

He thinks that the complex fluting process probably started out as an expedient way to thin the point's base, to make it easier to tie onto the shaft. But as in many human endeavors, once risk of failure increases, so does desire for supernatural assistance. That's why some of us cross our fingers for good luck.

Bradley thinks that flintknapping became ritualized during

△△△

Folsom times. After all, many contemporary Native American cultures include projectile points in sacred bundles, believing that stone points have their own spirit, that they can be used to secure supernatural power.

Life was risky in Folsom times—not only was fluting a tricky business, but so was putting meat on the table day after day. Could fluting one's Folsom points have become an integral part of some prehunt ritual, a way of making a lithic sign of the cross? Bradley thinks so.

△△△

evidence of repeated use for two or even three thousand years. On the basis of the age composition of the hunted herds, archaeologists figure that most such hunts took place in the late autumn and winter. On the northern Plains, surplus meat was probably frozen and cached for later use.

Folsom hunters were experts at using the natural topography to their benefit. Arroyos (arid land gullies) are a common feature of the Great Plains landscape, undergoing continuous cycles of erosion and deposition. Paleoindians knew how to stampede bison into deep, narrow arroyos, where sometimes the bottommost animals were crushed and left unbutchered. Paleoindian hunters also used natural barriers to help direct the stampeding bison, and, in at least one case, an artificial trap of logs barricaded an arroyo. Folsom hunters even knew how to use sand dunes to ambush bison.

THE RANCHOLABREAN EXTINCTION: TROUBLE IN PARADISE

The world of the Paleoindian hunter differed greatly from that of today. This is one reason why archaeologists have so much difficulty reconstructing Paleoindian hunting strategies: most of the game animals hunted by Paleoindians are today extinct. These first Americans were eyewitnesses to one of the world's most dramatic episodes of extinction. Before their eyes, Paleoindians saw native American animal species die out in droves.

To appreciate the magnitude of this mass extinction, take a walk on the path through the **Rancho La Brea Tar Pits,** near downtown Los

Angeles, California. These gooey asphalt beds both trapped and pre-served a huge range of prehistoric plant and animal life. La Brea is one of the world's richest sources of late Ice Age fossils, laid down between 11,000 and 36,000 years ago. So important is this single site that the animals faced by Paleoindian hunters are sometimes collectively called the *Rancholabrean fauna* because so many of them were excavated here.

Between about 10,000 and 12,000 years ago—that is, from Clovis through Folsom times—the Rancholabrean fauna was decimated. In North America alone, three dozen genera of mammals disappeared. The large herbivores were the hardest hit—twenty-foot-long ground sloths, giant beaver the size of modern bears, horses, camels, mammoths, mastodon, and musk oxen.

Survival of the meat-eaters, the carnivores, depended closely on the health of their prey. And as the herbivores began dying out, the carnivores were soon to follow—the saber-tooth cat (with its eight-inch canines), American cheetah and lion, the dire wolf, and the short-faced bear.

Rancho La Brea Tar Pits (Los Angeles, CA; Wilshire Blvd. and Curson Ave.) trapped some of America's best Ice Age fossils. Viewers can see how the fossils appeared when they were discovered.

George C. Page Museum of La Brea Discoveries (Los Angeles, CA; 5801 Wilshire Blvd.), adjacent to the Rancho La Brea Tar Pits, exhibits reconstructed fossils of the so-called Rancholabrean Ice Age fauna, including extinct wolves, birds, horses, and saber-tooth cats. Films and slides depict prehistoric life in the area. Visitors can observe fossils being prepared and studied. Phone (213) 857-6311.

Some paleontologists blame the Paleoindians for hunting the Rancholabrean fauna into extinction. Is it mere coincidence, they wonder, that the extinctions took place shortly after Clovis hunters first appeared in the Americas? Perhaps because the large herbivores had never before confronted a two-legged predator, these beasts lacked the necessary defensive behaviors, and the Paleoindians took merciless advantage. This explanation suggests that as Clovis people spread southward in what has been likened to a late Pleistocene blitzkrieg, they left in their wake the bones of animals rapidly passing into extinction.

Few modern scientists accept the "overkill" hypothesis. Most recognize that the Clovis people themselves were at risk during a period of massive global warming. During the period when these extinctions took place (between 10,000 and 12,000 years ago), the sea level rose. Winters became warmer and summers cooler, with less seasonal variability in temperature than today. Plant communities changed, and tall grasses covered today's short-grass plains. North America's vegetational zones shifted significantly and abruptly. Both snowfall and annual precipitation decreased significantly.

Many of the smaller mammals could adapt to these shifting conditions by modifying their ranges; the larger ones—the mammoths, mastodons, camels, and horses—placed greater demands on their environments. They could not cope with their transformed surroundings and were pushed beyond the brink to extinction.

Perhaps human hunters did play a role in wiping out certain animal populations. But most scientists now believe that the Rancholabrean fauna fell victim to a rapidly changing climate. Clovis people adapted to the changes. The extinct megafauna did not.

PRE-CLOVIS POSSIBILITIES

To this point, we have remained on fairly solid ground. Although scientists debate the role of Clovis hunters in exterminating the Rancholabrean creatures, nobody familiar with the evidence doubts the presence of Clovis culture in America 12,000 years ago. Clovis sites are the earliest well-documented archaeological remains in the New World.

But were Clovis people the very first Americans? Since the finds at Blackwater Draw in the 1930s, archaeologists have failed to turn up a single piece of undisputed pre-Clovis evidence anywhere in the Western Hemisphere. Numerous sites throughout North and South America offer tantalizing suggestions, but none provides ironclad proof acceptable to all archaeologists.

Many archaeologists, myself included, think that it's just a matter of time before solid pre-Clovis evidence turns up. In fact, many modern archaeologists have begun to acknowledge, if sometimes only privately, that Native Americans could easily have arrived as long as 40,000 years ago.

But if that were true, how could we tell?

ᐯᐯᐯ

ORAL TRADITIONS AND INDIAN ORIGINS: A NATIVE AMERICAN PERSPECTIVE

Roger C. Echo-Hawk (Pawnee)

The first people dwelt in a land of lingering darkness. In some Native American origin stories, humans emerged from this region to witness the sun's creation or the ordering of night and day. Thousands of years later, many Indians said that their ancestors entered the world from a dark place located underground. Other oral traditions, however—told in both Asia and America— describe the creation of earth from a watery world, and these stories do not typically associate darkness with the first people.

Many archaeologists believe that humans from Asia entered North America more than 11,000 years ago. As Ice Age glaciers absorbed water, sea levels fell hundreds of feet and "Beringia" appeared in the far north, linking Asia to Alaska. Some of the oldest human sites in eastern Beringia can be found above the Arctic Circle, where darkness lingers over the earth. Other scholars believe that humans followed the coastlines of Beringia by boat into the Americas—a route which does not pass through the Arctic Circle.

Climatologists believe that the Ice Ages were swept by wind-storms of much greater power than present-day hurricanes and tornadoes, and in one Indian tradition, the first people were created in the heavens and placed on earth by tornadoes. Other Indian stories say that the climate underwent a swift change when the animals (who reigned over the earth) caused summer to appear. Paleoclimatologists have found that a very sudden global warming event may have occurred 11,700 years ago at the end of the Ice Age. This date coincides with the earliest accepted archaeological evidence for the presence of humans in Alaska.

Many Native American oral traditions refer to the existence of dangerous "monsters" and giant animals in ancient times, and other stories are set in a period when animals and birds ruled the world. Paleontologists describe Ice Age America as a realm dominated by giant animals, or "megafauna." Mammoths, mastodons,

ᐯᐯᐯ

and giant sloths towered over human hunters; and fearsome short-faced bears, great cats, and other creatures could have made the New World a dangerous place for unwary people.

In many Indian traditions, a great flood covered the earth in ancient times, and some stories associate this event with the end of the age of monsters. Traditions of a mighty deluge can be found in oral and written literatures from around the world. The end of the most recent Ice Age, some 12,000 years ago, could have involved cataclysmic flooding. As the glaciers slowly melted, for example, the sudden release of a massive ice sheet into the ocean would have brought worldwide flooding. The end of the Ice Age also coincides with the extinction of many species of megafauna around the world.

The first Americans made artifacts and left sites that archaeologists can study for insights into the distant past. The ancient ancestors of modern Native Americans also created verbal documents about their experiences, and successive generations of Indians heard these stories as accounts of actual, not fictional, historical events. If Native American origin traditions shed light on the lifeways of people who settled in North America during the last Ice Age, then Indian literature preserves a remarkable legacy of documents about ancient human history in the New World.

THE CURIOUS CASE OF CALICO HILLS

It is an historical fact that unsupported claims of great human antiquity arise more frequently in California than in any other part of the New World. . . . Whether the Golden State produces more archaeological freaks, or whether the citizens of that element of the Union are simply uncommonly gullible, we do not know. But the situation does exist and it is likely to continue, and therefore it becomes an integral consideration in practicing and evaluating archaeology in California. Other states probably have their own special archaeological anomalies.

—THOMAS HESTER, ROBERT F. HEIZER,
AND JOHN GRAHAM,
FIELD METHODS IN ARCHAEOLOGY

The problems documenting pre-Clovis Americans can be seen first-hand in the Mohave Desert, not far east of Barstow, at the **Calico Early Man Archaeological Site.** Since the 1940s, avocational and professional archaeologists have scoured the ancient lake shorelines in the eastern Mohave Desert, finding what some think is evidence of very early human occupation in this area. But beyond the immediate participants, nobody paid much attention to these finds—until 1963, when the world-famous Dr. L. S. B. Leakey visited southern California.

Fresh from his triumphs at Olduvai Gorge—his world-shaking Paleolithic site in Tanzania, where fossil remains of very early humans were found associated with very primitive artifacts—Leakey became intrigued with the Mohave artifacts. Walking around the Calico Hills, Leakey determined that the site had promise, and suggested that subsurface testing would be profitable in a specifically selected area. Over a six-year period, two master pits and a series of trenches were meticulously excavated into the forty-foot-deep sedimentary deposits there.

These initial excavations encountered literally hundreds of thousands of chipped stone fragments, and about 600 of these were sorted out as "artifacts." At one point, excavators isolated a rock feature—

Drawings of some of the "best artifacts" recovered from early excavations at the Calico Hills site, California.

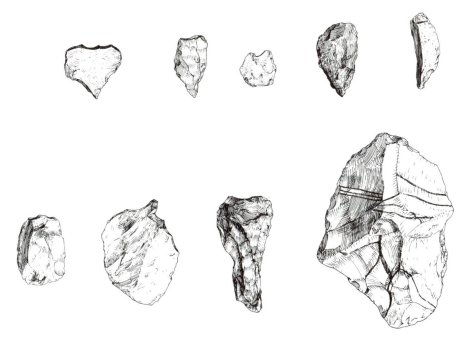

thirteen lime-coated stones arranged in a semi-circle—which investigators identified as an ancient hearth. Scientific examination of the encircling stones suggested that the interior had been heated. Radiocarbon dates processed on soil carbonates and a tusk fragment suggested an age older than 40,000 years—then the maximum limit of the radiocarbon method.

Calico Early Man Archaeological Site (Yermo, CA; 7 mi. NE via I-15 and Minneola Rd.) is jointly operated by the Bureau of Land Management and the Friends of Calico Early Man Site, Inc., a nonprofit, public benefit corporation established to support the excavation and interpretation of the site.

You will first encounter the Yermo alluvial fan, a cone-shaped deposit of mud, rock, and debris that flowed downslope, layer upon layer for thousands of years. Some flows brought rounded nodules of chalcedony and chert, broken off from outcrops upslope. Other flows brought finer materials, filling in with gravels and sands. The Calico Early Man dig is about halfway up the Yermo fan, which today stretches 8 miles long and 5 miles wide.

Visitors will see Master Pit I, the location hand-picked by Leakey. Excavations began here in November 1964 and the stratigraphic profiles here remain impressive. Four years later, in Master Pit II, excavators dug down and down, eventually encountering the controversial "fire hearth" at a depth of 23.25 feet. It is still there.

Some 6,000 to 8,000 visitors are annually guided through the major excavation pits and displays at the site's visitor's center. Recently, however, the Bureau of Land Management has expressed concern about earthquake dangers of visiting such deep, unshored excavation units, and visitors are at times not permitted to visit the subsurface areas. Funding difficulties have also surfaced recently, and the interpretive potential for this provocative site is, at this writing, uncertain. Prior to visiting, you should call ahead and see what services are available. Phone (909) 798-8570.

Initially, the project geologist believed the age of the alluvial fan—and its associated artifacts, if that is what they are—to be about 50,000 to 75,000 years old. More recent dating techniques suggest to excavators an age of about 200,000 years old. But many other highly qualified specialists think that even the revised estimate is highly conservative; the Calico Hills deposits may well be several hundred thousand years old, maybe even several million.

So, if these finds were authentic, then the site is not simply pre-Clovis in age. If valid, Calico Hills contains some of the oldest evidence of human activity anywhere in the world.

Supporters of the Calico site believe exactly that. Not long before his death, Leakey put it this way:

> We believe we have established the presence of man-made artifacts in a deposit much older than anything previously found and established in the New World. We believe in doing that we have given others, especially the younger people, something to aim for. Go and search for better information. Go and find places where similar material is associated with fossils. It can be done. It must be done . . . I think that the total picture leaves little room for doubt that man was at Calico when that part of the fan was being laid down. For me, after fifty years in the field, there is no doubt, whatsoever!

Since Leakey's death, this research has been carried on by a dedicated corps who today claim that Calico is the oldest prehistoric tool site yet discovered in the Western Hemisphere. They assert that more than 12,000 stone tools have been recovered to date, and argue for an age of 200,000 ± 20,000 years. According to Ruth DeEtte Simpson (a highly-qualified archaeologist and prime mover in the Calico project since its inception) "Calico is indeed a pioneer project . . . we have found the first clues to early, previously unknown chapters in American archaeology."

The problem is this: virtually every professional archaeologist today questions her claim. Most professionally trained lithic specialists who have studied the famed rock of Calico think that people had nothing to do with it: not the "artifacts," not the hearth, not the ancient fan itself.

Researchers have particularly scrutinized the alleged stone tools, seeking signs of human manufacture: artifacts or "nature-facts?" Specialists from both sides of the issue have tried about everything to prove their respective points. Flintknappers have worked over quarry samples from nearby roadways and mines, where vehicles and heavy equipment have caused breakage. Experimenters at the San Bernardino County Museum dropped a fifty-pound boulder onto a block of Calico chalcedony, shattered stones with dynamite, tumbled rocks for twelve hours, crushed them with an eight-ton roadroller, and passed them through mechanical rock crushers, all in the attempt to simulate geological forces through time. Others have measured the edge angles, looked for damage on the tools from ancient butchering activities, and about everything else conceivable that one can do to a rock.

The conclusion? Most modern researchers ridicule the Calico tools as "geofacts," created by natural fracture processes without human intervention. Most feel that the "stone tools" from Calico were the result of thousands of years of downhill soil creep, debris flow, and flash flooding within the Yermo alluvial fan.

This, then, is the issue: On the one hand, we have a cadre of hard-working, mostly avocational, archaeologists advancing claims for an extremely ancient Pleistocene occupation of the California desert. Yet nearly everyone in the professional archaeological community thinks they are incredibly motivated and terrifically methodical, but badly misguided—and certainly wrong. But will Calico ultimately, like the Folsom site in 1927, rouse an archaeological establishment too conservative and calcified to recognize the evidence at hand?

What happened at Folsom in 1927 was remarkable. The conclusions drawn from the Folsom site were immediately accepted by the scientific community because they satisfied the minimum criteria necessary to establish the presence of people in the archaeological and geological records.

These minimum requirements, best articulated by Paleoindian specialist C. Vance Haynes of the University of Arizona are straightforward. They are just as relevant to Calico Hills archaeology today as they were to Folsom site archaeology in 1927.

CRITERION I:

The primary requirement is to establish an unambiguous human presence, either *biological* (a recognizable human bone is the best way) or *cultural* (usually an assemblage of artifacts that are clearly of human manufacture).

Look at the Folsom points illustrated in this chapter. Nobody has ever seriously questioned that these exquisitely flaked spear points were made by the human hand. Obviously, they are.

Then look at the artifacts from Calico Hills—and these are among the best ones! Leakey himself selected these "prime tools." In his mind, these are unquestionable examples of human craftsmanship. Yet nearly everyone else who has seen them thinks they're geofacts.

So here's the first problem with Calico Hills: already, it has failed to pass Criterion I—the human presence is not unequivocally established. The Folsom artifacts do it. The Calico Hills artifacts do not (at least not yet).

CRITERION II:

This indisputable evidence of human presence must lie *in situ* (archaeological tech-talk meaning "undisturbed" or "as encountered") within datable geological strata. This is necessary in order to prove an ironclad association between humanity and geological stratigraphy.

A Folsom point—no matter how finely flaked—found lying in spoil dirt does not itself establish that association. But the fluted points found at the Folsom site were left *in situ*, still embedded in the Ice Age clays in which they were found.

The same is true at Calico. The deposits were beautifully excavated, using techniques Leakey developed at Olduvai. Selected finds were kept *in situ* for all to see. No problem here.

CRITERION III:

Finally, the minimum age of the site must be established either through (a) primary association with fossils of a known age or (b) from material itself suitable for reliable isotope age determination (such as radiocarbon dating).

In 1927, it was the first of these options that was satisfied: the Folsom points were undoubtedly associated with bones of extinct Ice Age bison (and hence a late Pleistocene age could be assigned to the artifacts). Since then, with the advent of radiocarbon dating in the 1950s, we know that the Folsom finds are about 10,500 years old.

But at Calico Hills, neither dating criterion has been fully met. Fossils of known age are lacking. And isotopic age determinations remain the matter of considerable debate.

DOES CALICO HILLS MEASURE UP?

These three simple criteria form the underlying logic necessary to evaluate ancient sites around the world. Using these minimum criteria for establishing human antiquity shows us exactly why the Calico Hills site has failed to convince so many.

The problem is not amateur versus professional. The issue is not orthodoxy versus free-thinkers. If Calico Hills is ever to enjoy the breakthrough status of a Folsom site, the data must pass the simple logical steps applied at Folsom three-quarters of a century ago.

Having said this, I still think that a visit to Calico is warranted. Take these three simple criteria with you. Judge for yourself whether the Calico artifacts and features are real. Is this dig an impartial, scientific enterprise or an exercise in hero worship? You decide.

At the very least, you'll have a chance to see the only archaeological site in America with its own freeway off-ramp—only in California!

WHERE ELSE TO SEE PALEOINDIAN ARCHAEOLOGY

The following is a list of sites and museums that feature some of the artifacts and/or remains discussed in this chapter. Complete information on each is listed in the appendix by state at the end of the book.

Arizona State Museum (Tucson, AZ)

Cleveland Museum of Natural History (Cleveland, OH)

Denver Museum of Natural History (Denver, CO)

Maine State Museum (Augusta, ME)

The Mammoth Site (Hot Springs, SD)

Mastodon State Park (Imperial, MO)

Museum and Art Center (Sequim, WA)

Museum of the Great Plains (Lawton, OK)

Museum of Texas Tech University (Lubbock, TX)

R. S. Peabody Museum of Archaeology (Andover, MA)

Royal Ontario Museum (Toronto, ON)

Sandia Cave (outside Albuquerque, NM)

University Museum (Fayetteville, AR)

University of Nebraska State Museum (Lincoln, NE)

Spreading Out Across America

PALEOINDIAN culture was destined to die out, replaced in many parts of North America by people following the *Archaic* tradition. This term "Archaic" has assumed a special meaning, referring to the non-agricultural adaptations that once flourished across large parts of native North America, from the Far West (the Great Basin, California, and the Pacific Northwest), through the Great Plains, and into the Deep South. Although the Archaic adaptations span 10,000 years and a continent, certain key characteristics tie them all together.

DEFINING THE AMERICAN ARCHAIC

As used by archaeologists, the term Archaic means those hunting-gathering-fishing people who are not Paleoindians. The term was initially so used during the 1930s to designate a preceramic, pre-agricultural culture discovered in New York State. The absence of pottery was considered to be the hallmark of this cultural period.

Over the years, as archaeologists expanded their excavations, they came to realize that similar Archaic materials could be found throughout North America. Today, the term Archaic has taken on two rather different meanings, both of which are used in this chapter.

In eastern North America, the Archaic defines a specific period of time between the earlier Paleoindian cultures and the later "Woodland" cultures (generally distinguished by ceramics, moundbuilding, and agriculture, as we'll see in **Harvesting America's Heartland**). Later

49

Location of the key Archaic sites discussed in this chapter.

in this chapter, you will encounter such Eastern Archaic people at Russell Cave (Alabama) and Poverty Point (Louisiana).

But in much of western North America—where agricultural Woodland adaptations did not develop—Archaic refers to a more generalized, nonagricultural lifestyle. In ancient California, the Northwest Coast, and the intermountain West, Archaic lifeways lasted perhaps 10,000 years—well into the period of initial European contact—with people never relying on agriculture in any meaningful way.

There is every reason to believe that Indians of the Archaic period descended directly from Paleoindian ancestors. But the extinction of the Pleistocene megafauna and the spread of the modern deciduous forest produced such significant environmental changes that Archaic people were required to adopt rather different lifestyles from their Paleoindian predecessors.

As Archaic people spread out, they learned to live off the land, and they prospered. Some Archaic groups, particularly those living in high latitudes, depended heavily on hunting for their livelihood. Others, such as the Northwest Coast groups, became experts at fishing. Some, like the Desert Archaic people discussed below, relied on seasonal harvests of wild plants, while Native Americans in the eastern Woodlands would eventually discard their Archaic lifeway in favor of farming. Each tradition of the Archaic was adapted to its particular corner of America, and the rest of this chapter explores some of this diversity.

The Hidden Past at Hidden Cave

Silhouetted at the mouth of the black, endless cave, he stood alone. Far down the desert hillside, his family packed up camp. Where we're going, he thought, we won't need this sheer fishing net I made last fall, or the priceless abalone ornaments given us by our friends from the western seashore.

And why bother lugging those obsidian dart points? While not as easy to work, the chert stream cobbles are everywhere in the mountains we're headed for. We're lucky, he grinned, having our own cave in which to hide our many possessions.

His wife, nearly breathless from climbing up the steep rocky slope, interrupted his thoughts. Wearily, she handed him a deer skin pouch containing the dozen shiny black spear points, the fish net bound with a twisted tule rope, and the string of her shell beads and abalone ornaments. As he stooped and crawled his way into the cool darkness, he whispered goodbye, then carefully placed the precious pouch in a grass-lined pit, covered it with a layer of fresh tule, then laid down the fish net and the ornaments. As he smoothed the cool, almost liquid dust over his cache, he found himself smiling, savoring the day when he would return to recover his valuables.

They would be like old friends, familiar yet novel, like his acquaintances from the faraway ocean. He could still feel the cool sharpness of the dart points he had knapped only last week. With that fish net, he could feed five families for an entire winter . . . and the beads, the ornaments, how they made his wife feel.

He wondered too what would happen before he returned.

Archaeologist Georgia Wheeler leaving Hidden Cave, Nevada, during the summer of 1940. (Courtesy of the Nevada State Museum.)

Would his daughters grow so tall that they, too, would have to stoop to enter this hidden cave? Perhaps, he shuddered, none of them would ever return. The dart points and the fish net might rest there forever. Who could know?

Instinctively, he shifted from future to present. How glad he was not to be hauling his valuables with them as they headed into the mountains.

A scene more or less like this may actually have taken place 4000 years ago at a place called **Hidden Cave** (just east of Fallon, Nevada). As fate would have it, the anonymous Indian man never did return to recover his dart points, his fish net, and the shell ornaments.

We do not know precisely what happened at Hidden Cave. Perhaps he starved because an early frost killed the pine nuts. Perhaps his family kept moving eastward, where the steep mountains provided firewood, more secure shelter, and protection. Perhaps he was killed hunting bighorn sheep high in the ranges to the north. Maybe he just never passed this way again.

Rarely does archaeology tell us much about individuals. But we do know for certain that he never retrieved his tools from this stone "attic" because we found them there, thousands of years later. The cave dust still covered the pit, and the tools were still wrapped in bulrushes. The grass lining had not even been disturbed by pack rats.

Hidden Cave still amazes. Although you must crawl and squirm through the tiny opening, the cave's interior opens up into a huge cavern the size of a modern gymnasium. Archaeologists started digging here in 1940. That summer, occasionally helped out by men from the local Civilian Conservation Corps, archaeologists S. M. and Georgetta Wheeler worked alone inside the pitch-black cave, bedeviled by the choking dust. They tried breathing through a variety of masks and moistened bandanas. They lit up the place with carbide and electrical lights, but nothing really beat the dust and the dark.

Ten years later, Gordon Grosscup and Norman Linnaeus Roust, two students from the University of California at Berkeley, resumed excavations at Hidden Cave. Again working virtually alone, they toiled inside Hidden Cave for two months, recovering hundreds of artifacts and excellent samples of animal and vegetal remains.

Dust and darkness also hampered Roust and Grosscup. Knowing that dust from bat guano posed a health hazard, they wore a succession of dust masks, air filters, and moistened cloths. Their 1951 field notes record that "none of these proved satisfactory and until some more capable experimenters produce the answer, the problem will remain annoyingly unsolved."

As it turned out, I tried to become that experimenter. Having taken my students to Hidden Cave throughout the 1960s and 1970s, I was anxious to see what, if anything, remained unexcavated. Exploring with a weak flashlight, I could see that despite decades of vandalism and illegal relic collecting, large portions of deposits still remained untouched. I decided to take another crack at Hidden Cave.

We spent the summers of 1978 and 1979 digging there, with my crew from the American Museum of Natural History. Much of our time was spent solving logistical difficulties. After installing generators, we experimented with several lighting schemes, settling on a combination of fluorescent and quartz-halogen aircraft landing lights. Finally, excavators could work in artificial daylight everywhere inside the cave.

But it wasn't the pitch black that our predecessors complained about so much, it was the suffocating clouds of dust. Thinking ahead, we acquired loads of surgical masks, only to find that sixty tramping feet raised outlandish clouds of dust. And, once stirred up, the particles stayed in suspension for hours.

So we struck back, installing a series of wooden ramps inside the cave, keeping busy feet off the fine-grained silts. We also drilled through the cave breccia to position a 24-inch electric blower that circulated fresh air throughout Hidden Cave. Although ever-watchful colleagues ribbed me about "air conditioning" our site, the ventilator kept the cave relatively dust free during working hours.

Hidden Cave (Fallon, NV; 12 mi. E. on US 50) is today part of the Grimes Point Archaeological Area. The Churchill County Museum and the Bureau of Land Management cosponsor guided expeditions inside Hidden Cave. By the way, nobody has to crawl their way inside anymore. Thanks to foresighted Bureau of Land Management engineers, you barely have to bend over to get inside. Visitors can also take a self-guided hike along a petroglyph trail outside Hidden Cave. Phone (702) 423-3677.

Working inside Hidden Cave was no picnic—as three generations of archaeologists can attest to. But the hassles of digging taught us some valuable lessons about how Hidden Cave must have functioned in the prehistoric past.

For one thing, whatever else Native American people did in Hidden Cave 4,000 years ago, it's a cinch they never lived there. People usually live in carefully selected places, chosen to satisfy minimal conditions of human life—accessible food, water, and firewood, relatively level ground, adequate shelter, and acceptable levels of heat and light.

Hidden Cave comes up short on all counts, and the archaeological excavations confirmed this: no habitation debris. Instead, we found the archaeological deposits to be riddled with dozens of ancient storage pits, most of them emptied of their contents millennia before we got there. Once in a while, we would luck out and find an unopened pit with its cargo intact.

Oftentimes, archaeology becomes little more than the study of other people's garbage—the science of the half-eaten lunch, broken artifact, and long-cold campfire. But because people did not actually live inside

Hidden Cave, the archaeological deposits did not contain habitation garbage; instead, we found hundreds of still-serviceable artifacts in temporary storage.

Hidden Cave was also like grandma's pantry, a place to stockpile canned goods and preserves. Such storage was part of an overall ecological strategy in which ancient desert people timed their movements to encounter food in sequence: fish spawn in the spring, hard-shelled seeds ripen in the summer, acorns and piñon nuts are abundant in the fall, and so forth.

But not every ecosystem cooperates so readily. What happens, for instance, when all the best resources mature at the same time, say during the springtime, with little available during summer and fall? One obvious way to cope with this feast-or-famine problem is to capture what you can in times of abundance, and store (cache) what you don't need immediately for use later on. In this sense, the food cache is something like a tool cache—it relegates temporarily expendable food surplus into a "passive" state until needed.

Hidden Cave showed us how this strategy worked 4,000 years ago. We recovered hundreds of human coprolites—desiccated human feces. One particular coprolite contained both cattail pollen and charred bulrush seeds. This combination is intriguing because cattail pollen is available only in midsummer, and the mature bulrush fruits can be harvested only six weeks later. Clearly, one or both resources must have been stored. In effect, the Desert Archaic people using Hidden Cave had lengthened the availability of key resources by storing them.

Another coprolite contained pieces of piñon nut hull, bulrush seeds, fish bone, and some unidentified seed parts. We know that piñon and bulrush both ripen in the fall—but not in the same place. Bulrushes grew in the marshy lowlands outside Hidden Cave, but the piñon pine woodland has always been at least twenty miles away (and probably much farther than that). This unlovely little coprolite from Hidden Cave thus conclusively demonstrates how long-distance transport of food helped people survive in the hostile desert habitat.

DESERT ARCHAIC ADAPTATIONS

Hidden Cave tells us how ancient desert dwellers survived in a dynamic, if sometimes malevolent, environment. Four thousand years ago, this well-known locale was utilized variously as a prehistoric attic where people hid tools to be retrieved later, and a pantry where temporarily abundant food items were stashed for future need. But

Hidden Cave is more than that because it documents how the ancient Desert Archaic lifeway worked in western North America.

During the Pleistocene, sporadic populations of Paleoindians inhabited the western American deserts, clustering along the shorelines of huge inland lakes. But as the climate warmed up and the lakes began to dry out, Desert Archaic people, like those at Hidden Cave, began using these marshes to their advantage, collecting bulrush, cattail, and insect larvae, and river fishing during rich spawning runs.

Other Desert Archaic people quit the disappearing lakes altogether, moving into upland mountain valleys. Here they hunted bighorn sheep and collected plant resources in the ever-changing post–Ice Age landscape. These Archaic uplanders survived by pursuing a scheduled seasonal round, commonly moving several times each year.

Piñon pine rapidly spread northward from the Southwest 6,000 years ago, adapting readily to the desert mountains of the intermountain west. Inside each piñon pine cone were dozens of nutritious pine nuts, which ripened over a brief period in the fall. Piñon nuts quickly became a staple wherever available, providing a high-bulk food which could be stored for two or three years.

Survival in these harsh desert conditions required an extraordinary degree of cooperation. Based upon what we know about foraging people of the historic period, we think that the Desert Archaic lifeway must have revolved around the nuclear family, the basic and irreducible unit of survival which was characterized by a simple division of labor according to gender.

Following their Paleoindian heritage, men remained the hunters. But in the Desert Archaic tradition, the economic burden shifted to women. Aside from their role as companion and mother, their abilities to forage and gather wild plant foods made them the principal providers. As one would expect, as woman's economic role became more important, her social status was enhanced. These women of the desert were honored and respected. Not only were they expert herbalists and botanists, but they also became virtuoso weavers, and sometimes even assumed the shaman's duties.

A particularly prosperous woman might take two or more husbands. Since losing a wife was a death sentence in the deserts, and if women were locally scarce, some men elected to share a wife rather than go without.

Brides in Desert Archaic society, where survival often depended on a woman's detailed knowledge of the local resources, were no longer required to move into their husband's home territory. Men, in fact,

Split willow-twig figures recovered from a cave near the Grand Canyon. They probably represent bighorn sheep and were manufactured by Archaic people some 4,000 years ago. Some have been pierced with tiny spears, suggesting that they were made for rituals conducted to ensure success on the hunt. (Courtesy of the American Museum of Natural History.)

commonly moved into the wife's home camp. Without agriculture, these foraging people persisted for thousands of years in their harsh homeland.

As befitted their highly mobile lifestyle, these Desert Archaic people did not individually own either the land or its resources. All comers were entitled to fish, collect plant foods, and hunt anywhere they wished. But good manners always dictated that visitors first request permission to hunt or collect in another's territory.

LIFE IN THE CALIFORNIAN ARCHAIC

Unlike their Paleoindian forebears—who tended to focus most subsistence efforts on a few select species—Archaic people in California exploited an immense array of environments. This broad-based lifestyle served them well because no single resource held the key to their survival. The resulting lifeway survived for millennia, shifting with changing conditions, but always maintaining a balance between people and the land.

Californians found plentiful sources of protein-rich seeds in the

△△△

WHEN DID THE BOW AND ARROW
ARRIVE IN AMERICA?

In the popular mind and the Hollywood film, American Indians are associated with bows and arrows. But archaeology tells us that this association has not always existed. Without doubt, the first Americans arrived *without* the bow and arrow.

The bow appears to have been invented somewhere in the Old World during the late Pleistocene. But nobody knows just where or when. Unmistakable wooden arrow shafts, preserved in archaeological sites in northern Germany, date about 9000 B.C. The bow and arrow was also in use in Africa at about the same time, or even earlier, judging from the rock art of the area. Preserved bow-and-arrow specimens firmly demonstrate the spread of this technology eastward across Asia, but the trail cools as one moves eastward into northeastern Asia, the presumed origin for the New World populations.

The earliest evidence for bow and arrow technology in North America turns up, as one might expect, in the Arctic—perhaps as early as 9000–6000 B.C., but certainly by 3000 B.C. Whatever the actual date of introduction, use of the bow and arrow spread eastward, reaching the Canadian Arctic by 2500 B.C. This new technology moved slowly to the south, reaching the Plains (and perhaps the Great Basin) by about A.D. 200, and spreading into the Pacific Northwest and California by about A.D. 500. Bows and arrows first appear in the so-called Basketmaker caves of northeastern Arizona between about A.D. 500–600, and apparently the atlatl had been entirely replaced in the American Southwest by roughly A.D. 750.

In other words, the bow and arrow seems to be an Old World invention that worked its way eastward across Asia, across the Bering Straits, then down into the Americas in an uneven progression from north to south.

But how—I hope you have been wondering—do archaeologists know all of this? The truth is that much of the above scenario is inference, even guesswork. Only rarely do archaeologists have the luck to actually find the organic remains of bows and/or arrows in an archaeological site. In the American Southwest, for

△△△

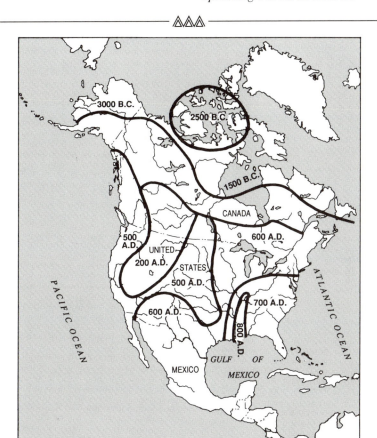

Suggested chronology depicting the spread of bow and arrow across Native North America. Although the general picture is probably correct, archaeologists still rely heavily on educated guesswork in tracking the course of this important invention (after a map by John H. Blitz in North American Archaeologist*).*

instance, numerous bow, arrow, and atlatl fragments have survived in arid caves and rock shelters. But even though these artifacts provide direct evidence of bow-and-arrow technology, the specifics remain rather sketchy because so few of the surviving fragments have been directly dated (by radiocarbon dating, for instance).

Even such preservation is rare. More commonly, archaeologists

△△△

must track the spread of bow-and-arrow technology inferentially. Note, for instance, that throughout this book, I've often used the general term *projectile point* rather than the more common "arrow-head," "spearpoint," or even "bird point." I do this to avoid making assumptions about how a particular artifact was used.

But such assumptions are required when tracking the spread of the bow and arrow. In general, archaeologists believe that the larger points were used on spears and atlatl darts, the smaller points were used to tip arrows. Of course this equation is not perfect, and it's always a judgment call as to what's "large" and what's "small." Still, most archaeologists agree with this assumption, and most of what we know about the spread of bows and arrows through the Americas relies on this inference.

△△△

chaparral, where they also hunted deer and smaller mammals. Along the Pacific coastline, they harvested countless species of fish, shellfish, seals, and even whales that periodically became beached. The mountains provided deer, bear, and elk, plus the plant foods that became available by midsummer. The major rivers served up huge quantities of spawning salmon, trout, and eel.

This ingenious adaptation can be appreciated today at **Chaw'se: Indian Grinding Rock State Historic Park**, located in the hilly and wooded Sierra Nevada foothills. Chaw'se contains a typical reconstructed Miwok village including bark houses, a ceremonial round-house, acorn granaries, shade ramadas (open porches), an Indian game field, and multiple demonstrations of traditional arts, crafts, and games. These reconstructions and demonstrations give present day descendents of the Miwok an opportunity to preserve their traditions and to share them with others.

Traditional Miwok houses were made by tying together cedar poles with wild grapevines, then covering the shelter with incense cedar bark. The bark, taken from dead trees, was overlapped to make the house waterproof; a hole in the top let the smoke escape from the cooking and heating fires. The village was the primary political unit in Miwok life, although on occasion several villages might form an alliance. Miwok villages varied in size from two dozen to several hundred people, each village owning a specific territory.

The California State Artifact, *an eight-thousand-year-old effigy depicting a grizzly bear, excavated from an archaeological site in San Diego County, California.
Recognizing the multicultural importance accorded the grizzly bear in California
mythology—from earliest Native American times through its enshrinement on
California's State flag—a coalition of archaeologists, professional museologists, and
representatives of the Native American community brought this unique artifact to
the attention of the California public. On June 24, 1991, Governor Pete Wilson
signed legislation recognizing this artifact as "The California State Prehistoric
Artifact," the first archaeological artifact so recognized in the United States. (Drawing of an artifact cast provided courtesy of Henry C. Koerper, Cypress College.)*

The park also includes numerous ancient rock carvings: circles,
spoked wheels, animal and human tracks, wavy lines and so forth.
Some are heavily patinated, suggesting an antiquity of perhaps 2,000 to
3,000 years. The key feature of this site is a monumental outcropping of
marbelized limestone with 1,185 mortar holes, the largest concentra-
tion of bedrock mortars in North America. *Chaw'se* is the Miwok word
for grinding rock, and this feature became the hub of Miwok village
life, a gathering place where women could relay news while they
ground the day's acorn meal.

Acorns were harvested in the fall, dried and stored in large granaries,
called *cha'ka*. Made of four or more poles arranged around a stump or
stone, then woven together with slender brush stems, these granaries
were sometimes eight feet tall or even higher and looked like huge
baskets. They were lined with pine needles and wormwood (also called
mugwort, an aromatic plant that warded off insects and rodents) and
thatched with white fir or incense cedar to shed snow and rain. Such
granaries could hold a family's winter supply of acorns—about 1,000
pounds. Properly stored, acorns could help the Miwok survive the
winter.

Like most nuts, acorns are rich in protein and fat, but they are bitter
because they contain tannin. To make acorns edible, the Miwok

Outstanding examples of the world-famous coiled Chumash basketry. Beginning with the European explorers and settlers, collectors have eagerly accumulated Chumash baskets, which are notable for their decoration and fine workmanship. (Courtesy of the American Museum of Natural History.)

cracked and shelled them, then placed the acorn meat into a mortar cup, and pounded it with a stone pestle into the texture of fine meal. After sifting the meal, the Miwok women repeatedly poured hot and cold water through the meal to leach out the tannin. This prepared meal was then mixed with water in a large, watertight cooking basket. Hot rocks were added to the acorn mush, and it was stirred with paddles

---

Chaw'se: Indian Grinding Rock State Historic Park (Volcano, CA; ½ mi. off SR 88 at 12881 Pine Grove-Volcano Rd.) is a 135-acre preserve where ancient Miwok Indians carved out hundreds of mortar cups in limestone as they ground acorns for food. A ceremonial roundhouse, the largest in California, and recreated village are featured. The *Chaw'se Regional Indian Museum* includes artifacts, presentations, exhibits and audiovisual programs representing nine Sierran Indian tribes. Phone (209) 296-7488.

---

until the meal was cooked. Soup, biscuits, and bread were also made of acorn meal.

Archaic Californians managed their homeland with a gentle hand. Lightning fires have always been a threat to the indispensable acorn harvest, and Archaic people clearly understood the principles of fire ecology. They knew that the chaparral became ecologically unstable when it was overly mature. When fire finally did erupt, it could be catastrophic. They took preventive action by deliberately setting brushfires to burn off older growth, litter, and seedlings. Periodic torching of the underbrush eliminated the danger of destructive crown fires—which all too often darken today's California summer sky.

Californian Archaic people also understood that a managed burn of chaparral vegetation promoted new growth. Tender new sprouts appeared within a month of a spring burn, providing attractive browse for deer; fall burning was certain to provide springtime fare for the Indian people. Judicious burning also increased the available grazing lands for deer, elk, and antelope, and facilitated the gathering of acorns that ripened after the burning took place. Fires were sometimes deliberately set in oak groves to clear the ground for easier acorn gathering, to decrease the effects of pests such as the acorn weevil, and to kill other kinds of tree seedlings that could eventually out-compete the valuable oaks. Through time, native Californians exploited additional resources and spread into areas that had been previously unsettled.

THE NORTHWEST COAST ARCHAIC

In 1970, tidal erosion exposed a group of ancient Makah houses in the cliff bank facing the Pacific Ocean. This was *Ozette village*, where Makah people had lived in their year-round homes into the late nineteenth century. About 500 years ago, the village of Ozette had been

Tobacco-smoking pipes from the Northwest Pacific Coast. The broken pipe (middle-left) has a human figure on one end and a thunderbird on the other. The bottom-left pipe is made of sculpted and inlaid steatite, a soft and easily carved stone. The figure at the front of the pipe is probably a dog in harness; the figure at the rear is probably a turtle. At the far right is a pipe decorated with a human figure surmounted by another human head. (Courtesy of the American Museum of Natural History.)

flattened by a destructive mudflow that crushed entire houses, and buried thousands of artifacts beneath a ten-foot-deep mantle of blue-gray clay. Working with archaeologists from Washington State University, the Makah people assisted in reconstructing their own rich history as whalers, sealers, fishermen, hunters, craftsmen, and warriors.

In archaeological parlance, Ozette is a "wet site," meaning that the deposits are so water-saturated that destruction by fungi and bacteria has been radically reduced. Finding a "wet site" is phenomenal good luck for an archaeologist because instead of digging up merely stone and bone remnants, fragile materials made of wood and fiber will also be recoverable. In effect, what Pompeii had preserved by volcanic ash, Ozette protected with mud.

The artifact inventory from Ozette is truly phenomenal, numbering in excess of 50,000 items. Planks from the cedar houses were preserved, as well as the narrow sleeping benches that once lined the house interior. There were woven cedar bark pouches containing harpoon

A selection of Northwest Coast artifacts of stone and abalone shell from beaches of the Columbia River. The notched stones on the left, sometimes decorated, were used as net sinkers. The pendant (center-right) is made of abalone; the incised bowl (upper-right) is made of sandstone. (Courtesy of the American Museum of Natural History.)

— ⚠⚠ —

HOW TO READ ANCIENT ROCK ART

Nobody knows how many rock art sites exist in North America. The count for the American West alone approaches 25,000 individual sites; by contrast, only a few hundred rock art sites are known from east of the Mississippi. Numerous sites have been protected and interpreted for the public, and several of these are listed in the Appendix of this volume.

The most basic technical distinction is between a *petroglyph* (an engraving on stone) and a *pictograph* (a painting on stone). Petroglyphs, the most common form of Native American rock art, occur by the thousands, particularly in the West. They are produced by pecking, incising, carving, scratching, or abrading; sandstone, welded tuff, and granite are particularly common substrate surfaces.

By contrast, pictographs are painted, most commonly with red ocher pigment, usually hematite (an oxide of iron). In a few areas—particularly near Santa Barbara, near the Four Corners, and in western Texas—true polychrome paintings have been produced, with blues, greens, yellows, and black added. In some locales, it is clear that petroglyphs have also been painted.

Rock art specialists define "styles," with varying degrees of success. The most general descriptive scheme distinguishes between *naturalistic* and *abstract* styles. Naturalistic (or "representational") rock art, usually depicting simplified human or animal forms, is widespread across North America, with several clearly regional variants. Abstract rock art, with little recognizable referent, is largely restricted to the American Southwest, California, and the Great Basin.

Dating rock art is notoriously difficult. The most obvious dating technique is *superposition*, in which elements of one style clearly overlap an earlier style. In the Great Basin, for instance, some archaeologists believe that the scratched technique usually overlies pecking, suggesting that scratched styles are later; others disagree.

Often, the mineral pigments used in pictographs are mixed with an organic binder, such as grease, fat, or even blood; when applied thickly enough, flecks of this ancient paint can be col-

— ⚠⚠ —

lected and directly dated by radiocarbon methods. Particularly in the arid West, a kind of *desert varnish* accumulates on petroglyph surfaces, making the older elements much darker than those added later. This is called dating by *patination*, and recent research suggests that the degree of patination itself might be datable using new, high-tech methods.

In particularly fortunate cases, datable archaeological deposit overlaps the rock art surface; thus, when the archaeological deposit is dated (by radiocarbon or some comparable method), one knows that the rock art must be older. Or sometimes, inside caves, pieces of the painted ceiling have spalled off and become incorporated in archaeological strata, once again providing a "minimum age" estimate for the rock art.

Finally, researchers can sometimes date naturalistic rock art styles by content. At several western locales, hunters are shown using bows and arrows. Since we know that the bow is a relatively recent introduction to native North America, any rock art style

Pecked anthropomorphs near Dubois, Wyoming. These deep-cut images show men disguised as bison and in bird costumes. (Courtesy of the American Museum of Natural History.)

Geometric and realistic representational petroglyphs, located along a rock escarpment behind Pueblo San Cristobal, New Mexico. (Courtesy of the American Museum of Natural History; photographs by N. C. Nelson.)

Petroglyph of a huge bear figure, on a rock ledge behind Pueblo Largo, in the Galisteo Basin of New Mexico. (Courtesy of the American Museum of Natural History; photograph by N. C. Nelson.)

Petroglyphs of human figures wearing kachina face masks at Pueblo San Cristobal, New Mexico. (Courtesy of the American Museum of Natural History; photograph by N. C. Nelson.)

This pecked animal, probably a cougar, is one of dozens evident on the sandstone boulders in the Petrified Forest National Park, Arizona. (Courtesy of the American Museum of Natural History; photograph by N. C. Nelson.)

incorporating bow hunting must also be "late." Conversely, rock art depicting atlatls (or spearthrowers) is thought to be "early." But all such dating attempts are discouragingly general and error prone; the failure to establish firm stylistic chronologies has severely hampered interpretive analysis.

So how do you read rock art? The simplest answer to this question is "you don't." For decades the question has bedeviled rock art researchers. Explanations of specific panels and styles vary considerably: the images were aids to memory (recording maps or myths), accounts of important events (such as astronomical occurrences or battles), simple doodling, ancient decoration, child's play, or that great archaeological catchall—works of ceremonial significance.

There is no simple explanation for most Native American rock art because it served so many purposes. Moreover, once in place, rock art panels take on a life of their own and sometimes acquire new and entirely different explanations through the ages, each successive culture incorporating the petroglyphs and pictographs into new images for their own purposes.

One final word is in order here. Rock art, by its nature, is extremely vulnerable to destruction and defacement. Petroglyphs often occur on small boulders, which may be carried off by the thoughtless visitor. Sometimes, even huge rock art panels are "collected," the vandals blasting or jack-hammering away the matrix. Often rock art panels occur on flat, soft stone surfaces, and successive generations of visitors often feel compelled to deface the earlier symbols with modern graffiti.

When visiting a rock art site, your best move is to *keep hands off*. Do not make rubbings. Do not enhance the rock art with chalk outlines. Do not collect any artifacts that might be scattered about. Also keep in mind that many ancient rock art sites are considered to be *sacred sites* by some modern Native American people. Please respect their customs and beliefs when you visit the sites of their ancestors.

Paired horned serpents and Kachina-style mask at Pueblo San Cristobal, in New Mexico's Galisteo Basin. The checkerboard collar on the left-hand figure is typical and thought to signify corn. (Courtesy of the American Museum of Natural History; photograph by N. C. Nelson.)

blades, wooden clubs for dispatching seals and fish, fine tools for woodcarving, pendants, hats, baskets, toys, and weaving equipment, and an extraordinary life-sized wooden effigy of the dorsal fin and back of a killer whale, studded with more than 700 sea otter teeth. Because the deposits contain still-green alder leaves and cedar bark, excavators know that the site was destroyed in June.

Thus, instead of piecing together the past from indiscriminate discards, archaeologists working at Ozette had before them the entire range of Makah household items. Some archaeologists think that Ozette is the most significant archaeological find in North America—an American Pompeii. Washington State University excavated there for eleven field seasons until they shut down operations in 1981.

Makah Cultural and Research Center (Neah Bay, WA; on SR 112) exhibits the heritage and archaeology of the Makah people. Many items on display were recovered during archaeological excavations at the village of Ozette, which contained the largest precontact Northwest Coast Indian collection in the country. Reconstructions of the Ozette cedar longhouse and the oceangoing canoes are displayed. Phone (206) 645-2711.

Unfortunately, the Ozette site is inaccessible today. But the public is welcome at the **Makah Cultural and Research Center**, located about fifteen miles from Ozette, on present-day Neah Bay, Washington. Owned and operated by the Makah Indian Nation, this is the sole repository for archaeological materials discovered at the important coastal village of Ozette.

BISON HUNTERS OF THE NORTHERN PLAINS

The Great North American Plains—a flat land of cold winters and hot summers, of sparse and unpredictable precipitation—cover three-quarters of a million square miles. Here Paleoindians hunted mammoths and other now-extinct Ice Age game. Then at the end of the Pleistocene, the primeval northern conifer forest was gradually replaced by deciduous forest. Sometime between 8000 B.C. and 6000 B.C., these forests were in turn replaced by a postglacial vegetation cover of perennial grasses. Trees occur today only in stream valleys, scarp lands, and hilly localities.

Plains Archaic people prospered for hundreds of generations by following their natural cycle of hunting game of all kinds, gathering seeds, tubers, nuts, and berries. While the Plains Archaic lifeway emphasized variety and broad-based subsistence, bison hunting was always critical for survival.

Early Europeans exploring the Great Plains were astounded by the countless numbers of "wild cows," American bison that roamed across an endless "sea of grass." Nobody knows how many bison once populated the Great Plains, but estimates run as high as 60 million at the time of European contact. The concerted effort of Euro-Americans to drive the American bison into extinction was nearly successful, with fewer than 1,000 animals surviving by the late 1800s.

Long before the European horses came to the Plains, Native American hunters developed highly successful ways of harvesting these huge beasts. Although sometimes they hunted buffalo individually, they learned the hard way that driving a stone-tipped arrow or spear through the tough buffalo hide was no easy task. Many arrows were lost before one struck home. This is why the Plains Archaic hunters developed the art of "buffalo jumping," a singularly successful way to take large numbers of bison without the dangers and uncertainties of individual stalking. Buffalo jumps employ a highly sophisticated hunting technique, and archaeologists are only beginning to understand their complexity.

The hunts began spiritually, with medicine men and women carrying out elaborate and time-honored rituals necessary to ensure that buffalo would come close enough to the camp to be easily taken by hunters. This was considered a deadly-serious venture, ultimately controlled by the supernatural. Every Plains tribe had specific songs, charms, dances, ritualistic offerings, and prayers for calling in the bison. Among the Blackfeet, certain buffalo songs could be sung only during times of near starvation.

On the night before the buffalo drive, a medicine person would slowly unwrap a pipe, and pray to the Sun for success. The next morning, the man assigned to call in the buffalo arose very early. He told his wives that they must not leave the lodge, or even look outside, until he returned. They should burn sweet grass and pray to the Sun for his success and safety. Without eating or drinking, he joined the others and went up on the prairie.

Then the "buffalo runners" were sent out to locate the herd, and begin driving the bison toward the jump. Disguising themselves in buffalo hides and wolf robes, the runners passed near the herds, mostly females, cautiously luring the game toward the cliffs. One specially trained buffalo runner tried to entice the herd to follow him by imitat-

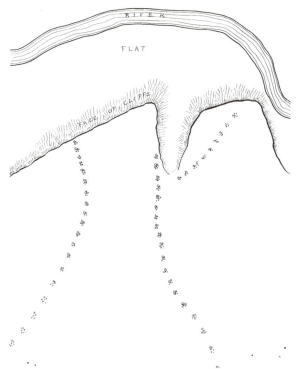

Field sketch by ethnologist Clark Wissler of an ancient bison drive site on Two Medicine River, south of Browning, Montana. From the highest part of the bluff, a series of boulder piles were built outward across the grassland. The left-hand line extended for about two miles. The bison were driven between the rock alignments and then propelled over the cliff, free-falling for about ten feet before landing on the sharp slope of broken rock, where the survivors were dispatched with stone mauls. (Courtesy of the American Museum of Natural History.)

ing the bleating of a lost calf. Several days might be required to position the animals for the kill.

The herd was also directed toward ambush by a cleverly constructed V-shaped drive lane, edged with hundreds of stone men (also called "soldier cairns" or "dead men"). Such drive lanes can extend for miles, usually forming a V-shape toward the cliff edge. Because bison can only dimly perceive such features on the horizon, they mistook the soldier cairns for human hunters, and instinctively moved toward the center of the drive lane.

Once the drive actually started, dozens of people hid behind brush piled on the cairns, keeping the animals from turning back by shouting and waving buffalo hides. As the herd concentrated in the drive lane, hunters rushed up from behind, trying to panic the beasts into a thundering reckless rush over the steep cliff. This stampede must have been a frightening sight, since buffalo can reach speeds of thirty-five miles per hour. These drive lanes usually ended abruptly at the edge of a steep cliff. Often, such cliffs faced into the prevailing winds, so bison were prevented from scenting the hunters.

As they reached the cliff's edge, most buffalo plunged blindly downward. The fall killed many outright; others were disabled by broken legs and backs. Because the barricades prevented escape, hunters could easily dispatch the living with arrows. This step was particularly important because Plains Indians believed that any escaping animals would warn the other herds, and the buffalo would go away.

Today, the best place to see how a bison jump worked is at the **Head-Smashed-In Buffalo Jump** in Alberta, Canada, one of the oldest, largest, and best-preserved bison jump sites in North America. According to Piegan Indian legend, Head-Smashed-In got its name 150 years ago, when a young hunter wanted to see for himself the dramatic plunge of the buffalo over the steep sandstone cliffs. Standing below the cliffs, like somebody behind a waterfall, he saw hundreds of beasts hurtle to their deaths. But because the hunt that day was so successful, the carcasses piled up in front of him, and he became trapped beneath the cliff. When his people arrived to begin the butchering, they found him with his skull crushed beneath the weight of the dying buffalo.

The Olsen Creek Basin, an area about 2,500 acres, served as the "gathering basin" for the Head-Smashed-In buffalo jump. A natural grazing area, the basin attracted huge buffalo herds particularly in the early fall, when bison could graze on the nutritious late-maturing grasses. Nearly 500 people were required to operate Head-Smashed-In.

Not far from the cliff and bison jump at Head-Smashed-In, on the flatlands below, is the campsite where bison parts were processed. A few tipi rings (stones used to anchor the hide tents against the wind) can still be seen on the prairie surface today.

The buffalo provided Plains Indians with life—food, clothing, and shelter. Nothing was wasted. Because successful buffalo jumps provided considerably more meat than could be consumed immediately, several steps were taken to preserve the meat for the future. Much of it was sliced into thin strips and hung on racks to dry in the sun. Many times, this dried meat was then converted to the food staple, pemmican. This was done by pulverizing the sun-dried meat with a stone maul. Buffalo fat and grease were then added and, sometimes, to enhance the flavor, chokecherries. The mix was placed in a hide container, then pounded to remove all the air. So stored, pemmican could keep for many

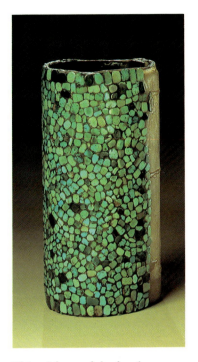

Deer bone spatula or scraper, inlaid with turquoise and jet, was excavated at Pueblo Bonito. (Courtesy of the American Museum of Natural History.)

This wickerwork basket from Pueblo Bonito was encrusted with a worked turquoise mosaic. (Courtesy of the American Museum of Natural History, photograph by P. Hollembeak and J. Beckett.)

This frog effigy, made of jet and inlaid with turquoise, was recovered from Pueblo Bonito in 1897. Pueblo people sometimes consider the frog as a ritualistic symbol of water and perhaps such symbolism operated during Anasazi times as well. (Courtesy of the American Museum of Natural History.)

Painted sandstone mortar from Pueblo Bonito. (Courtesy of the American Museum of Natural History.)

Three black-on-white mugs recovered from a single room at Pueblo Bonito, New Mexico. (Courtesy of the American Museum of Natural History, photograph by P. Hollembeak and J. Beckett.)

Overview of Pueblo Bonito, Chaco Canyon, New Mexico. (Courtesy of the American Museum of Natural History, photograph by Russ Finley.)

Plaited basket with herringbone design, from Granch Gulch, Utah. It was found stuffed to the brim with red and yellow corn kernals. (Courtesy of the Wetherill-Grand Gulch Project and the American Museum of Natural History, photograph by Bruce Hucko.)

Assorted Basketmaker artifacts collected in the 1890s from Grand Gulch, including clockwise from top center: coiled basket, siltstone tablet with incised cross design, wooden crook-necked staff, bone flute, turkey feather blanket, and Olivella shell necklace. (Courtesy of the Wetherill-Grand Gulch Project and the American Museum of Natural History, photograph by Bruce Hucko.)

This painting, by George Catlin, shows two Sioux hunters disguised in wolf skins. This stalking technique was highly effective because the bison were so accustomed to prowling wolves that they took little notice, allowing hunters to creep within bow-shot. (Courtesy of the American Museum of Natural History.)

Stone axes, hafted in willow handles and tied with yucca binding, recovered from a Basketmaker cave in Allen Canyon, Utah. (Courtesy of the Wetherill-Grand Gulch Project and the American Museum of Natural History photograph by Bruce Hucko.)

Two thousand year-old tule duck decoys from Lovelock Cave, Nevada. (Courtesy of the National Museum of American Indian.)

Human effigy jar in the form of a hunch-backed squatting female, from Alkali Ridge, Utah. (Courtesy of Wetherill-Grand Gulch Project and the American Museum of Natural History, photograph by Bruce Hucko.)

Some of the enormous Clovis points recovered from the Richey-Roberts cache near Wenatchee, Washington. (Photograph by R. M. Gramly.)

Anthropomorphic stone sculpture from the Puget Sound area, Washington. (Courtesy of the American Museum of Natural History.)

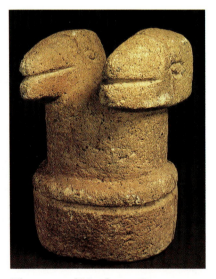

This unusual Northwest Coast stone bowl from the Lillooet River area has two protruding birdlike or fishlike projections. (Courtesy of the American Museum of Natural History.)

The Great Kiva at Casa Rinconada in Chaco Canyon, New Mexico. (Courtesy of the American Museum of Natural History.)

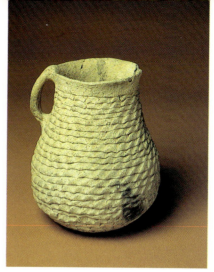

This corrugated ceramic pitcher from Chaco Canyon was manufactured during the Pueblo I-II period. (Courtesy of the American Museum of Natural History, photograph by P. Hollembeak and J. Beckett.)

Excavated ruins of "Yellow House" at Kin Kletso, Chaco Canyon. (Courtesy of the American Museum of Natural History, photograph by Russ Finley.)

A modern pathway leads visitors through the impressive circular ruins at Tyuonyi, in Bandelier National Monument, New Mexico. (Courtesy of the American Museum of Natural History, photograph by Russ Finley.)

Aerial view of Aztec Ruin, a Chacoan outlier in northwestern New Mexico. (Courtesy of the American Museum of Natural History, photograph by Russ Finley.)

This rare 1917 photograph shows the freshly completed excavations and reconstructed Great Kiva at Aztec Ruins, New Mexico. The print was later hand-tinted. (Courtesy of the American Museum of Natural History, photograph by Earl Morris.)

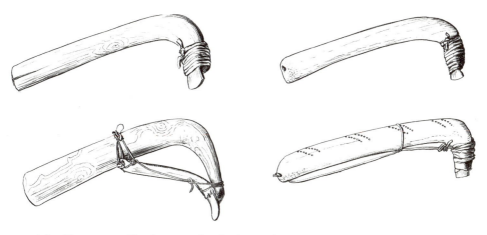

Adze-like scrapers like these, made of either antler or wood, were used by Blackfeet artisans for scraping and removing hair from hide. (Courtesy of the American Museum of Natural History.)

months. Buffalo tongues were often awarded to those responsible for ensuring the success of the hunt, particularly medicine men and women.

Nearly every scrap of the flesh was eaten, of course, but that was only the beginning. Dressed with the hair left on, buffalo skin protected from winter's cold; once the hair was removed, it became a summer sheet or blanket or was made into moccasins, leggins, shirts, and dresses. Tanned buffalo skins covered the lodges, the warmest and most comfortable portable shelters ever devised. Using rawhide with the hair shaved off, Plains people made parfleches, trunks in which to pack and transport small items. The tough, thick hide of the bull's neck became a war shield capable of stopping an arrow, turning a lance thrust, or even deflecting the ball from an old-fashioned, smooth-bore gun. The green, untanned hide became a kettle for boiling meat. The skin of the hind leg made moccasins and boots. Other parts were fashioned into cradles, gun covers, whips, mittens, quivers, bow cases, and knife-sheaths. Strands of hide were braided into ropes and lines. Buffalo hair was stuffed into cushions, and later, saddles. Buffalo horn provided spoons, ladles, and small dishes. Horns also decorated war bonnets. Glue was rendered from the hoofs, and used to fasten back and belly sinew to bows to strengthen them. Ribs became scrapers for dressing hides, and runners for small sleds drawn by dogs. Lashed to a wooden handle, the shoulder blades became axes, hoes, and fleshers. Fitted on a stick, the skin of the tail became a fly brush.

Head-Smashed-In Buffalo Jump Interpretive Centre (Ft. Macleod, AB; 18 km. NW on Hwy. 785, off Hwy. 2) presents exhibits on the ecology, history, and excavations at one of America's best-preserved Plains Indian buffalo hunting areas. The interpretive center, built into a grassy hillside, blends into the surrounding landscape. Highly qualified native interpreters explain the site and its significance to the visitor. Phone (403) 553-2731.

So it was that Head-Smashed-In, and dozens of other places, provided the northern Plains people with a way to procure huge numbers of bison. In places, the buffalo bones created deposits almost thirty-five feet deep at the base of the cliff. Consisting of dirt, stone rubble, and bison bones, these deposits were eventually covered with windblown dirt ("loess") and by boulders that fell from the overhanging cliff.

Radiocarbon dating suggests that Head-Smashed-In was first used as a buffalo jump about 5,700 years ago. Two Scottsbluff spear points found at Head-Smashed-In suggest that the site even might have been used in Paleoindian times, although there is no direct evidence linking

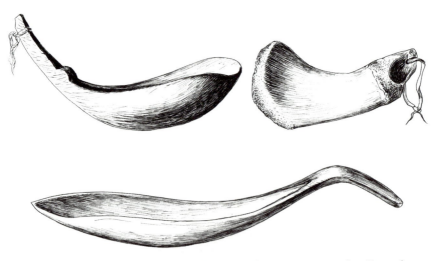

Blackfeet spoons and dippers. Although most such spoons were made of bison horn, the example at the upper-right was crafted from the pelvis of a calf. (Courtesy of the American Museum of Natural History.)

the prepared buffalo jump to these artifacts. The uppermost strata at Head-Smashed-In contain metal arrowheads, confirming that the jump was used into postcontact times. But once the horse and gun became readily available, Plains tribes ceased using buffalo jumps like Head-Smashed-In.

THE SOUTHEASTERN ARCHAIC

A rather different version of the Archaic adaptation can be seen at **Russell Cave National Monument**, less than a mile south of the Alabama/Tennessee State line. At the end of the Pleistocene, this area still experienced severe winters. The freeze-thaw cycles cleaved the large rock masses, and torrents of water carved out this magnificent shelter, one of America's most important Archaic sites, a long tubular tunnel in the limestone that makes up the Cumberland Plateau.

American Indians first visited Russell Cave about 9,000 years ago, probably in the fall and winter. Although these first visitors had a passing acquaintance with domesticated plants, they ate mostly wild plant foods. During the winter months, when fruits and berries were unavailable, nuts and seeds became their important plant foods. They also depended heavily upon hunting deer, plus the occasional gray squirrel, raccoon, rabbit, black bear, and bobcat. Although porcupine no longer live in the area, the presence of their bones in Russell Cave provide biologists with valuable clues for reconstructing the biodiversity of the forest during pre-Columbian times. Meat from these animals was roasted immediately or stored for later consumption. Animal skins were fashioned into clothing, and the bones crafted into a variety of awls and needles for coiling basketry and sewing hides into clothing. Even tiny fishhooks were crafted from bone slivers.

These first visitors probably numbered fewer than two dozen, and left behind only a sparse record of their passing. Nearby, they collected carefully selected chert cobbles and fashioned many spearpoints sitting inside the protected reaches of Russell Cave. Both the broken spear points and the byproducts from their manufacture littered the cave floor. They also discarded grinding slabs for processing nuts and seeds, and distinctive "nutstones" with their small circular depressions perfect for holding a nut steady so that it could be cracked with another rock. Mats were sometimes spread out on the clay floor, leaving impressions for archaeologists to find.

Undoubtedly, a great variety of tools and other artifacts were used inside Russell Cave. But the damp cave environment did not allow preservation of things like basketry, and articles of wood and hide. We also know that from time to time, people died near Russell Cave, and they were reverently buried in shallow pits scooped into the cave floor.

For millennia, people living in this Archaic tradition used Russell Cave as both a habitation and a sheltered workshop. Then, starting about 1000 B.C., during the Woodland period, the character of Russell Cave changed markedly as farmers from a nearby settled village began to visit the site.

Water continued to drip from the ceiling, and gradually pieces of the roof fell in, burying the Archaic cultural debris beneath twelve feet of rubble. Over the years, other groups camped at Russell Cave, drawn there by the natural protection from the elements. Because of the moderate temperatures inside the cave, water flowing through Russell Cave did not freeze in the winter, providing a reliable source of water. So it was that layer by layer, the sediments inside Russell Cave piled up. This remarkable record of human history was slowly sealed beneath a cap of animal droppings, windblown leaves and dust, plus limestone chunks spalling off the cave roof.

The first of the ancient artifacts was discovered in 1953, when avocational archaeologists began digging in Russell Cave. Their test excavations soon revealed the depth and remarkable stratigraphy. They realized that the site held important clues about those who had lived in northern Alabama millennia before. Fortunately, they passed along their findings to scientists at the Smithsonian Institution, who conducted three field seasons of excavation at Russell Cave. In 1961, Russell Cave was declared a national monument and the National Park Service conducted further excavations there.

Russell Cave National Monument (Bridgeport, AL; 8 mi. NW via CRs 91 and 75) is a cave located where the Tennessee River Valley traverses the Cumberland Plateau. This cave is part of a larger cavern that extends about 7 miles into the side of a limestone mountain. Using objects recovered from the excavations, the visitor center portrays the various Native American lifestyles represented in Russell Cave. In the nearby shelter, visitors can see the exposed cave wall rock layers. Nature trails wind through the site. Interpreters demonstrate the Archaic people's tools and weapons. Films and slide shows are presented in the visitor center upon request. Phone (205) 495-2672.

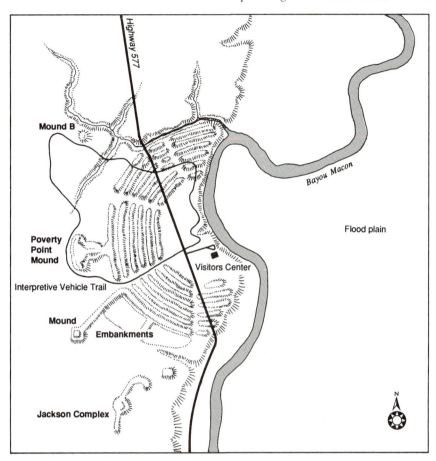

Distribution of earthworks at Poverty Point, Louisiana. The Jackson site post-dates the late Archaic geometrical earthworks (after Jon L. Gibson, Poverty Point: A Culture of the Lower Mississippi Valley).

POVERTY POINT: AN ARCHAIC OMEN OF THINGS TO COME

Another spectacular expression of the eastern Archaic can be seen at the **Poverty Point** site, constructed between about 1800 B.C. and 500 B.C. Poverty Point is best known for the striking earthworks still visible there: one large mound and three smaller ones, interrelated to six concentric low ridges arranged in the shape of a partial octagon. The largest mound looks like a bird with wings outspread; it measures 710 by 640 feet, and stands 70 feet high. Although the smaller, conical mounds superficially resemble the burial mounds of the subsequent Woodland cultures, no human burials have been found in the Poverty

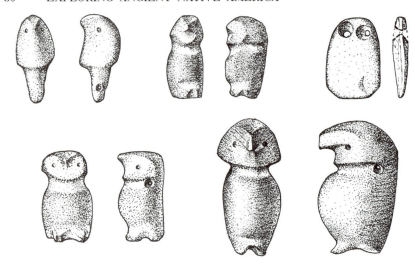

Tiny owl effigies made of jasper, from the Poverty Point site; the largest stands ¾" high. Most have small drilled holes through the head for stringing. (Courtesy of the American Museum of Natural History.)

Point mounds. Instead, one of the Poverty Point mounds was underlain by a bed of ashes and burnt human bone, suggesting that an important personage may have been cremated there, and the mound erected over the charred charnel house.

Millions of cubic feet of earth were required to construct the six concentric ridges, the outermost having an exterior diameter of two-thirds of a mile. So extensive are these earthworks that, when first reported in 1873, investigators thought they were natural levee formations. Only when archaeologists took to the air, in the 1950s, was it discovered that these embankments were man-made artificial ridges. Some of the embankments had houses built on top of them, while others seem only to have served to connect the mounds, or perhaps to mark alignments of some sort.

And more surprises were still to come. Until very recently, archaeologists thought that the Poverty Point earthworks originally formed a symmetrical circle or octagon, and that the eastern side was eroded away by the Arkansas River. But recent geological investigations have established that the bluff along the eastern margin of the site was there for thousands of years before construction began. In other words, the enclosure was deliberately designed in its semicircular, amphitheater-like form from the beginning.

The artifacts from Poverty Point demonstrate not only a high degree of craftsmanship, but they also establish a new pattern of long-distance trade: copper from the Great Lakes, lead ore (galena) from Missouri, soapstone (steatite) from Alabama and Georgia, and various tool stones (used for dart points and knives) from Arkansas, Tennessee, Mississippi, Alabama, Kentucky, Indiana, and Ohio.

The people of Poverty Point did most of their cooking on open hearths or in watertight baskets. To boil water in a basket, Native Americans simply heated up some stones, and dropped them in. But Poverty Point was built on alluvial soil, which lacked the stones commonly used for boiling and for baking. Poverty Point people solved this problem by substituting "artificial stones," ingeniously molded and decorated clay balls—called Poverty Point objects—for the stones they lacked.

Poverty Point people were by no means homogeneous; rather, they were divided into a number of politically, socially, ethically, and linguistically distinct groups, sharing a suite of distinctive artifacts: Poverty Point objects, clay figurines, microflints, plummets, and the extraordinarily well crafted stone beads and pendants. The common denominator is the preference for exotic materials, imported from faraway regions, and use of ground and polished stone artifacts, especially ornaments and other emblems of status.

Baked clay figurines (top) and balls (bottom) from the Poverty Point site. One investigator has estimated that the entire Poverty Point site might have originally contained more than 24 million such baked clay objects. (Courtesy of the American Museum of Natural History.)

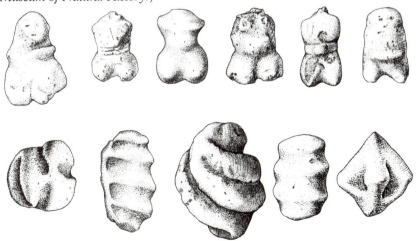

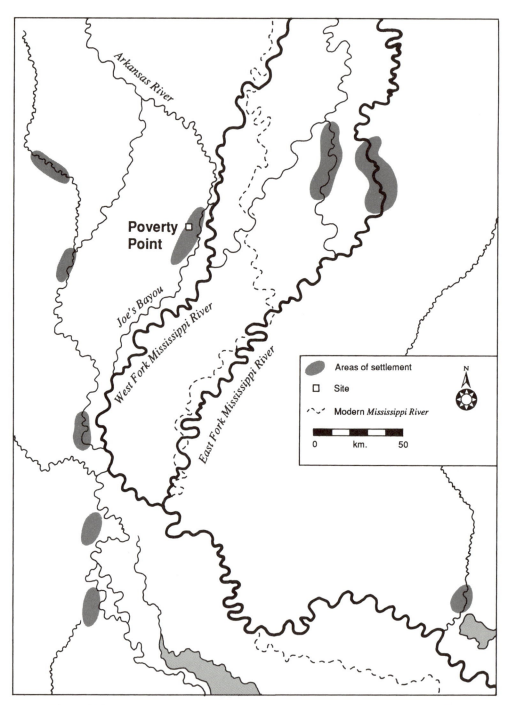

The probable topography of the Lower Mississippi Valley about 1000 B.C. The suggested distribution of Poverty Point community territories is also indicated (after Jon L. Gibson, Poverty Point: A Culture of the Lower Mississippi Valley).

During its peak, about 1000 B.C., people of the Poverty Point culture lived in about ten population clusters, ranging in size from an acre to more than 100 acres. The largest settlement was the Poverty Point site itself, which may have been home to several thousand people. Each population cluster was linked to the others by waterways.

Poverty Point has long posed a problem for American archaeologists. In the traditional view, Native Americans during this time period are believed to have been nomadic hunters and gatherers, living in small bands or rudimentary tribes. Such "unsophisticated" people were thought to have been incapable of joining together for large-scale community projects—such as building the huge earthworks at Poverty Point. According to this conventional wisdom, such monumental construction efforts are possible only after relatively large human populations started living in permanent villages, which were in turn supported by a food-producing, fully agricultural economic base. Because Poverty Point appears to satisfy neither condition, it became enigmatic.

Some archaeologists question this premise. Some think that the distinctive Poverty Point lifeway might have arisen without any agricultural base. Others think that the Poverty Point people did farm, but they farmed in a different manner from most American Indian groups. Instead of growing maize (an import from Mexico), perhaps the fields supporting Poverty Point contained plants native to the American Southeast, like sunflower, sumpweed, and goosefoot. Some evidence also suggests that Poverty Point groups might have cultivated small garden plots of bottle gourd and squash, both for use as containers and for their edible seeds.

Perhaps equally important is the fact that Poverty Point has been viewed until recently as a cultural isolate. We now know that the Poverty Point lifeway extended far beyond the boundaries of the site itself. The Poverty Point culture existed in the lower Mississippi Valley between 2000 and 700 B.C. Today, more than 100 Poverty Point sites

Poverty Point State Commemorative Area (Epps, LA; 4-1/4 mi. E. on SR 134 and 1 mi. N on SR 577) is a 400-acre archaeological site that preserves one of America's earliest and largest prehistoric earthworks. The site has a museum, observation tower, and interpretive walking and vehicle trails. On occasion, visitors can watch excavations in progress. Phone (318) 926-5492.

have been recognized in Louisiana, Arkansas, and Mississippi; so-called Poverty Point influences can be traced as far as Florida, Tennessee, and Missouri. Clearly the Poverty Point phenomenon existed over a huge region, encompassing many people and multiple sites. Granted, the Poverty Point site itself remains unusual, but it is no longer the archaeological mystery of three decades ago.

This elite center was eventually abandoned, and a thousand years passed before eastern North America again saw such elaborate ceremonial spaces. But Poverty Point remains important because it foreshadowed the creativity soon evident elsewhere in the eastern Woodlands.

LESSONS FROM AMERICA'S ARCHAIC PEOPLE

Native Americans would eventually occupy one-quarter of the world's habitable surface, spreading to every terrestrial habitat in the Americas: to the mountains, the deserts, the woodlands, and the prairies of America. As time passed, their varied and sometimes colorful lifeways would anticipate the extraordinary diversity that became modern America.

These were America's foraging people, those living in Hidden and Russell caves, the acorn harvesters of California and the buffalo hunters of Alberta, the whale hunters of the Olympic Peninsula and the moundbuilders at Poverty Point. There are those who would dismiss these Archaic people as simply "primitive," irrelevant to modern concerns because they did not become farmers and they did not live in cities. Today, some think that to be "primitive" is to be backward, shabby, ailing, and famished.

Western civilization has constructed its own past, a perception of history based on platitudes projected backwards in time. Nineteenth-century scholars wrote of the three major stages of human culture: a progression from "savagery" to "barbarism" and finally to "civilization." Later social historians characterized the technological innovations of the past as somehow "rescuing" human beings from the "pressures" of simpler lifestyles and "permitting" new, more progressive customs to unfold. This view assumes that people must always attempt to get ahead, to wrest an edge. It assumes that people must invent agriculture as a natural culmination of human evolution. But does this "civilized" lifestyle necessarily bring with it improvements in the health and well-being of its members? Does this really imply "progress?"

△△△

WHERE CAN I DIG?

There is no substitute for personal field experience, and no textbook or classroom exercise satisfactorily simulates the field situation. Learning to excavate means getting your hands dirty. It all boils down to going on a dig, and there are three ways to do this.

Most archaeologists get their first taste of fieldwork by enrolling in an organized archaeological field school. Major universities and colleges generally offer such opportunities, sometimes on weekends but more often during the summer session. Field schools are conducted on virtually every kind of archaeological site, and living conditions vary from pup tents to relatively plush dormitories. Many instructors require only a passing classroom familiarity with archaeology, whereas others accept only relatively advanced graduate students.

It is increasingly possible to join a dig as a volunteer. Many large research and cultural resource management projects rely on nonpaid participants to supplement the paid staff. A number of overseas excavations rely almost exclusively on volunteers who pay their own transportation, and exchange their on-site labor for room and board. Earthwatch is an organization that pairs selected archaeological projects with motivated volunteers willing to help out. Although somewhat more expensive than the average archaeological field school, Earthwatch excavations provide rare opportunities to become involved in worthwhile (and sometimes glamorous) archaeological fieldwork.

Avocational ("amateur") archaeological societies also offer numerous opportunities to excavate. In many cases, these nonprofessional groups are well trained and adequately supervised. The best ones coordinate their own excavations with ongoing professional-level research.

But some caution is advised here. Current ethical standards discourage private collectors from digging up artifacts. In many instances, "pothunting" is illegal, and the courts have recently upheld a number of convictions for such looting. Although most archaeological societies discourage illegal and unethical destruction of archaeological sites, a few outlaw groups still sponsor "digs" for the sole purpose of obtaining artifacts. If you have any

△△△

━━━━━━━━━━━━━━━ ΔΔΔ ━━━━━━━━━━━━━━━

question about the integrity of an archaeological society, a local university or museum can usually clarify the situation. As a rule of thumb, you might ask a couple of key questions: What professionally trained archaeologists are involved in the excavations, and what happens to the artifacts once they have been dug up? If no responsible archaeologist is involved, and/or if the artifacts end up in private hands, you are advised to steer clear of the dig.

Below are listed several sources for obtaining information on current fieldwork opportunities in archaeology. But a couple of additional warnings are in order. Fieldwork opportunities vary from year to year, and you should obtain the most current information before making plans. And having supervised a dozen such digs, let me enter a personal plea: Before signing on with any expedition or field school, be certain you know what you are getting into. Archaeological excavation is physically taxing, and field camps can be socially intense. Neither you nor the dig will benefit if you are unable or unwilling to participate fully. If you have specific questions, by all means talk to the archaeologist in charge before making a commitment. Do not get in over your head.

CLEARINGHOUSES

Archaeology magazine publishes a list of "classifieds" which include entries for archaeological field schools, both domestic and abroad. Other dig possibilities may be advertised elsewhere in the magazine (address: P.O. Box 928, Farmingdale, NY 11737).

"Field Opportunities Bulletin" is published annually by the Archaeological Institute of America; there is a charge (53 Park Place, New York, NY 10007).

━━━━━━━━━━━━━━━ ΔΔΔ ━━━━━━━━━━━━━━━

America's Archaic past tells us that the answer is no. Today's short-sighted view of "progress" ignores the fact that specialization can itself be destabilizing. How many people realize that farmers often must work much harder than hunters, gatherers, and fishing people? Typical preindustrial farmers spent four to six days working the fields. The California and Northwest Coast foragers may have needed to work only two days a week to feed their families. Farming people usually require that even their children help out in the fields. Children in foraging societies are not typically part of the labor force.

———————————— △△△ ————————————

"Your Career in Archaeology" is available from the Society for American Archaeology (808 17th Street, N.W., Suite 200, Washington, DC 20006).

The American Anthropological Association provides information regarding field school opportunities (1703 New Hampshire N.W., Washington, DC 20009)

PAY-AS-YOU-GO ARCHAEOLOGY

Earthwatch helps paying volunteers join two-week archaeological expeditions throughout the world (617/926-8200).

University of California Research Expeditions Program allows the general public to join small University of California research excavations around the world; no experience necessary. Partial student and teacher fellowships available (University of California, Desk K5, Berkeley, CA 94720).

Crow Canyon Archaeological Center allows nonexperienced participants to join excavation teams working on thirteenth-century Anasazi pueblos. Adult programs of a week or more are available June through October (800/422-8975).

Several museum and independent travel groups offer specialized travel packages to archaeological sites, often with professional archaeologists as guest lecturers. Although few offer hands-on possibilities, several visit ongoing excavations; be certain to find out the exact itinerary before joining up. A partial listing is available in *Archaeology* and *Natural History* magazines.

———————————— △△△ ————————————

Native people of California achieved the highest aboriginal population density in North America, without an agricultural base. The nonagricultural people of the Great Plains and the Northwest Coast crafted ecologically viable alliances capable of weathering the long-term storm. Desert Archaic people maintained a virtually unchanged adaptation to the harshest of environments for 10,000 years.

We have much to learn from nonagricultural foraging people. These generalizing economies have a demonstrated longevity, a degree of long-term cultural stability and survival unknown in today's world.

WHERE ELSE TO SEE ARCHAIC ARCHAEOLOGY

The following is a list of sites and museums that feature some of the artifacts and/or remains discussed in this chapter. Complete information on each is listed in the appendix by state at the end of the book.

Alaska State Museum (Juneau, AK)

Anderson Marsh State Historical Park (Kelseyville, CA)

Chumash Painted Cave State Historic Park (near Santa Barbara, CA)

Coyote Hills Regional Park (near Fremont and Newark, CA)

Glenbow-Alberta Institute (Calgary, AB)

Hearst Museum of Anthropology (University of California, Berkeley, CA)

High Desert Museum (Bend, OR)

Hueco Tanks State Historical Park (El Paso, TX)

Idaho Museum of Natural History (Pocatello, ID)

Illinois State Museum (Springfield, IL)

Kwagiulth Museum & Cultural Center (Quathiaski Cove, BC)

Los Angeles County Museum of Natural History (Los Angeles, CA)

Madison Buffalo Jump State Historic Site (Three Forks, MT)

Maine State Museum (Augusta, ME)

Malki Museum (Banning, CA)

Mammoth Cave National Park (Cave City, KY)

Museum of Anthropology (University of British Columbia, Vancouver, BC)

Museum of Man (Balboa Park, San Diego, CA)

Nevada State Museum (Carson City, NV)

Newfoundland Museum (St. John's, NFL)

Patrick's Point State Park (Trinidad, CA)

Port Au Choix National Historic Park (Port Au Choix, NS)

Providence Mountains State Park (near Blythe, CA)

Sheldon Jackson Museum (Sitka, AK)

Strathcona Archaeological Centre (Edmonton, AB)

University of Alaska Museum (Fairbanks, AK)

University of Oregon, Museum of Natural History (Eugene, OR)

Valley of Fire State Park (Overton, NV)

Writing-on-Stone Provincial Park (Milk River, AB)

AGRICULTURAL
IMPERATIVES IN THE
AMERICAN SOUTHWEST

THE AMERICAN Southwest is classically defined as extending roughly from Durango (Colorado) to Durango (Mexico) and from Las Vegas (Nevada) to Las Vegas (New Mexico). Although this area contains a range of environmental diversity, the Southwestern cultural area has a predominantly arid to semiarid climate, and this aridity has conditioned the nature of human existence here over the past 11,000 years.

When early European explorers entered the Southwest, they encountered diverse Native American groups, some of them subsisting by hunting and gathering natural resources, others relying upon agriculture for their subsistence. Native people of the American Southwest did not adopt full-blown agricultural lifestyles overnight. For a thousand years, maize and other cultivated plants were integrated with the traditional hunting and collecting economies of the preceding Archaic period, without wide-ranging or immediate changes in the environment, economy, or sociocultural context of the people involved.

By about 3,000 years ago, such casual agriculture was well established in the Mogollon Highlands of New Mexico, and these farming people had become increasingly dependent upon it for a significant portion of their diet. Then, between about A.D. 200 and 700, southwestern ecology changed forever—for both farmers and non-agriculturalists.

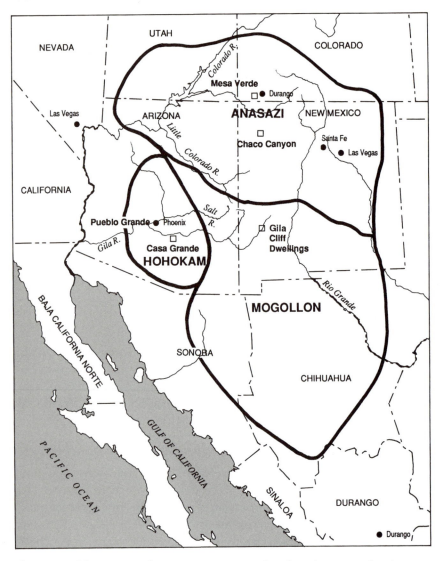

Location of key sites and major precontact cultural traditions in the American Southwest.

Adopting agriculture is hardly an inevitable process, and the archaeological record documents a 2,000-year history of experimentation and population expansion and contraction, shifting population densities within limited areas that subsequently dispersed across the landscape. Sometimes, such expansions succeeded, and stable farming societies lasted for centuries. Elsewhere, the experiment failed, and the land was temporarily abandoned.

But once agriculture took firm hold in the Southwest, exclusive reliance on hunting and gathering was no longer a viable option. High-risk farming, by people showing ingenuity and remarkable technological skill, survived for millennia. This persistence is both an important lesson in itself and a preamble to the achievements that were to follow.

Ceramics and agricultural crops ultimately arrived from the Mexican southland, but they did not travel together. Each would greatly en-

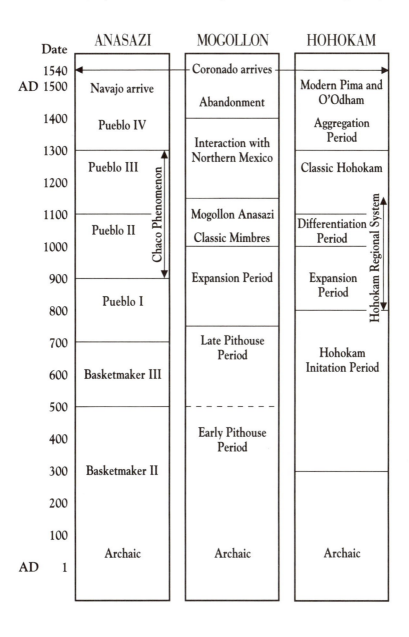

△△△

EARLY MAIZE AGRICULTURE
IN THE SOUTHWEST

Prehistoric American Indians introduced four domesticated plants to the Southwest: maize, squash, beans, and bottle gourd. These are all upland plants, initially domesticated in Middle America.

The most important of these, maize, was the staff of life throughout much of precontact America. Over a 7,000-year period, American Indians domesticated hundreds of varieties of maize, beginning in the semiarid highlands of Mexico with a common wild grass (*teosinte*).

Over the millennia, wild *teosinte* cobs evolved into larger and larger forms, from the thumbnail-sized cob of 5,000 years ago to the massive ears sold in modern markets. In this process, people came to depend increasingly on this plant community, and conversely, teosinte reproduction required that humans physically remove the husks so that seeds could propagate. Such domestication effectively converted a wild species to one dependent upon human intervention for survival. Full-blown agricultural domestication took place when practices like weeding, irrigation, and plowing created new opportunities for plant evolution.

Not only were plant genetics modified, but human behavior was affected as well. Becoming a farmer means taking care of cultivated plants, although the adoption of farming does not necessarily mean that only domestic species are eaten. During the historic period, the Pueblo and O'odham peoples of Arizona, for instance, relied on domesticated foods for perhaps 50–70 percent of their diet. But in some years, they ate little or no domesticated

△△△

hance an already rich Native American heritage in the Southwest.

Archaeologists conventionally divide the late precontact period of the Southwest into three major cultures—the Anasazi, the Hohokam, and the Mogollon—each occupying a distinctive ecological niche within the mosaic of southwestern environments.

These traditions in the American Southwest have conventionally been viewed as societies characterized exclusively by egalitarianism. That the Southwest supported an obvious lack of economic stratification was taken as a reflection of the relatively low level of overall

━━━━━━━━━━━━━━━━━━━ ∆∆∆ ━━━━━━━━━━━━━━━━━━━

food; other years, they lived almost exclusively on their domesticated crops. When crops failed—as they did from time to time—the pueblos broke up into smaller family foraging groups, which were quite capable of living off naturally available foodstuffs.

Early southwestern farmers experimented for centuries with growing various genetic strains of maize at the northern limit of its range. Many archaeologists think that these early southwestern farmers may have lived like historic western Apache people of east-central Arizona, where some of the earliest use of cultivated plants in the Southwest occurred. Seasonally, they moved into the mountains and planted small gardens, which they apparently did not attend with much vigor. Perhaps one-quarter of their diet derived from plant domesticates, with hunting supplying maybe 35–40 percent of their food.

The maize fields were small, less than a half acre or so. Each household owned four to six fields, but usually planted only two or three of them each year. It took a month to prepare and plant the fields, with all family members helping out. When the corn was about three feet tall, most of the people moved away for the summer, to harvest various wild plant foods. In early fall, they returned to harvest and store the crops, which took another month's time.

In effect, these agricultural products began as backups, buffers against failure of key wild foodstuffs such as mescal, piñon nuts, cactus fruits, and juniper berries. Because maize could be stored, it was readily available in time of nutritional stress. Although cultivation was also relatively inexpensive, taking only a couple of months each year, domesticated crops formed the basis of southwestern subsistence and ritual life for thousands of years.

━━━━━━━━━━━━━━━━━━━ ∆∆∆ ━━━━━━━━━━━━━━━━━━━

environmental productivity. But in recent years, Southwestern archaeologists have begun to recognize that in certain key areas—particularly in the Chaco Canyon and Sonoran desert regions—prehistoric systems developed that were not only internally differentiated but which extended their influence far beyond their own boundaries. It has been increasingly difficult to support arguments that Chacoan and Hohokam regional systems retained an essentially egalitarian structure. Below, we explore several alternative models to account for previously unrecognized complexity.

ANASAZI ADVANCEMENTS

The high deserts of the Colorado Plateau comprise the Anasazi home-land. The name *Anasazi* derives from a Diné (Navajo) word mean-ing "enemy ancestors." Although proto-Anasazi people lived in pit houses, between A.D. 700 and 1000 the Anasazi began constructing their distinctive multiroom apartment complexes that would give

TREE-RING DATING

Like many of archaeology's dating techniques, *tree-ring dating* (also called *dendrochronology*) was developed by a nonarchaeolo-gist, A. E. Douglass, an astronomer by training. Because each ring represents a single year, it is, in theory, a simple matter to deter-mine the age of a newly felled tree: just count the rings.

Douglass took this relatively common knowledge one step further, reasoning that because tree rings vary in size, they may preserve information about the environment in which individual trees grew. Because environmental patterning affects all the trees maturing there, these regular patterns of tree growth (that is, ring width) should fit into a long-term chronological sequence.

Schematic diagram showing how a tree-ring chronology is constructed, starting from a sample of known age and overlapping successively older samples until the sequence extends back into the archaeological past.

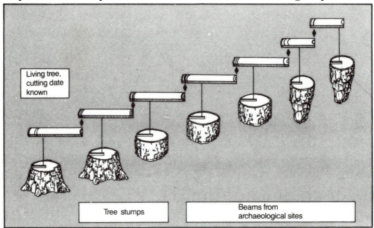

Living tree, cutting date known

Tree stumps

Beams from archaeological sites

their descendents, the Pueblo Indians, their name.

The chronology in the Anasazi area is extraordinary, due primarily to the widespread availability of tree-ring dating. At one site in Chaco Canyon alone (Chetro Ketl), more than 500 tree-ring dates have been compiled thus far, making Chetro Ketl one of the most precisely dated sites in the Americas. The Anasazi chronology is also buttressed by a solid sequence of dates from radiocarbon and other methods.

Douglass began his tree-ring chronology with living specimens; he would examine a stump (or a core from a living tree), count the rings, then overlap this sequence with a somewhat older set of rings from another tree. But the dead trees and surface snags went back only 500 years or so. Further back, dendrochronology had to rely on the prehistoric record.

Fortunately, Douglass was working in the American Southwest, where arid conditions enhance preservation. By turning to archaeological ruins, Douglass began mining a vast quarry of tree-ring data. Sampling ancient beams and supports, he slowly constructed a prehistoric "floating chronology," spanning several centuries but not tied into the modern samples. Douglass could use his floating sequence to date various ruins *relative to one another*, but the hiatus between prehistoric and modern sequences meant that his chronology could not be correlated with the modern calendar.

This "gap"—the unknown span of time separating the ancient, prehistoric sequence from the known, historically grounded chronology—plagued Southwestern archaeologists for years, until finally, in 1929, an expedition at Showlow, Arizona, found a specimen that neatly bridged the gap. The sequences were united, and almost overnight, Douglass was able to tell Southwestern archaeologists when their most important sites had been built: Mesa Verde was erected between A.D. 1073 and 1262, Pueblo Bonito in Chaco Canyon between A.D. 919 and 1130, the Aztec ruin between A.D. 1110 and 1121, plus dozens of others.

Since then, the dendrochronological sequence has been extended back millennia, and many other areas are building their own sequences, including Alaska, the American Arctic, the Great Plains, Germany, Great Britain, Ireland, Turkey, Japan, and Russia.

THE ANASAZI OF MESA VERDE

The evolution of the distinctive Anasazi lifeway can be seen at *Mesa Verde*, Colorado. The term *mesa verde*, Spanish for "green table," refers to the comparatively flat tablelands here, heavily forested with juniper and piñon trees. **Mesa Verde National Park** encompasses eighty square miles, rising 1,800 to 2,000 feet above the valley along the north side and slopes gradually down to the cliffs bordering the Mancos River canyon on the south. A score of spacious canyons cut into Mesa Verde, and some of the world's most famous archaeological sites were constructed in the shelter provided by the hundreds of alcoves that eroded into these cliffs. Only a few of these spectacular ruins have been professionally excavated by archaeologists, and visitors are welcome to only a select few of these.

Anasazi roots extend back into Paleoindian times, at least 9,000 years ago. By about A.D. 600, the first Anasazi settlers—often designated as the so-called Basketmakers—arrived in the Mesa Verde area. Although very little evidence for this early occupation can be seen in Mesa Verde proper, the village of Twin Trees (on Chapin Mesa) contains eight pit houses, two of which have been excavated. These Basketmaker pit houses were sunk a few feet below ground, with four main timbers supporting the roof. A fireplace was set inside, protected with a well-placed air deflector. The people who lived here were sedentary farmers, who raised maize, beans, and squash.

Although the early Basketmakers were agricultural, they did not make pottery. Beginning about A.D. 450, the later Basketmakers made mostly gray and black-on-white ceramics, and they lived in shallow pit houses with antechambers frequently constructed of upright stone slabs. Lined storage containers ("cists") are common inside and outside the structures. Clusters of these pit houses formed small villages; at Mesa Verde, one of these late Basketmaker villages, Step House Cave (on Wetherill Mesa), was built between A.D. 600 to 610; six pit houses were built beneath the overhang. Twin Trees likewise has a late Basketmaker occupation (located not far from the earlier pit houses). Significantly, Twin Trees also contains a larger-than-average pit house which lacks the usual domestic features and strongly suggests the beginnings of village-wide religious observances—for perhaps both villages.

The pit houses in these Basketmaker villages probably each sheltered an extended family—relatives from grandparents through grandchildren. The middle generation most likely formed the core of these

Cliff Palace, at Mesa Verde, is the largest cliff dwelling in the Southwest, containing more than 200 rooms and nearly two dozen kivas. This view was taken in 1931. (Courtesy of the American Museum of Natural History.)

households, with each subhousehold occupying specific living quarters within the pit house, and cooperating to provide a fair share of daily necessities. The Basketmaker village population probably ranged between 40 to 150 people.

Then, throughout the Colorado plateau, the Anasazi entered the *early Pueblo* phase (A.D. 700–900), marked by the transition from pit houses to surface dwellings. Instead of storing supplies in cists and living strictly in pit houses, these Pueblo people built a series of storage rooms behind the pit areas, with ramadas in front of them. Walls were made by weaving branches through uprights, then plastering the foundation with mud. As these wattle-and-daub walls were connected to one another, large habitation spaces were created above ground, presaging the pueblo style of architecture that continues to this day in the American Southwest.

At least some of these Anasazi people continued to utilize pit houses, for the most part in the winter. Sometimes called "protokivas," these pit houses became deeper and in some cases had a *sipapu* (or entrance to the spiritual world), suggesting a gradual change in function away from purely secular domestic activities. (See **The Anasazi Kiva**)

Black-on-white Anasazi mugs. (Courtesy of the American Museum of Natural History.)

The transition to surface habitation was completed during the next phase of Pueblo life, between A.D. 900–1050. By this point, the pit house of earlier Basketmaker times had evolved into the ceremonial kiva. Most such sites consisted of single-story, linear pueblos, often standing in two tiers, with storage rooms in back and habitation rooms toward the front, facing the kiva.

Some of these kivas were huge, exceeding forty feet in diameter. These Great Kivas probably evolved from the ceremonial pit houses of earlier Basketmaker times, serving as centers for key ceremonial activities that united smaller and larger communities. An excellent example can be seen at *Far View Ruins*, an eleventh-century style site on Mesa Verde (four miles north of the Chapin Mesa Museum). Although Far View resembles many of the later pueblos at Mesa Verde, it was used for centuries before the existing walls were constructed. The Anasazi first settled Far View about A.D. 900; their numbers increased to about 500 people by the A.D. 1100s. They built an artificial reservoir at Mummy Lake—capable of storing a half-million gallons of water—draining into the key agricultural areas through canals into terraced fields.

By about A.D. 1100, the population of this area shifted away from Mesa Verde, toward places like *Lowry Ruins*. Pueblo towns grew to more than 1,000 inhabitants, living near Great Kivas or distinctive tri-wall structures (such as that evident at *Aztec Ruins*); both seem to have provided communal meeting areas and places for conducting secret rituals.

About A.D. 1200, people from places like Far View moved ten miles southward, into a larger community of thirty-some cliff dwellings in Cliff and Fewkes canyons. At eye-catching sites like Cliff Palace, Sunset House, New Fire House, and Mummy House, they occupied more than 500 rooms, perhaps 600 to 800 people sharing close, if well-protected quarters. Cliff Palace, the largest and best known of cliff dwellings, was built into an alcove in the east wall of Cliff Canyon; it is best seen from Sun Temple, the D-shaped ceremonial structure directly opposite on the west rim. At Sun Temple—on the promontory formed by the confluence of Cliff and Fewkes canyons—the Anasazi people worshipped. These cliff dwellers farmed fields a walkable distance away. The mesa top contained fertile soil, although less piñon grew here in Anasazi times.

Mesa Verde National Park (southwestern CO) is one of the premier archaeological refuges in the world. During the summer season, visitors can drive along a 12-mile access road to Wetherill Mesa, where two cliff dwellings and four earlier mesa-top villages are open.

Ruins Road makes two 6-mile loops and provides views of about forty cliff dwellings from canyon-rim lookout points. Two pit houses and six pueblos show the architectural sequence of the Mesa Verde structures. Several ruins can be viewed at close range from points along the cliff edge.

Spruce Canyon Trail, a 2-mile round trip, starts from the Spruce Tree House Trail, follows the bottom of Spruce Tree Canyon, and ends in a picnic area around the headquarters. To use this trail, register in the chief ranger's office near the museum.

Two excellent videos are shown to provide some background necessary to interpret the complex history of Mesa Verde. *Anasazi* is a multi-image presentation dealing with the prehistory and discovery of the ruins; *Ta'a Anasazi Ho'Lo'* depicts the lifestyle of Native American people still living in the Four Corners area. Both are shown at Far View Lodge (15 mi. S. on US 160; phone 303/529-4421 or 303/529-4465).

The ruins in Fewkes Canyon—consisting of four intriguing cliff dwellings visible from the encircling road—cannot be entered because of deterioration. Near the head of the canyon is Fire Temple, one of the most remarkable of the ruins. Nearby is New Fire House, composed of two alcoves. In the upper alcove are a number of living rooms; the lower one contains a few living rooms and three kivas. Down the canyon a short distance in a deep, arched alcove is Oak Tree House, with more than fifty habitation rooms and seven kivas. South of this building (directly below Sun Temple) is Mummy House, also in a bad state of disrepair, except for a single, well-preserved room high on the face of the cliff.

THE CHACO PHENOMENON

About A.D. 900, the Anasazi of northwestern New Mexico generated a sustained burst of cultural energy in Chaco Canyon, a place that still amazes visitors today: hundreds of contiguous rooms of beautifully shaped and coursed stonework, three or four stories high, form huge sweeping arcs. Within its thirty-odd square miles, the canyon contains more than 2,400 archaeological sites: nine full-blown towns (the "Great Houses"), each with hundreds of rooms, along a nine-mile stretch.

This is the Chaco phenomenon—large planned towns next to hap-hazard villages; extensive roadways built by people who relied on neither wheeled vehicles nor draft animals. Although affluent enough to import luxury items by the thousands, the Chaco Anasazi eventually packed up and moved elsewhere.

But prior to this, Chaco Canyon was a very unusual place. Between A.D. 1050 and 1300, the Chacoan people defined themselves as some-how special. During these so-called classical times, two distinct kinds of sites appeared. Throughout the Anasazi area, numerous smaller pueblo sites dotted the landscape. What made Chaco unique was the regional system that arose there. Some sites in Chaco Canyon proper, and a few other places on the Colorado plateau, became huge, with both room and kiva size and frequency increasing dramatically.

So arose the Chacoan towns, the most famous of which is Pueblo Bonito (Beautiful Town). It once reached five stories into the sky and could house a thousand people. America would not witness a larger apartment building until the Industrial Revolution of the late nineteenth century. Each of these Great Houses was centrally located amidst a cluster of smaller sites, defining a community.

The Chaco regional system probably originated to solve economic problems, possibly a food shortage triggered by environmental factors in the tenth century. Some view this response as *extensive*—emphasizing the drive to put more and more land under cultivation, for instance. Others feel it was an *intensive* response, as seen in efforts to develop communal ways of controlling water. This latter explanation suggests why the Chaco system developed where it did—in resource-poor Chaco Canyon, rather than elsewhere where resources were better, and where existing population densities were higher.

The key to spiritual and economic good fortune at Chaco may have been turquoise which, by the early A.D. 1000s, was valued across a huge regional network. Although the nearest source is more than 100 miles to the east (at Cerrillos, near present-day Santa Fe), large quantities of turquoise turn up in Chaco Canyon, where it was processed into finished jewelry and other ritual necessities.

Towns that could control and manipulate the turquoise trade seem to have been amassing capital. Chaco people started banking their

Rare photograph of Pueblo Bonito, taken in 1895, prior to excavation. "Threatening Rock," a great 30-ton stone monolith can be seen towering over the site. Ancient Anasazi builders attempted to stabilize it with pine pole props and a wide stone terrace. For years, National Park Service engineers precisely monitored its movements until, during the afternoon of January 21, 1941, Threatening Rock buckled and fell, crushing 65 rooms along the north wall of Pueblo Bonito. (Courtesy of the American Museum of Natural History.)

⟁⟁⟁

THE ANASAZI KIVA

Agriculture fueled the Anasazi lifestyle, and summer rain was necessary for the crops to grow. Anasazi people expected both rainfall and harvests to respond to their prayers and solicitations. Part of the ritual was confined to the underground kiva. Other parts were designed for the open plaza aboveground. In the privacy of the kiva, people sang and prayed and prepared for more public participation. Such ceremonies could last more than a week.

Kivas reflect the Pueblo belief that people emerged from a previous world into this one, and this process was symbolically reflected as they came from the kiva into full view of the plaza. Ritual derived its power from its degree of secrecy. Gradually, from initial induction into Pueblo secret societies to the growing obligations of later adult life, the mysteries of belief were revealed.

The kiva is an earthly representation of the original, primordial homeland, built in darkness underground. Into this, the ultimate cave, Anasazi people descended through the smoke hole by ladder. Set into the ground was the round, shallow, navel-like *sipapu*, symbolic of the place where the Corn Mothers emerged from the earth, assuring spiritual access to still another world deep below.

Kivas are an omnipresent part of the contemporary Puebloan world. But the Great Kivas of the Chaco towns and their outliers (such as Aztec Ruins) were different. Each Chacoan town had a Great Kiva, and several others are found up and down the canyon. The Great Kiva at Chetro Ketl, just down the road from Pueblo Bonito, is more than fifty feet in diameter. Its great curving walls held special niches, each filled with strings of stone and shell beads, then sealed with masonry. There is the encircling bench, the central raised square firebox, the paired rectangular masonry "vaults," and the stair entryway. Massive sandstone disks supported equally huge roof-support timbers, carried, amazingly enough, by hand from mountains forty miles away.

Although the smaller kivas served the local clans, the Great Kivas involved larger social units—perhaps half an entire pueblo. And the largest of these may have nurtured the town as a whole.

⟁⟁⟁

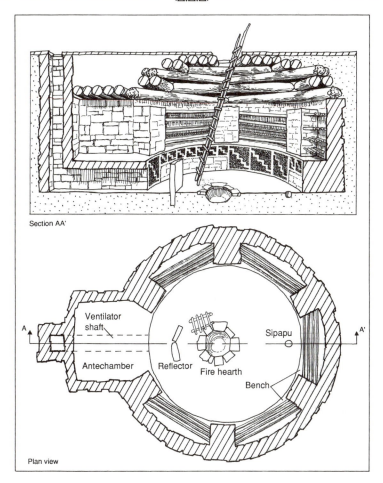

Schematic diagram of some common features contained within pre-contact Anasazi kivas. According to Pueblo religion, the characteristic sipapu is considered to symbolize the place of emergence from the underworld (modified from Peter Nabokov and Robert Easton, Native American Architecture).

Centrally placed for all to see, the greatest of the Great Kivas dominated all directions. So built, the Great Kivas required that ritual extend beyond the human-scale to the natural world beyond.

Characteristic geometric designs on the interior of black-on-white Anasazi bowls.
(Courtesy of the American Museum of Natural History.)

prosperity, storing up resources, and carefully redistributing them to other places under their domain. Before long, a ritual hierarchy took over. Social distinctions began to separate the people living in Great Houses in Chaco from the commoners who lived in scattered villages.

By A.D. 1100, nine large and formal Chaco towns had sprung up. Yet despite the frenzy of building and the long distances required to bring in structural roof supports, it may be that the actual full-time population of Chaco did not increase much. Throughout this extraordinary century, perhaps 2,000 people made Chaco Canyon their home on a permanent year-round basis. But a room-by-room analysis shows that the Chacoan towns could have readily housed three times that number.

In other words, the human population of Chaco Canyon must have fluctuated dramatically. Archaeologist James Judge has suggested that

Some designs painted on Anasazi black-on-white pottery, including the flute player
(Kokopelli), deer, bird forms, and a butterfly. (Courtesy of the American Museum
of Natural History.)

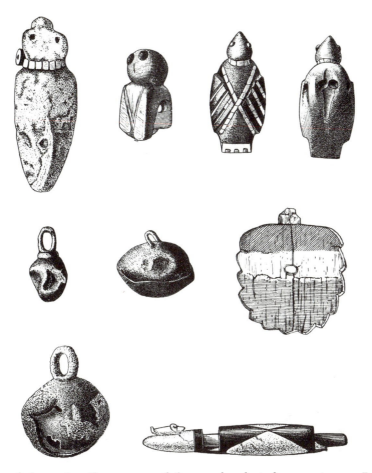

Assorted Anasazi artifacts recovered from archaeological excavations at Pueblo Bonito. Across the top are stone effigy figures; the bird on the right is made of hematite inlaid with turquoise. The carved wooden plaque (center-right) has been painted red, yellow, and green. The copper bells were imported from Mexico. (Courtesy of the American Museum of Natural History.)

floods of relatives showed up in Chaco Canyon during so-called pilgrimage fairs, when Chacoan people from the hinterlands periodically visited the canyon to trade for turquoise, which had become increasingly important in their ritual and ceremonial lives. In good years, travelers may have brought extra food on the pilgrimage, perhaps to trade it for exotics such as turquoise, macaws, or copper bells from Mexico. But if a local community was drought-stricken, and it arrived at the pilgrimage festival hungry, perhaps turquoise wealth could be exchanged for more immediate needs, like food for the clan.

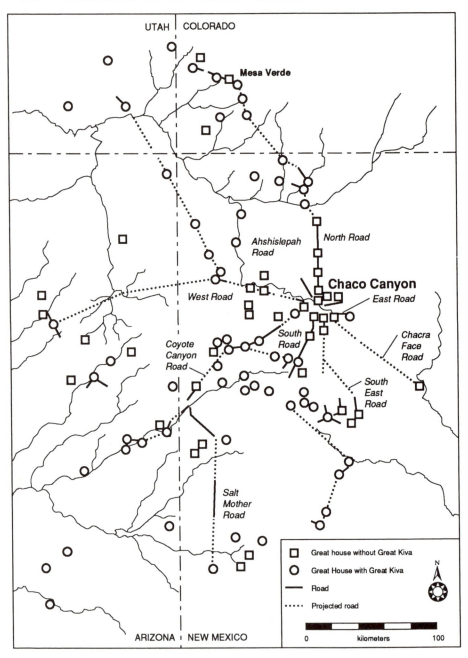

Schematic diagram of Chaco road system as it may have existed by A.D. 1050. Seven major road segments appear to have led into Chaco Canyon, although precise reconstructions are still problematic (after Kathryn Gabriel, Roads to Center Place).

How did all these people get to Chaco Canyon? Archaeologists poring over satellite-produced photographs may have discovered the answer—an elaborate system of arrow-straight roads running hundreds of miles into the surrounding desert. The entire Chacoan system was physically integrated by an infrastructure of roads that spread across three states. The longest and best-defined roads, constructed between A.D. 1075 and 1140, reach more than 50 miles into the hinterland. In some places the Chacoans constructed causeways, and elsewhere they cut stairways into sheer cliffs.

The well-built Chaco roads could have served for communication as well as transport. Several related mesa-top signal stations have been found near Chaco that provide for line-of-sight communication—presumably by smoke, fire, or reflected light. The roads tied far-flung regions together, moving the goods and people required to build and maintain extensive public works. Officials and bureaucrats could travel along the public roads to inspect, to coordinate, and to supervise. The roads themselves may have become symbols of authority, linear banners proclaiming affinity and cooperation, signifying participation in a system whose importance far exceeded the sum of its parts.

The formalized trade fairs were probably scheduled well in advance. Both production and distribution of goods were carefully timed to anticipate the next festival. Although people came from throughout

Various black-on-white ceramic Anasazi animal effigies, including a parrot and a goose with distorted bill. (Courtesy of the American Museum of Natural History.)

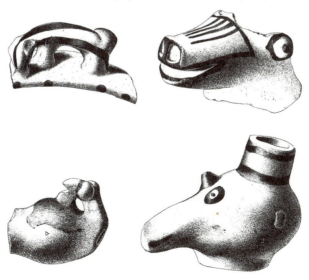

the land, primed to trade their goods and services, they were all identified as Chacoan people. The festivals reinforced this common bond with rituals of belonging. As time passed, ever more pilgrims showed up at the fairs, as spiritual and economic ties bound them more tightly into the Chacoan sphere.

Chaco Canyon was largely abandoned by A.D. 1140 (at least the tree-ring dates suggest that no new construction took place after this date). If people kept living in the canyon after this time, there is little evidence for it. Perhaps the Chaco Anasazi reorganized socially. Or maybe they just moved out, shifting northward, to the San Juan River. Whatever happened, by the mid-twelfth century, the Chaco system had been devastated, due at least in part to the severe drought conditions that gripped the countryside.

Then, about a century later, there appears to be a migration of people from Mesa Verde to Chaco. They brought their classic black-on-white pottery with them, reoccupied some of the old Chacoan sites and constructed others (some of which were actual cliff dwellings). This occupation lasted relatively briefly, the people probably continuing to move eastward. Finally, Diné (Navajo) people moved in during the 1700s and stayed there until 1947, when Chaco Canyon National Monument was fenced off by the National Park Service.

Two views of an Anasazi human effigy, sitting with arms crossed and knees elevated. The ear is pierced and facial painting consists of black dots with parallel margins. A large diamond-shaped pattern covers the backside. (Courtesy of the American Museum of Natural History.)

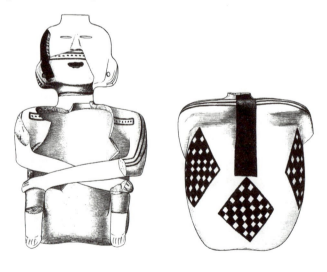

Chaco Culture National Historical Park (northwestern NM; reached from the town of Thoreau by taking SR 57 about 60 mi. N; it is 26 mi. S. of Nageezi Trading Post and 29 mi. S. of Blanco Trading Post via SR 44) preserves the ruins of the major Great Houses and several thousand smaller sites. The park is accessible only over dirt roads that are rough and sometimes impassable in wet weather, visitors should check on local conditions.

Self-guiding trails explore seven of the park's ruins, including Pueblo Bonito, Chetro Ketl, Pueblo del Arroyo, Casa Rinconada, and three village sites. Four other trails lead into the back country; free permits, available at the visitor center, are required.

The visitor center is 1½ mi. from the south entrance. Phone (505) 988-6727 or 988-6716.

THE HOHOKAM OF THE SONORA DESERT

Throughout the blistering deserts of southern Arizona and northern Sonora lived the Hohokam people. The name *Hohokam* is a O'odham word meaning literally "all-used-up," but usually is given the more generic translation of "ancient" or "old ones."

Hohokam communities straddled major continental trade routes, from the California coast to the Great Plains, from the high civilizations in Mexico to the resource-rich Rocky Mountains. Intrepid Hohokam middlemen bartered and transported merchandise as diverse as buffalo and deer skins, sea shells, turquoise, obsidian, rare minerals, finished textiles, salt, exotic feathers, and ceramics.

After looking at the precise year-by-year chronology available for much of the Anasazi area, Southwestern archaeologists have become a bit spoiled, at least in terms of temporal controls. In the Hohokam area, specialists complain bitterly about the second-rate chronology available for Hohokam sites. And to a great extent, they are correct. Chronological problems have indeed dominated Hohokam archaeology for years. This difficulty is easily understood because desert woods are unsuitable for tree-ring dating. Hohokam chronology has been built from a host of less precise techniques, including radiocarbon and paleomagnetic dating, augmented everywhere by less satisfactory ceramic stylistic dating methods. Still, the chronology available for Hohokam sequences is far superior to that available in other parts of this continent. In truth, it is only by comparison with the various

Hohokam stone palette with lizard patterns in bas-relief. Some palettes like this one are stained with lead silicate, which liquifies and turns red when heated; it may be that these palettes were involved with cremation rituals, perhaps as censers or altar pieces. (Courtesy of the American Museum of Natural History.)

Anasazi microchronologies that the Hohokam sequence suffers. By general North American standards, the Hohokam archaeologists have it easy.

It has been only within the past decade that archaeologists have transcended chronological issues to look deeper into the meaning of Hohokam as a behavioral phenomenon. As it turns out, the chronological deficiencies are more than offset by the excellent data available documenting Hohokam demography and intracommunity patterning.

Hohokam archaeologists have recently sketched a picture that is nothing short of astounding: the complexity seen in these parched Hohokam desert sites clearly rivals—and at times uncannily mirrors—contemporary Anasazi developments, particularly those in Chaco Canyon. In a sense, there is a Hohokam phenomenon as well.

Archaeologists long believed that Hohokam origins went back to the late Archaic hunter-gatherer lifeway, with maize agriculture very slowly coming to supplement a traditional diet of game, piñon nuts, cactus fruit and hard-shelled seeds. But recent research along the floodplain of Tucson's Santa Cruz River has changed this view. Archaeologists working along the right-of-way of Interstate 10 through Tucson found several deeply buried sites that have forced archaeologists to reconsider the transition to farming-based village life. Dating to between 1200 B.C. and A.D. 150, these new sites suggest that maize, beans, and squash (and possibly tobacco and cotton) may have arrived during a large in-migration of already agricultural people.

At the Santa Cruz Bend site, archaeological teams found nearly 200 pit structures, including a "Big House" (8.5 meters in diameter) and associated plaza; these public areas may have been used for religious rites and political gatherings, serving as the central focus of the 300 B.C. settlement. Extended families lived in circular house groups, sharing courtyards and storehouses.

By A.D. 700, the end of this so-called Pioneer period of the Hohokam, farming communities prospered along the major river systems of the Phoenix basin, and the Hohokam heartland covered roughly 4,000 square miles. Communities probably ranged in size from a few extended families to more than several hundred people. Already, they were avid traders, exporting cotton textiles, worked stone (particularly obsidian), salt, pigments, turquoise, and other desert resources as far as central Mexico. From the southland, they received stone mosaic mirrors, marine shells, birds with flamboyant plumage, and carefully crafted copper bells. They also traded with

Hohokam red-on-buff jar. (Courtesy of the American Museum of Natural History.)

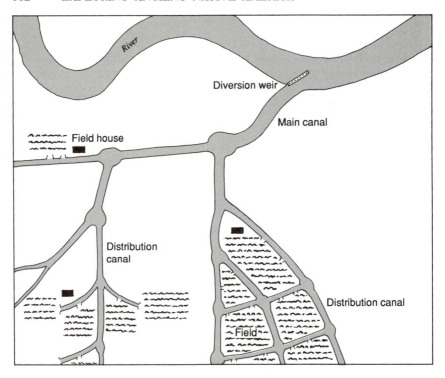

Schematic diagram showing the major components of Hohokam irrigation systems, as mapped in the Phoenix Basin, Arizona (after W. Bruce Masse, Chaco and Hohokam).

their distant Anasazi and Mogollon contemporaries.

A new feature of Hohokam architecture, distinctive large earthen mounds, appeared sometime before A.D. 800; these slope-sided accumulations of trash and dirt may have once served as dance platforms. Hohokam of this period also started a long-lasting trend by cremating their dead.

Between A.D. 700 and 1100, there was an upsurge in population, village size, canal irrigation, and ceremonialism. Trade networks expanded far beyond previous frontiers, funneling scarce and expensive resources to talented Hohokam artisans. Artistic excellence was increasingly expressed in stone, bone, shell, and ceramics.

The largest Hohokam villages during this period were more than 500 acres in size, hosting perhaps a thousand people. Such villages—each with its own ball court—were spaced evenly, at about three-mile intervals, along the main irrigation canals. A privileged elite class seems to have emerged, living in large and exclusive house clusters, enjoying their wealth, and burying their dead in richly accompanied cremations. At this point, understanding Hohokam archaeology depends upon how well one understands the meaning and distribution of two key facilities in Hohokam society: irrigation networks and ball courts.

Particularly impressive was the increasingly advanced technology that harnessed the most scarce Hohokam resource of all: water. Their system of canal irrigation was unrivaled in native North America. Agriculture moved from the flood plains—where nature provided—to the terraces, where considerable human ingenuity was required. During this period, more than 900 miles of main canals were excavated to water the Salt River valley. Some of these canals were massive even by today's standards—seventy-five feet across at the top and several miles in length. Hundreds of smaller ditches snaked across the Sonoran desert, further expanding the horizons of the Hohokam agricultural base. The modem city of Phoenix employs a canal system virtually superimposed on the early Hohokam plan for diverting water from the Salt River, a mute and unintentional tribute to the Native American engineers who came before.

This was a time of awesome human investment, much like the period of feverish building that took place in Chaco Canyon at exactly the same time. Archaeologists have estimated that building just the primary Hohokam canals would have taken 100 laborers—each working a month a year—at least 420 years to construct the main canal systems watering the Salt River valley.

Canal irrigation required not only a tremendous investment in backbreaking labor but, once built, these artificial drainage systems called for constant monitoring and maintenance. Floodgates had to be opened and closed; downstream, the canals had to be periodically mucked out; flood damage had to be rapidly repaired, else the year-round crops would wither. In short, elaborate social mechanisms must have arisen to provide the necessary leadership and coordination to meet the demands of effective water management in the parched desert setting. Particularly challenging must have been the redistribution of agricultural products among villages of vastly unequal rank, to say nothing of overseeing and coordinating the far-flung Hohokam trade network.

During this period, the boundaries of the Hohokam regional system were, in a real sense, defined by the distribution of ball courts. The two are one and the same. It is true, of course, that the distribution of ball

Hohokam ballcourt in Snaketown, Arizona. Only the west half had been excavated in 1935. (Courtesy of the Arizona State Museum.)

courts across Arizona and Sonora corresponds roughly to the distribution of Hohokam red-on-buff pottery and highly distinctive shell ornaments. Still, there is something very special about the way Hohokam people played their ballgame, and where they chose to play it.

Hohokam ball courts appeared about A.D. 800 or so, and proliferated until about A.D. 1150, after which no more ball courts were built. Adobe embankments surrounding the largest ball court—at Snaketown, Arizona—stood 16 feet high and stretched nearly 200 feet on a side. At least 500 people could have stood on these elevated sidelines to watch the goings-on. Two similar ball courts can be seen today at **Pueblo Grande**, in downtown Phoenix, Arizona.

The Hohokam ballgame probably began as an imitation of the ritual athletics in central Mexico, where perhaps Hohokam traders observed the proceedings firsthand. But once back home, the Hohokam developed their own version, including the unique construction of their ball yards.

We cannot deduce what activities and events were specifically associated with these ball courts. While it seems likely that both intramural and intervillage contests took place, we do not know the rules, or the social mechanisms that tied Hohokam populations living in communities without ball courts to communities that had them. Still, on one level at least, ball courts must have provided a socially sanctioned mechanism for legitimizing face-to-face interaction between distant yet somehow related Hohokam populations. By A.D. 1050, the ball court network contained more than 200 venues, all of which appear to be somehow connected to trade. Moreover, some contained cremation burials, the significance of which is unclear.

The ballgame transcended the individual community, the political alliance, and economic cooperative. It probably served a critical latent function of facilitating greater dissemination of goods, services, and presumably marriage partners. Like the irrigation systems, the ball court organizations reinforced the social controls necessary for basic Hohokam survival. The demise of the Hohokam regional network, after about A.D. 1150, corresponds closely to the collapse of the ball court system, which died out and was abandoned by A.D. 1200 or so.

Despite many parallels to contemporaneous Chaco Canyon, what happened next is uniquely Hohokam. Rather than abandoning its core, Hohokam society reorganized itself, leaving the bulk of its population in place. During the Classic Hohokam period, between about A.D. 1100 and 1450, many traditions fell into decline: some of the traditional centers of Hohokam life were abandoned, some groups stopped cremating their dead, craftsmanship trailed off, and few new ball courts were built.

But, curiously, moundbuilding surged during the Classic period, with more and larger mounds being built. More than forty mound sites have been detected in Hohokam territory, the largest of which, at Pueblo Grande, contains up to 32,000 cubic yards of fill. Such an achievement would have taken 100 workers, each laboring a month each year, up to twenty-four years to complete.

Pueblo Grande Museum (Phoenix, AZ; 4619 E. Washington St.) is a large Hohokam ruin along the north bank of the Salt River. The primary ruin is a large, rectangular platform mound of caliche-adobe; elite families may have lived in residences or special-purpose rooms built atop this elevated platform. Two or three ball courts once stood here, as well as a multistory building, numerous room blocks and compounds. The occupation spans the entire Hohokam culture sequence. Phone (602) 495-0900.

The site of Pueblo Grande covers more than 1,000 acres, the central mound framed on the north and south by ball courts. The large compound enclosure contains multiple stores, and many rooms extended in all directions from the mound. Agricultural fields and irrigation ditches must have spread out to the south and west. Two thousand people lived at Pueblo Grande, but most villages at this time were probably much smaller.

By A.D. 1300, some of the Hohokam elite took the unusual step of moving their dwellings to the top of platform mounds, perhaps expressing in architecture their newfound power. At **Casa Grande Ruins**, between Phoenix and Tucson, we see the culmination of this trend in platform-mound architecture. The ground floor of this remarkable four-story house was constructed on a six-foot high earthen platform. In addition to using Casa Grande as their residence, the elite occupants probably used it as a storehouse and astronomical observatory. Most Hohokam villagers still lived in small adobe houses or pit houses.

Casa Grande Ruins National Monument (Coolidge, AZ; 1 mi. N. SR 87) features the *Casa Grande* (Big House) built by Hohokam Indians more than 650 years ago. Partially ruined, the four-story structure is formed of layers of caliche mud and represents the height of Hohokam architecture. Around the main building are the remains of a walled village; vestiges of other prehistoric villages are nearby. Casa Grande was abandoned for unknown reasons in the early 1400s, after the Hohokam had used it for only a century. The visitor center offers interpretive exhibits. Phone (602) 723-3172.

Ceremonialism during Classic Hohokam times became distinctly less public. Compounds, mounds, and walled plazas suggest that a heightened sense of secrecy and seclusion crept into elite lives. Moundtop houses were brightly painted with symbols of power and social status, and elite individuals adorned themselves with exotic turquoise, worked marine shells, and gaudy feathers.

Disaster must have struck the Hohokam heartland about A.D. 1400: once-flourishing towns were stripped and burnt, or they were gradually forsaken. Nobody is sure why. It may have been an environmental problem—floods, increasing salt buildup in the soils, deteriorating climate. Or perhaps the problem was more cultural in origin: maybe the strutting elite were brought down by civil warfare, maybe trade routes were disrupted (remember the problems in the Anasazi area at the same time), maybe the centers of power shifted south of the international border. Some archaeologists would even extend the Classic period to A.D. 1600, suggesting it may have been undermined by introduced

Schematic representation of Hohokam trade routes and materials. This network, which reached its peak between A.D. 800 and 1100, linked the various ballcourt communities along the Little Colorado River (to the north) with their counterparts along the international border (after David E. Doyel, Chaco and Hohokam).

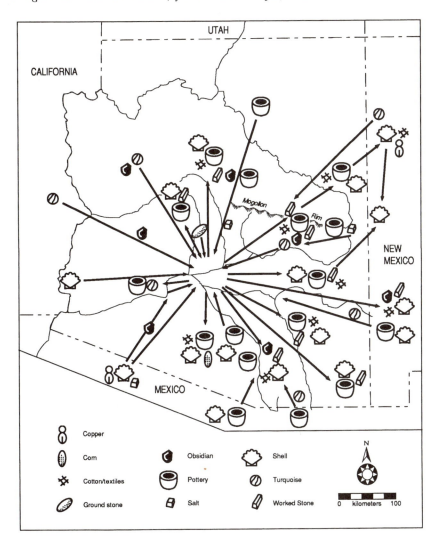

European diseases. We do know that by the time Jesuit Father Kino said mass at Casa Grande in 1694, this great village already lay in ruins.

There is no consensus about whether the Hohokam were ancestors of the O'odham Indians who greeted the first European explorers in the Sonoran Desert. The Hohokam and historic-period O'odham built similar dwellings and council houses, participated in ballgames, had a similar subsistence base, and buried their dead in similar ways.

Perhaps 5,000 O'odham people lived in the Phoenix basin during the seventeenth century. But only two centuries earlier, the population must have been between 40,000 and 50,000 people. Whatever the cause, it is clear that such a drop in population must have drastically simplified the post-Hohokam lifestyle—perhaps simplifying directly into the historic O'odham existence.

As one might expect, the O'odham people see their own history somewhat differently. They deny that the ancient ones, the Hohokam, were their ancestors. O'odham oral tradition holds that those who built the mound sites were an evil people they call the *civanos*. The O'odham believe that their ancestors arrived from the East, driving the wicked *civanos* out of the Phoenix basin. These two mechanisms— warfare and migration—would indeed seem to explain the dramatic population decline between about 1400 and 1700. Increasingly, archaeologists are recognizing the truth contained in such oral traditions.

FARMERS OF THE MOGOLLON HIGHLANDS

The Southwest's third major cultural tradition—called *Mogollon* (after the distinctive Mogollon rim that forms the northern limit of Arizona's central mountains)—remains more controversial. In fact, over the years, the Mogollon tradition has been treated like the poor stepchild of Southwestern archaeology.

The initial idea of a distinct Mogollon tradition first was proposed by archaeologist Emil Haury in 1936. Many Southwestern archaeologists were reluctant to accept Mogollon as truly distinct from its two universally recognized neighbors, the Anasazi and the Hohokam. It also irked archaeologists from adjacent areas that ceramics seemed to be more ancient in the Mogollon area than among the well-studied Anasazi.

Today, archaeologists universally recognize the distinctive Mogollon culture of the prehistoric farmers who lived in the forests and upland meadows along the Arizona–New Mexico border. In the most basic sense, it is now clear that living in the mountains required an ecological adaptation distinct from either desert dwellers (such as the Hohokam) or plateau inhabitants (such as the Anasazi).

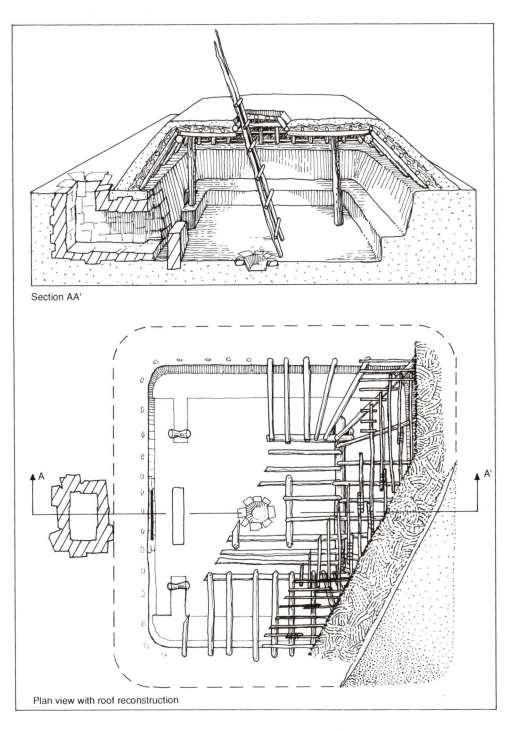

Section AA'

Plan view with roof reconstruction

Schematic diagram of a domestic pithouse, such as those built by Mogollon people (modified from Peter Nabokov and Robert Easton, Native American Architecture).

Three Mimbres bowls (ca. A.D. 1000–1200). The "kill" hole in the bottom, made when the bowl was included as a mortuary offering, helped release the vessel's spirit into the next world. (Courtesy of the American Museum of Natural History.)

The basic Mogollon pattern emerged from its late Archaic roots about A.D. 200 and survived until A.D. 1400. The best visitable archaeological site in the Mogollon tradition is **Gila Cliff Dwellings**, north of Silver City, New Mexico. Protecting more than 500 acres, this national monument contains an early Mogollon pit house typical of those inhabited prior to A.D. 1000. The Mogollon people who dwelled in such pit house villages made distinctive plain brown and red-slipped pottery. These earliest villages, usually adjacent to good farmland, were apparently occupied year-round. Many were fairly large; sometimes fifty or more pit house depressions are evident on the surface. Many were situated for defensive purposes.

Then, beginning about A.D. 1000, Mogollon individuality merged with the Anasazi tradition, as people began to construct aboveground dwellings. People of the so-called Mogollon Pueblo tradition lived in Anasazi-style aboveground apartments focused inward toward a plaza. They constructed rectangular ceremonial rooms (or kivas) within regularized pueblo room blocks. Mogollon Pueblo parents commonly bound the skulls of their offspring against stiff cradle boards, producing the distinctive flattened crania that were considered attractive.

The most visible archaeology at Gila Cliffs belongs to this Mogollon Pueblo tradition. There are seven caves along a side-canyon cliff reaching 150 feet above the canyon floor; five of these contain forty masonry rooms built into the recessed rock-shelters 150 feet above the canyon floor. The roof timbers show that these rooms were built about 1275 or so. The Mogollon Pueblo retained a distinctive culture despite increased trade and actual co-residence with Anasazi people after A.D.

1000. But unlike their Anasazi neighbors, the Mogollon tradition did not survive as a recognizable cultural entity into the historic period.

Within the southern Mogollon territory of southwestern New Mexico, a distinctive variant emerged known today as Mimbres. More than 100 pit houses and over 400 Classic Mimbres surface rooms have been excavated. An extensive research effort, most of which was directed at a narrow time range (the period A.D. 650–1150) took place during the 1920s and 1930s, however, very little is available for public viewing.

And yet, these Mogollon people have become world famous as makers of the legendary Mimbres pottery. Painted with long brushes of yucca fibers, the intricate motifs range from complex geometric designs to stylized human forms, birds, bats, bighorn sheep, rabbits, and insects. The earliest Mimbres pottery, dating from about A.D. 750 to 1000, is painted in the classic black-on-white tradition. Later pots, made between A.D. 1050 and 1200, employ polychrome designs, particularly blacks and reds. Mimbres pottery commonly accompanied the dead, and these pots were often "killed" with neat holes punched through the bottom, symbolically releasing the spirits of the painted figures.

Unlike the Chaco and Hohokam areas, Mogollon territory shows little evidence of significant social stratification. Although the Mogollon practiced irrigation, the effect was nothing like that seen among the Hohokam: no exceptionally large sites, no even spacing of villages

Line drawings of various Mimbres bowls showing a range of human and animal depictions. (Courtesy of the American Museum of Natural History.)

along river courses, no settlements controlling a disproportionate amount of wealth (as measured in exotic turquoise and sea shell artifacts).

Instead, the Mogollon cultural tradition seems to reflect an unbroken, village-based development lasting more than nine centuries. Then, about A.D. 1400, Mogollon sites were inexplicably abandoned—a curious development given the abundance of rich agricultural land and water that seemed everywhere available.

Gila Cliff Dwellings National Monument (near Silver City, NM; a 2-hour drive 45 mi. north of Silver City via SR 15) features Mogollon ruins near the west fork of the Gila River. A 1-mi. trail leads from the parking area to the dwellings. The visitor center is 2 mi. from the entrance. Phone (505) 536-9461.

WHERE ELSE TO SEE SOUTHWESTERN ARCHAEOLOGY

The following is a list of sites and museums that feature some of the artifacts and/or remains discussed in this chapter. Complete information on each is listed in the appendix by state at the end of the book.

Acoma (Sky City, NM)

Anasazi Heritage Center (Dolores, CO)

Arizona State Museum (Tucson, AZ)

Aztec Ruins National Monument (Aztec, NM)

Bandelier National Monument (outside of Santa Fe, NM)

Bryce Canyon National Park (Panguitch, UT)

Casa Malpais (Springerville, AZ)

Capitol Reef National Park (Torrey, UT)

Denver Museum of Natural History (Denver, CO)

Edge of the Cedars State Park (Blanding, UT)

Heard Museum (Phoenix, AZ)

Hovenweep National Monument (Utah/Colorado boundary)

Lowry Ruins (Cortez, CO)

Maxwell Museum of Anthropology (Albuquerque, NM)

Montezuma Castle National Monument (near Camp Verde, AZ)

Museum of New Mexico (Santa Fe, NM)

Museum of Northern Arizona (Flagstaff, AZ)

Navajo Tribal Museum (Window Rock, AZ)

Newspaper Rock State Park (Monticello, UT)

Petrified Forest National Park (outside of Gallup NM)

Puye Cliff Dwellings and Communal House Ruins (Española, NM)

Salmon Ruin (Bloomfield, NM)

Southwest Museum (Highland Park, Los Angeles, CA)

Tonto National Monument (Globe, AZ)

Tusayan Ruin and Museum (Grand Canyon National Park, AZ)

Tuzigoot National Monument (Clarkdale, AZ)

Walnut Canyon National Monument (Flagstaff, AZ)

Wheelwright Museum (Santa Fe, NM)

Wupatki National Monument (Flagstaff, AZ)

HARVESTING THE EASTERN WOODLANDS

THE PALEOINDIANS of eastern North America followed a more generalized ecological adaptation than their western counterparts, one not as easily disrupted by the disappearance of one or two key resources. As it turned out, this broad-spectrum lifestyle laid the foundation for the versatile plant collecting economies that characterized the eastern Woodlands during later periods. As their population increased, people of eastern North America became more efficient, intensifying their own food collecting strategies, increasing economic exchanges with others, and improving their ability to store food for the future. In this way, even as their food-producing economy escalated, they learned to protect themselves against year-to-year resource fluctuations.

Inevitably, some groups harvested more effectively and produced more food than their neighbors. Others excelled at trade and barter. As time passed, primary access to the more valued "exotic" items came to rest in the hands of a relatively small elite. In response to growing competition over scarce resources, the older, more egalitarian social forms came to be more rigid and controlled.

Poverty Point (considered in chapter 2) foreshadowed the creativity that would soon be evident elsewhere across the eastern Woodlands. Between 2000 and 1000 B.C., native people began a long-term interaction with local plant species they found growing wild—especially squash, sumpweed (or marsh elder), sunflower, and goosefoot. As people harvested the wild bounty, they usually selected only the best plants

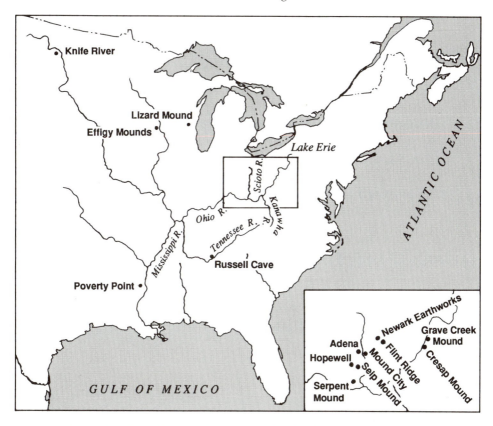

Some key archaeological sites in the Eastern Woodlands.

and kept only the best seed for replanting. Given sufficient time, such selection would activate genetic pressures for seeds to germinate more quickly than did untended plants in the wild.

Farmers of eastern America came to be inextricably involved in the life cycles of these plant crops. Their gardens, informally planted at first, became increasingly significant by providing a dependable, managed food supply that could be stored for late winter use and even into early spring.

So it was that the native annual plants of the eastern Woodlands were incidentally domesticated. Seasonally occupied campsites, surrounded by organically rich trash deposits, provided ideal habitats for wild plants and incidental domesticates. These new and vigorous seedbeds in turn attracted further human attention. Tethered to the major river valley trenches, Native American people reoccupied special places and key locales over extended periods of time. As human

△△△

THE WOODLAND TRADITION: WHAT IS IT?

Most of the cultures introduced in this chapter fall under the umbrella term *Woodland*. But wherever possible, I have avoided this term because it tends to confuse many people unfamiliar with the peculiar usages of archaeology. Still, like Archaic and Paleoindian, Woodland has a special meaning in American archaeology, so an aside about its various meanings is probably in order.

The Woodland tradition has historically been defined by the presence of three key traits, or hallmarks:

- Manufacture of distinctive ceramics,
- The incipient development of agriculture, and
- Construction of funerary mounds.

Throughout much of eastern North America—including the Midwest, the Southeast, the Northeast, and the eastern Great Plains—the Woodland period follows on the heels of the Archaic.

Although the time frame for the Woodland period varies considerably by location, most Woodland characteristics appeared by 1000 B.C. (or somewhat earlier) and lasted until replaced by other cultures—such as the Mississippian in the Southeast and the Plains Village Tradition on the Great Plains—between A.D. 700 and 1200.

Elsewhere, as in the Far West, where so-called Archaic lifeways continued into the historic period, the suite of Woodland characteristics never appeared at all.

One reason I sidestep this Woodland terminology is to avoid confusion with the quite useful term "eastern Woodlands," which generally denotes the eastern half of native North America, those billions of acres of primeval forests, cut by countless coursing "river roads."

△△△

populations increased, the interactions between people and plants intensified.

Note something special here. We used to hear about the so-called Neolithic Revolution, a time of rapid change when humans took control over nature, domesticating plants and animals to provide a predictable and secure food source, and to escape the uncertainties of nature. By inventing agriculture, the thinking went, the requirements of storing grain created a demand for durable, heat-resistant storage vessels—therefore, some genius thought up pottery. So viewed, agriculture and pottery were seen as co-paving the road to the great civilizations of the past.

No such overnight, food-producing rebellion ever happened—at least not in eastern North America. The entire process of initial plant domestication was extremely casual, without any radical change in human diets or human habits.

The effects of such incidental plant domestication can readily be seen at a place like Russell Cave, Alabama, where foraging Archaic people lived and worked beneath the huge overhang for thousands of years. Then, sometime between about 1000 B.C. and A.D. 500, the character of Russell Cave changed markedly as the site became tied into the changing lifestyles of settled village farmers. Just as agriculture did not develop overnight, neither did the manufacture of fired pottery. Pottery showed up in parts of South Carolina, Georgia, and the Florida coastal lowlands during the late Archaic period (roughly 2500 B.C.).

The earliest ceramic vessels look like flowerpots, remarkably similar to the earlier steatite (stone) bowls from the same area. Some of these early ceramic pots were even tempered with steatite fragments, and it is tempting to assume that early southeastern potters were consciously imitating these early stone bowls. Although the evidence is difficult to interpret, many archaeologists think that these early northeastern ceramics were invented locally, then spread throughout the eastern Woodlands between 2500 B.C. and 500 B.C.

Although most of the pottery found at Russell Cave is plain, sherds are sometimes decorated with incised patterns or impressions from fabric applied while the clay was still wet. Other changes took place in the artifact inventory as well. The smaller projectile points during this period suggest use of the bow and arrow. Bone tools were more finely finished, and people decorated themselves with ornaments of bone and shell.

Russell Cave reflected the changes that characterize much of the eastern United States during this time. Apparently these farming people left their settled villages when food supplies ran low and transformed Russell Cave into a temporary winter campsite. When they quit the cave in the springtime, they probably rejoined other Woodland groups at summer encampments, settlements far larger than any known during the preceding Archaic period.

THE ADENA CULTURE (1000—100 B.C.)

Like agriculture and pottery, the third defining Woodland characteristic—burial ceremonialism—actually shows up during the late Archaic period (at Poverty Point, for instance). Before long, the funerary
mound complex was to sweep across the eastern United States. In fact,
one burial mound of this period stands only a few hundred feet from the
entrance to Russell Cave.

The *Adena culture* is the most visible manifestation of the new American ceremonialism. Distributed across the American midlands to the
Atlantic coast, at least 500 Adena sites have been documented, most of
them dating after 500 B.C. In the early Adena period, burial ceremonialism was relatively simple. The deceased was commonly laid out in a
shallow, sometimes bark-lined pit; then an earthen mound was erected
over the spot; during later Adena times, the dead were commonly
interred in more elaborate log tombs. The original mound often grew in
size as subsequent burials were interred and covered over. Sometimes
burials were sprinkled with red ocher or other colored pigment.

The Adena Mound, excavated in 1901, was located near Chillicothe, Ohio. Its earlier stage began with construction of a large, subsurface bark-lined tomb containing extended and cremated burials, and
continued with the addition of log tombs and more burials. The second
stage was composed of distinctly different soil which had been heaped
over the dead who were not buried in log tombs.

Although the Adena Mound cannot be visited today, you can see a
similar Adena period structure at the **Grave Creek Mound State Park**
(in Moundsville, West Virginia). Also known as Mammoth Mound,
Grave Creek is the largest known Adena-period construction, originally standing nearly seventy feet tall, with a flattened top sixty feet in

---

Grave Creek Mound State Park (Moundsville, WV; 801 Jefferson
St.), is a 69-foot mound originally surrounded by a moat crossed
by two passageways. When the mound was tunneled into in 1838,
two burial chambers housing numerous relics were discovered.
The adjacent *Delf Norona Museum* named after a former director,
tells the story of the Grave Creek Mound and contains an impressive display of Adena materials. Phone (304) 843-1410.

diameter; it is considered by some to be the largest prehistoric Indian burial mound of its kind in the world. Its base was surrounded by a circular ditch, perhaps a moat. Excavated early in the nineteenth century, Grave Creek Mound yielded up a rich array of Adena materials, and an engraved stone tablet that caused quite a flurry of interest. Several earthworks and smaller mounds occur nearby, including the Cresap Mound, excavated by the Carnegie Museum of Pittsburgh, and the Natrium Mound, excavated by representatives of the Smithsonian Institution.

Adena grave goods are well represented in the museums of America, and deservedly so. At first, the Adena people were buried with mostly utilitarian items—tools of stone and bone, ceramics, and items of personal ornamentation—presumably the personal possessions of the deceased. Destined for duty in the afterlife, they are both lavish and ornamental. Long-distance exchange networks brought in mica from North Carolina, native copper from Lake Superior (fashioned into a variety of ornaments and tools). The best display of Adena material culture can be found in the **Ohio Historical Center**, in Columbus. Particularly striking is a bird in flight, cut out from a sheet of hammered native copper.

Significantly, these burial mounds contain no sign of differential treatment of the dead. Most archaeologists believe that Adena mortuary ritual reflects a basically egalitarian societal organization.

Ohio Historical Center (Columbus, OH; jct. I-71 and 17th Ave.) is an immensely important facility displaying artifacts and dioramas illustrating Ohio's colorful prehistoric past. Many of the treasures of American archaeology are displayed here, particularly Adena and Hopewell materials. The museum also houses the Ohio Historical Society's administrative offices, a historical research library and the state archives. Phone (614) 297-2300.

THE HOPEWELL COMPLEX (200 B.C.–A.D. 500)

Another major mound-building complex was first recognized at a sprawling mound group near Chillicothe, Ohio. This astonishing site initially contained at least thirty-eight conical mounds, most enclosed by an extensive, geometric embankment, obviously laid out with great precision. As nineteenth-century investigators began to explore the

‪△△△‬

OHIO'S VENERABLE SERPENT

One of America's most intriguing archaeological artifacts does not fit inside a glass museum case. It is a monumental mounded serpent, mysteriously crawling along a bluff overlooking Ohio's Brush Creek. The ancient builders of **Serpent Mound** carefully planned this oversized effigy by first outlining a monstrous snake nearly one-quarter of a mile long with small stones and lumps of clay. Then they piled up countless basket loads of yellow clay over the outline, burying their markers.

The result is a flawlessly modeled serpent, forever slithering northward. Many observers think the snake may be trying to swallow an egg, judging from the oval earthwork near the mouth. Some suggest that the oval is a symbolic representation of the reptile's heart, or perhaps an enlarged and highlighted eye.

The meaning of the strange Serpent Mound has puzzled visitors ever since the site was first surveyed by Ephraim Squier and Edwin Davis in 1848. When Frederick Ward Putnam, then of Harvard University, visited in 1885, he was shocked to see that the sinuous mound was being destroyed by repeated plowing. Putnam set out to save the site by purchasing the land for Harvard University. He spent three field seasons excavating the effigies and nearby conical mounds. After restoring each to its original contours, Putnam saw to it that Harvard turned the site over to the Ohio Historical Society, which has maintained it ever since.

The snake has always been the most mysterious of creatures. Alone among the animals, it is swift without feet, fins, or wings. Serpent lore permeates Native American belief systems— sometimes the snake is a symbol of evil, sometimes a benevolent deity. The rattlesnake is slow to attack, but venomous in the extreme. It is like lightning: the quick spring and rapid flash, its mortal bite, its zigzag course, the sudden strike of released intensity.

The snake sheds its skin every spring. Thus to some ancients, it symbolized eternity, recalling the annual renewal of life. For many Indian people, the cast-off snakeskin has power to cure and heal. To others, it is the teeth, or the flesh that holds the creature's power.

‪△△△‬

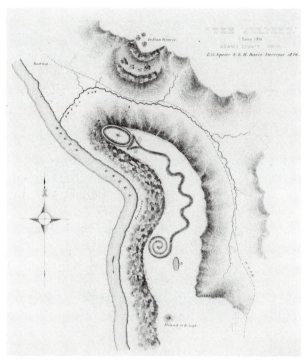

Squier and Davis engraving (1846) and 1930s aerial photograph of Ohio's celebrated Serpent Mound. (Courtesy of the Smithsonian Institution; photograph by Dache M. Reeves.)

△△△

The Ohio Indians of generations ago saw the snake as symbolic of Ursa Major and Ursa Minor, the Big and Little Dipper. Some scholars have found astronomical alignments in the various wriggling curves of Serpent Mound. An astronomer studying Serpent Mound has pointed out that the serpent's body is congruent with the shape of the Little Dipper, that the movement apparent in the serpent's tail reflects the progress of the constellation around the North Star.

No single, satisfying answer explains Serpent Mound to us. In fact, even assigning a chronological date to the serpent effigy is problematical; it does not contain any burials, and no artifacts have been found in the fill, so the serpent's construction cannot be cross-dated or associated with any particular culture.

One guess is that Serpent Mound is coeval with the conical burial mounds nearby. If these mounds were built by the same people as those who constructed Serpent Mound, then the snake effigy could be ascribed to the Adena builders, sometime during the first millennium B.C. But making this connection requires a considerable leap of faith. Alternatively, one might note that, beginning about A.D. 1000, the area around Serpent Mound was occupied by the later Fort Ancient people, and it could be that the spectacular effigy is only 1,000 years old.

During the summer of 1991, a team of archaeologists returned to Serpent Mound, relocating a trench excavated more than a century earlier. Like previous archaeologists, they found no diag-

△△△

Serpent Mound (Locust Grove, OH, 4 mi. NW on SR 73) is one of the finest remaining prehistoric Indian effigy mounds. Museum facilities and a viewing tower are located on-site. Phone (513) 587-2796.

strange constructions, it became immediately clear that the ancient people who had built these mounds had cared deeply about their ancestors. Not only had they built huge earthen monuments to encase their dead, but their respect was reflected in the magnificent objects prepared especially for the graves. Mica was brought in from the distant

△△△

nostic artifacts in the fill, but they were able to recover several tiny charcoal samples, which were then subjected to radiocarbon analysis.

The results were a surprise, falling about A.D. 1070. If these results hold up, then it would appear that the Great Serpent Mound was *not* built by Adena or Hopewell people, but by much later Mississippian architects.

The excavators, including Brad Lepper (of Great Hopewell Road fame), have gone even further, pointing out that this new ^{14}C date, corresponds almost exactly to two amazing astronomical events. In A.D. 1054, light from the supernova that produced the Crab nebula first reached the earth, remaining visible during daytime for at least two weeks. Then, in A.D. 1066, Halley's Comet appeared in its brightest manifestation ever, visible around the world.

Could it be that some Native American observers in the Ohio River valley set out to create a permanent memorial to these remarkable celestial events? Maybe the wriggling earthwork is not a serpent at all; could the oval (the "egg") actually represent the head of Halley's comet, with the "serpent's body" actually representing its fiery tail?

Have we heard the final word about the Great Serpent Mound? Probably not. But one thing is certain. Serpent Mound remains pure art. It still bewilders. It still has magnetism. And if we continue to protect its fragile profiles, it always will.

△△△

Appalachian Mountains, volcanic glass from Yellowstone, chert from North Dakota, conch shells and sharks teeth from the Gulf of Mexico, copper from the Great Lakes. They fashioned mystical and exotic artworks from these raw materials, then placed these offerings inside tombs to memorialize their dead. Many of the Ohio mounds were mined and looted for their treasures.

The late nineteenth century enjoyed a pitched debate over Moundbuilder origins. Finally, the myth of a mysteriously lost race was laid to rest by a series of carefully planned, concerted archaeological excavations in the 1890s. One of these digs took place at the farm of Mordecai Hopewell, west of Chillicothe, Ohio. When these astonishing artifacts were exhibited at the World's Columbian Exhibition in

Chicago in 1893—and their proper context was known—the answer was clear: the mysterious Moundbuilders never really disappeared—they simply became today's American Indians.

One of the neat things about being an archaeologist (even today) is that you get to name the things you find. So, because nobody knew what these ancient Ohioans called themselves, archaeologists decided to name them the Hopewell Mound Group after Mordecai Hopewell's farm, the place where they were first discovered.

Hopewell Culture National Park (Chillicothe, OH; about 3 mi. N. SR 104), established in 1923, protects a group of Hopewell mounds and a 13-acre square enclosure. On May 27, 1992, the president signed legislation authorizing the National Park Service to acquire land at several Hopewell culture sites in this area: *High Banks Works, the Seip Earthworks,* and *the Hopeton Earthworks.* A visitor center contains exhibits and public facilities. An observation deck provides an outstanding view of the area, as well as a recorded description and history. There are marked trails and trailside exhibits. Phone (614) 774-1125.

Neither a particular culture nor a political power, Hopewell was North America's first Pan-Indian religion, stretching from Mississippi to Minnesota, from Nebraska to Virginia. Today, the term *Hopewell* describes this broad network of contacts among different native American groups between about 200 B.C. and A.D. 500. For the first time these native people, who shared neither language nor culture, were drawn together by a unifying set of beliefs and symbols. For centuries, Hopewell dominated eastern North America.

Mound City preserves one of the greatest concentrations of Hopewell burial mounds. Curiously, Mound City was not a city at all. It was a village and mortuary site for Hopewell people living along the Scioto River during the first two centuries A.D. Here, the modern visitor can get a sense of the dramatic funerals and everlasting monuments that Hopewell people erected for their deceased elite.

In *Mica Grave Mound*, a spectacular trove of artifacts was excavated in 1921: elk and bear teeth, copper ornaments, large obsidian projectile points, and a cache of 5,000 shell beads. Two copper headdresses were recovered, one with three pairs of copper antlers, the other represented a bear, with hinged ears, and legs riveted on. Today, part of Mica Grave

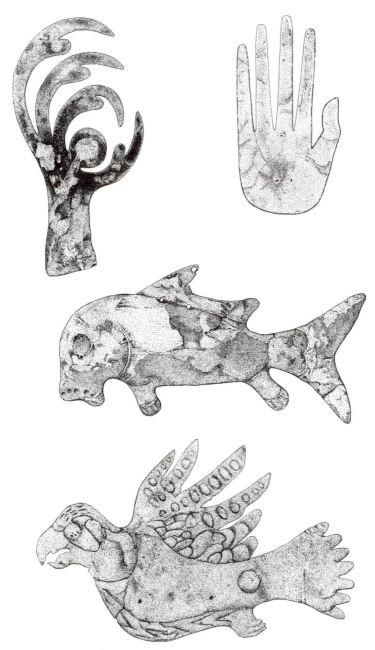

Miscellaneous Hopewell artifacts from Ohio. The sheet mica for the powerful bird talon (upper-left) was imported from North Carolina. The oversized mica hand (upper-right) still glistens after centuries of burial in a Hopewell mound. The naturalistic copper fish (center), representing a redhorse sucker or buffalo fish, may have been regarded by the Hopewell people as a symbol of the underworld. Finery such as the hammered copper hawk (bottom) accompanied the Hopewell elite to the afterlife.

Mound has been removed to exhibit the elaborate multiple burial contained within. As was the custom at Mound City, all the four individuals were cremated. Amidst the ashes, archaeologists found obsidian tools, effigy pipes depicting a raven and a toad, and a copper headpiece fashioned into a human form.

When the *Mound of the Pipes* was first excavated in the mid-nineteenth century, more than two hundred effigy smoking pipes were recovered, depicting various animals, birds, and reptiles. Some think that the Mound of the Pipes was a lasting monument to a master carver of sacred pipes, and a fitting monument it would have been. Hopewell artists are famous for making pipes such as these from locally available pipestone. Best known are the platform pipes, which have a cylindrical bowl resting upon a straight or curved base. Sometimes the bowls depicted birds and animals. Archaeologists are unclear as to just what was smoked in the pipes, since tobacco is not native to the area, and there is little record of its use in eastern North America prior to European contact. But whatever they were smoking, the archaeological evidence clearly demonstrates that pipe smoking was a critical aspect of Hopewell ritual.

Inside *Death Mask Mound*, the largest and oldest of the two dozen mounds in this compound, were found the remains of thirteen people, accompanied by copper falcon effigies. This mound contained an original subterranean charnel house, later replaced by one built on the surface. Such charnel houses were often used to store the body of the deceased person. Sometimes, a mound was erected atop the charnel house of a particularly important individual.

Mound City demonstrates how the system of social ranking worked in Hopewell society. The mounds themselves became visible reminders of the power of particular individuals and their families. The long period of planning, engineering, and execution involved in erecting such effective and long-lasting monuments was a cumulative group investment toward maintaining their own social order.

The rich grave goods of Mound City, presumably emblems of rank or status, also reflect Hopewell sociopolitical organization. Some archaeologists believe that animal effigies, such as those from Mica Grave Mound, represent long-vanished clans or lineages among the Hopewell people, similar to clans named after ravens and other animals by some later Native American groups. According to this interpretation, Hopewell society was divided into a series of rank-ordered lineages, perhaps similar to the ruling families of Hawaii in the early nineteenth century. If so, then each of the primary burial centers such as Mound City may have been used by one or more of the lineages as the final resting place for its most exalted individuals.

While Mound City is one of the most spectacular sites left to us by the Hopewell people, it represents only the mortuary aspect of the Hopewell lifeway. At other archaeological sites, such as the **Seip Mound**, in nearby Bainbridge, Ohio, one gets a better glimpse of the religious and the civic aspects of Hopewell society. Mound City cannot be taken as typical of Hopewell life any more than Arlington Cemetery is typical of late twentieth-century life in the United States.

Seip Mound State Memorial (Bainbridge, OH; 10 acres 3 mi. E. on US 50), contains the great central Hopewell mound (250 ft. long, 150 ft. wide, and 30 ft. high). A pavilion has related displays. Phone (614) 297-2300.

At least thirty mounds once stood at Seip, within and near a large geometric earthwork west of Chillicothe. Several large mounds have been scientifically excavated, revealing Hopewell civic and ceremonial structures, in which a number of activities took place. When the buildings were no longer used, a separate mound was erected over each section, one of them is the second largest of the Ohio Hopewell mounds.

THE HOPEWELL INTERACTION SPHERE

While the Hopewell people enjoyed a certain degree of agricultural productivity, even this marginal abundance created problems. By A.D. 400, the Hopewell population had grown so large that it threatened to outstrip and degrade its environment. Towns got bigger, and as new communities sprang up, they built on top of the critical agricultural hinterland. No longer was there plenty of unused land encircling each village. Living in sedentary villages became a risky strategy, particularly because the Hopewell did not store up much extra food. What if the gardens failed? What if the local acorn crop did not mature? What if a particularly harsh winter killed off the local deer herd, or if the local fish run failed because of droughts or floods? Every community experienced, at one time or another, occasional shortages. Starvation was not unknown.

As their new lifestyle posed more problems, the Hopewell people

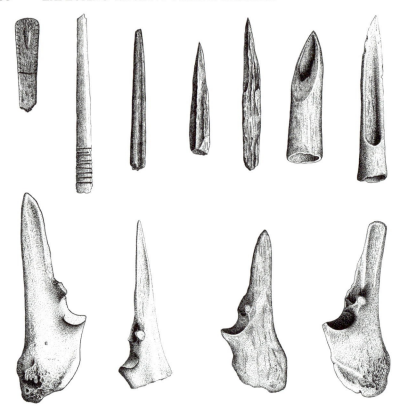

Bone and antler tools from the Greenhouse site, near Marksville, Louisiana. At the upper-left are two bone pins, perhaps used as hair decorations. The sharpened awls (upper-right), made from split deer bone and antler, were used for piercing skins and probably also as chisels. The bone awls at the bottom were probably used for skin dressing, with the tips deliberately rounded to avoid puncturing the delicate deerskins. (Courtesy of the American Museum of Natural History.)

responded by banding themselves into huge networks of reciprocal trading partners. Far-flung communities joined forces, looking to one another for support in lean years.

Generation upon generation of Hopewell traders would load their dugouts for distant destinations, carefully packing their Ohio pipestone, highly valued flint from the **Flint Ridge quarry** (only a few miles from Newark, Ohio), and freshwater pearls, planning to return laden with a precious cargo of grizzly bear teeth, maybe even sharkskin, mica from the Smoky Mountains, silver from Ontario, alligator teeth, and barracuda jaws from the Gulf of Mexico.

These exotic raw materials were funneled into regional Hopewell centers, where artists crafted them into fine objects of art, some of the

Flint Ridge State Memorial And Museum (Brownsville, OH; 3 mi. N. of US 40 on SR 668) encompasses an important outcrop of Vanport flint. Numerous quarry pits can be seen, where this material has been removed, from prehistoric times to the present. The museum contains a flint pit and traces the mineral from its raw state to its many uses. Phone (614) 787-2476.

most impressive Native American art ever made. These items were in turn distributed to distant leaders. Food may also have been traded, following the lines of trade already established.

This so-called Hopewell interaction sphere developed into the first large-scale trade network in precontact North America. It not only forestalled famine, but also dispersed tons of exotic items across the eastern half of the continent.

REGIONALIZED INTERACTIONS: THE GREAT HOPEWELL ROAD?

The physical distribution of these distinctive Hopewell artifacts came to reflect the realm of Hopewell ideology and religion. Yet despite this widespread commonality, there was no single person or individual group who ruled the entire Hopewellian kingdom. Instead, each individual territory remained under local control.

It is curious, then, that archaeologists seem to know more about long-distance Hopewellian exchange than about ritual and interaction at the local level. How did the individual Hopewell polities interact?

One possibility is suggested by the practices of Native American tribes during the historic period. Tribes often gathered together for feasts, ceremonies, and contests of skill, while individuals conducted their own private business on the periphery. We know that the Hopewell erected several different kinds of earthworks: village, defensive, burial, and some apparently used for other purposes, probably religious ceremonies and games or commercial or political transactions. Can we see this regional ritual interaction in these nonmortuary earthworks?

Recent research being conducted at the **Newark Earthworks** suggests an intriguing possibility. These earthworks, on the west side of Newark, Ohio, were once one of the most extensive in North America. Today, urban Newark has sprawled over large parts of the Hopewell earthworks, obliterating walls and mounds. But important sections are still preserved in *Octagon State Memorial* and *Moundbuilders State Memorial*.

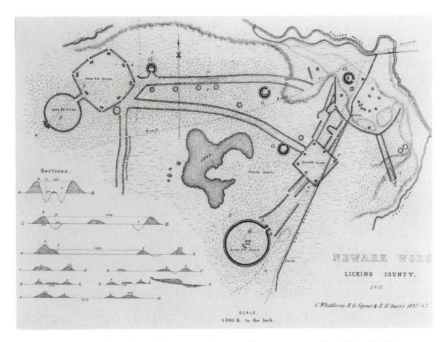

The Newark Earthworks, Ohio, sprawl across four square miles. This 1846 engraving of the Grave Creek Mound, West Virginia, appeared originally in the classic Ancient Monuments of the Mississippi Valley *by E. G. Squier and E. H. Davis (1846).*

The geometric constructions at Newark and elsewhere in Ohio must have formed an important part of Hopewell religious and social life, not only as the residences of high-ranking Hopewell leaders, but probably also for periodic rites of renewal. The earthworks may have been used for formal meetings of state, religious ceremonies, and perhaps also as a venue for private individuals to meet face-to-face and conduct their own private transactions. The Newark Earthworks were assembled on a grand scale, presumably reflecting the importance of the activities held within their confines. The original earthworks covered four square miles, including several large compounds connected by causeways.

Bradley Lepper, archaeologist and curator of the Newark Earthworks, has recently come up with a startling theory. Well aware of the newly discovered road system connecting Chaco Canyon to its outliers (discussed in the previous chapter), Lepper began looking for a similar system of roads that might once have connected the important ceremonial centers of the Hopewellian heartland. And he may have found it. Digging through various nineteenth-century accounts, Lepper turned

Newark Earthworks (Newark, OH) comprises preserved portions of a system of prehistoric Indian mounds and earthworks, much of which has been destroyed by city development.

Moundbuilders State Memorial (1 mi. SW of SR 16 on SR 79) preserves what is left of the Newark earthworks. It contains a circular earthwork 1,200 feet in diameter with grass-covered earthen walls ranging from 8 to 14 feet in height. In the center are three lower connected mounds.

Ohio Indian Museum (on the Moundbuilders State Memorial grounds) exhibits the prehistoric cultures of Ohio in various media. Museum staff can provide directions to nearby *Octagon* and *Wright Earthworks*. Phone (614) 344-1920.

up an unpublished map and notes that documented parallel walls of earth running for at least six miles in a perfectly straight line. Although cultivation and construction in the Newark area subsequently obliterated the end of this ancient earthwork, Lepper thinks that this might have been the remnant of a Hopewell period road that once connected the major monuments of Newark and Chillicothe, sixty miles apart.

Rare 1934 photographs seem to show this same linear feature—two distinct lines cutting an arrow-straight path across a patch of Licking County farmland. Combining standard archaeological surveys with aerial reconnaissance across the suspected route, Lepper was electrified to find that the two elevated earthen walls are still there—in precisely the same location as in the 1934 photographs. He now had his first tangible evidence of the Great Hopewell Road.

How would such a ritual road system work? Perhaps, as when leaders of the modern world meet, the ancient Hopewell exchanged presents, particularly gifts representative of the crafts and handiwork of their home countries. Through such visits, new contacts can be established between nations, and also between several sectors of same nation: bureaucrats, businessmen, religious leaders, and private citizens. Often, what begins as symbolic exchange between rulers can trickle down to establish formalized patterns of commerce between the two countries.

The same may have been true in Hopewell times. Some archaeologists think that certain of the amazing artifacts recovered from places like Mound City, may have been exchanged in just this way, to establish commercial and diplomatic ties between two distant political groups. Perhaps the ritual roads at Newark were once used for processions carrying such diplomatic items. Impressed by the straight lines visible from the air, Lepper is pursuing the idea that the major Hopewell centers were once connected by straight ceremonial pathways. Of course, Lepper's findings remain tentative, and many archaeologists are suspending judgment until more convincing data are available.

Still, the possibility of the Great Hopewell Road remains exciting. After all, what Southwestern archaeologist in the 1950s would have dreamed that the Chacoan outliers were connected by arrow-straight roads running hundreds of miles into the surrounding desert?

The great Hopewell enterprise ceased by about A.D. 500. Perhaps this breakdown was due to a collapse in traditional trading relationships. Or, perhaps the Hopewell demise came about from outright warfare and social unrest. But whatever the cause, it is clear that the Hopewellian traders paved the way for cultural achievements yet to come. Within a few centuries, the Hopewell territory would be united again, this time under a fully agricultural and politically more structured society that archaeologists term *Mississippian*.

THE ENIGMATIC EFFIGY MOUNDS (A.D. 350–1300)

In some parts of the upper Mississippi Valley, the attitudes toward ancestors began to change. Although the Hopewell worldview held for a short while elsewhere, Native Americans of southern Wisconsin decided to save their precious copper and obsidian to fashion into tools for the living. No longer crafting decorations for the dead, they venerated their ancestors instead with awesome and artistic monuments.

Here, on high ground bypassed by the Ice Age glaciers, ancient Americans erected huge earthen likenesses of lynx, panther, bison, water birds, eagles, lizards, and turtles. Although continuing to construct more conventional mounds in conical and linear configurations, these people are best known for their virtuoso construction of immense animal-shaped effigy mounds.

Lacking a better term, archaeologists speak of the Effigy Mound Culture to denote the builders of this great Native American artistic tradition. Restricted to the relatively small area of northeast Iowa, southwestern Minnesota, and western Wisconsin, this complex dates between about A.D. 350 and 1300. Perhaps as many as 10,000 such mounds once stood here, but urban expansion and intensive agriculture have erased all but a handful. Although many Native American cultures erected earthen mounds—and we have examined some very impressive ones earlier in this chapter—these effigy mounds still capture the imagination, and archaeologists still puzzle over their meaning.

At **Lizard Mound County Park**, Wisconsin, for instance, visitors can view one of America's best-preserved effigy mound groups. This small area apparently once contained about sixty mounds, and thirty-one survive today. A self-guiding trail winds around two dozen of the most spectacular earthworks.

Lizard Mound County Park (West Bend, WI; 4 mi. N. on SR 144, then ¼ mi. E. on County A) is named after the most prominent effigy mound surviving here. Designed in animal, bird, and geometric shapes, the park's mounds and earthworks are accessible on a self-guiding tour and nature trail. Phone (414) 335-4445.

Most of these mounds rise three or four feet above the ground's surface, and their shape is surprisingly crisp, demonstrating the great care taken in the original construction. Many assume conical or cigar shapes, but about half are true effigies, including several panthers and two birds. The identity of these effigies is, of course, a matter of considerable speculation. In fact, the famous "lizard effigy" of Lizard Mound County Park may not be a lizard at all. Some think it should be interpreted as an alligator or a turtle.

At **Effigy Mounds National Monument**, a 1,475-acre site in northeastern Iowa, there are more than 200 mound sites, dating to the last 2,500 years. Included in the monument are twenty-six animal effigies. Some of these mounds are monumental in size. Great Bear Mound is 70 feet across at the shoulders, reaching 137 feet in length. But perhaps most impressive are the huge birds and the Marching Bears at Effigy Mounds, where a group of thirteen individual effigies still cluster along an arc, nearly symmetrically spaced around an east-west line. Why were these effigies built? Why here? What do they mean?

As with the Hopewell burial mounds, early European visitors took them as emblematic of some "vanished race" of pre–Native American groups. Then, for a while, the effigies were considered to be an exotic form of burial mound, until excavation proved that—unlike their Hopewell counterparts—these so-called treasure houses were mostly empty.

Today, some archaeologists think that the effigies served as gigantic territorial markers, separating several groups from potential competi-

Aerial photograph of the Great Marching Bear Group, containing ten "bears," three "birds," and two linear mounds. These dynamic representations, probably built

tion and conflict over the same resources. Others point out that effigy mounds were built in distinctive groups, ranging from two or three mounds to more than 100. While several conical or linear mounds in a group might contain human burials, those depicting an effigy shape are almost always empty, containing neither human remains nor artifacts. This suggests to some that the effigies defined sacred, ceremonial ground rather than mortuary areas. Or maybe they were designators for meeting places before or after the winter breakup into smaller groups.

Perhaps it was the effigy shape itself that held the greatest significance. Some have suggested that animal effigies might represent clan totems, earthen symbols depicting related family groups. Perhaps these monumental ground figures were an attempt, through ritual means, to

between A.D. *600–1300, comprise one of the largest groups of effigy mounds still surviving. (Courtesy of the National Park Service.)*

connect with specific animal spirits, to ensure a consistent and regular food supply. The lack of artifacts contained within suggests to some that *the actual building of the mound* is what's important, not unlike the contemporary Diné (Navajo) sand paintings, which are made and then destroyed.

Still others emphasize the importance of the heavens in traditional Native American cosmology. Many American Indian groups paid close attention to what was overhead, intertwining their cultural rhythms with the perpetual cycles of sun, moon, planets, and stars. They observed eclipses and the conjunctions of planets, devised calendars for festivals, and established dates for planting. All this was vital knowledge.

Today's astronomers capture this wisdom in books and scientific journals. Ancient Americans did the same thing through myths, rituals and festivals, symbolic architecture, dance, and costume. The Anasazi have left us their sacred spaces, the organized rocks of architecture, and markings on canyon walls as records of their astronomy. In the eastern Woodlands, we have the effigy mounds.

Is it significant that on early spring evenings the Big Dipper is located precisely over the top of the main mounds at Effigy Mounds National Monument? Does it matter that during late summer you can see the Big Dipper exactly over the bottom position of the effigies? Could it be that the earthen Marching Bears represent the march of the Big Dipper around Polaris—the north star? Some astronomers think so.

There is no single satisfying answer to these questions. Whatever they meant to the people who made them, the enigmatic effigy mounds today provide an archaeological Rorschach test against which to project one's personal beliefs about the past and those who lived it.

Curiously, we know more about the Effigy Mound people than about the effigy mounds they are named for. Archaeological excavations of the more prosaic habitation areas suggest that the Effigy Mound people lived in dispersed family groups during the winter, a time of scarce resources. Then, during the spring and summer as resources became more abundant, they coalesced into larger, more sedentary villages. Studies of refuse in such camps suggest a reliance on white-tailed deer, bear, and elk. They also collected wild plant foods, and kept gardens.

Unlike their Hopewellian contemporaries, these people manufactured native copper into actual tools, rather than simply decorative ornaments such as those made by Hopewell artisans. And they buried their dead with few if any offerings for the afterlife. Yet despite such differences, the builders of the effigy mounds probably differed little in terms of economics and everyday life from the Hopewell peoples.

Ultimately, the Effigy Mound builders were displaced about A.D. 1400 by intensive agriculturalists, who lived in much larger villages.

Effigy Mounds National Monument (Marquette, IA; 3½ mi. north of Marquette on SR 76) extends for 6 mi. along the bluffs of the Mississippi River, with the Yellow River bisecting the monument. At the visitor center a film and museum explain the history of the mounds.

THE PLAINS VILLAGE INDIANS

Several more complexes also flourished on the Great American Plains. Although their material culture and ceremonialism seems less elaborate than that of their northeastern counterparts, these Plains people manufactured ceramics, constructed mortuary mounds, and beginning about 1000 B.C., carried out rudimentary forms of agriculture—the hallmarks of this lifestyle.

Then, about A.D. 1000, the eastern and northern Plains people developed a more sedentary lifeway. The term *Plains Village Indians* is traditionally applied to these people who dominated the northeastern Plains for nearly 1,000 years. They constructed permanent, year-round earth lodges and developed a full-blown horticultural economy. Their descendants became the Mandan and Arikara people.

At the **Knife River Indian Villages National Historic Site**, in North Dakota, one can walk along the three interpretive trails that link the major village sites. Here one gets a rare chance to view an unrestored and largely unexcavated series of archaeological sites: their huge earth lodge depressions, extensive fortification ditches, cache pits, and artifacts scattered across the ground. In this relatively young park—only approved by Congress in 1974—modern travelers can imagine for themselves the human history that still lies buried beneath their feet.

The archaeology of the Knife River villages constitutes an unbroken record of 500 years of settled village life from the time when people arrived here about A.D. 1300. These five villages along the banks of the Knife and Missouri rivers were home to the Hidatsa, numbering perhaps 3,000 to 5,000.

Their summer villages—ordered communities containing as many as 120 earth lodges—were built on the natural terraces above the Missouri River and its tributaries. These sturdy dwellings were admirably suited to the environment, each comfortably housing from ten to thirty people. The villages often were strategically located for defense, built on a narrow bluff with water on two sides, and a protective palisade erected on the third. In wintertime, the inhabitants moved into smaller lodges located along the bottom lands. There, they were protected from the icy winds, with plenty of firewood at hand.

Although these Knife River villagers hunted bison whenever possible, they relied on a basic farming lifestyle, raising squash, pumpkins, beans, sunflowers, and a tough, quick-maturing variety of corn in their rich flood-plain gardens. The first corn of summer was celebrated by the

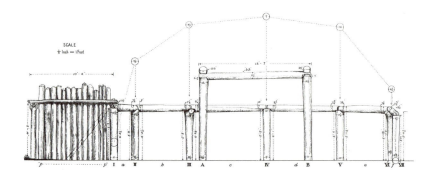

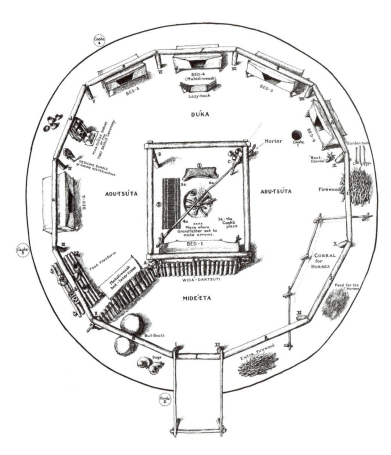

Sketch by Gilbert Wilson, who worked among the Hidatsa of the Fort Berthold Reservation between 1906 and 1918. This drawing depicts the spatial structure of a twelve-post Mandan earthlodge at Knife River, as described by Buffalo-bird-woman. This particular lodge was that of Small-ankle, her father, as it appeared about the time of her own marriage. (Courtesy of the American Museum of Natural History.)

Green Corn Ceremony (like that discussed in the next chapter). Berries, roots, and fish supplemented their diet.

The upper Missouri River was a lifeline winding across the northern Plains. Situated as they were, the Knife River people often served as intermediaries between other groups, and they dealt in a wide variety of goods: obsidian from Wyoming, Great Lakes copper, shells from the Gulf of Mexico and the Pacific Northwest.

It was here that the Mandan and Hidatsa people cordially hosted the Lewis and Clark expedition in the winter of 1804–05. As a result of such European contact, the Knife River people began trading in fire-arms and horses. These same villages attracted growing numbers of non-Indian traders who, in turn, inadvertently introduced devastating European diseases. Key villages were abandoned after smallpox ravaged the tribes in 1781. Considerable shuffling of village locations ensued, and the weakened Mandans and Hidatsas became easy prey for Sioux raiders. The Arikara joined the Mandans and Hidatsas in 1862.

Finally, the survivors were removed from the Knife River villages in 1885 and taken to the Fort Berthold Reservation. Today, the Three Affiliated tribes—the Arikara, the Mandan, the Hidatsa—preserve their traditional ways.

Knife River Indian Villages National Historic Site (Stanton, ND; 3 mi. N. on CR 37) contains the remains of three Hidatsa Indian villages, with visible lodge depressions, cache pits, and fortification ditches. Wintering at nearby Fort Mandan, Lewis and Clark stopped at this site in October 1804, when Sacajawea and her husband joined the expedition. A visitor center has exhibits and a slide program. Interpretive programs and cultural demon-strations are offered. Phone (701) 745-3309.

WHERE ELSE TO SEE WOODLAND-STYLE ARCHAEOLOGY

The following is a list of sites and museums that feature some of the artifacts and/or remains discussed in this chapter. Complete informa-tion on each is listed in the appendix by state at the end of the book.

Caddoan Mounds State Historic Site (Alto, TX)
Cleveland Museum of Natural History (Cleveland, OH)
Flint Ridge State Memorial and Museum (Brownsville, OH)

Fort Ancient (Lebanon, OH)

Garvies Point Museum and Preserve (Glen Cove, NY)

Grand Mound Interpretive Center (International Falls, MN)

Indian Mounds Park (St. Paul, MN)

Institute for American Indian Studies (Washington, CT)

Ka-Do-Ha Indian Village (Murfreesboro, AK)

Lizard Mound County Park (West Bend, WI)

Miamisburg Mound State Memorial (Miamisburg, OH)

Mitchell Prehistoric Indian Village (Mitchell, SD)

Mound Cemetery (Marietta, OH)

Ohio Historical Center (Columbus, OH)

Pawnee Indian Village State Historic Site (Courtland, KS)

Pinson Mounds State Archaeological Area (Pinson, TN)

Pipestone National Monument (Pipestone, MN)

Provincial Museum of Alberta (Edmonton, AB)

Ska-Nah-Doht Indian Village (London, ON)

Sheboygan Mound Park (Sheboygan, WI)

Wyandotte Cave (Leavenworth, IN)

MISSISSIPPIAN
TRANSFORMATIONS

BY *Mississippian*, archaeologists mean the hundreds of late precontact societies that thrived between about A.D. 750 and 1500 (or later) throughout the Tennessee, Cumberland, and Mississippi river valleys.

The Mississippian emergence can be characterized by a number of distinctive features:

- Characteristic pottery (usually tempered with crushed mussel shell),
- Village-based maize horticulture,
- Construction of large flat-topped mounds, commonly situated near the town plaza, and
- Stratified social organization embodying permanent (and probably hereditary) offices.

Mississippian people also adopted the bow and arrow, explicitly connected their religion to agricultural productivity, often worshiped a fire-sun deity, and engaged in intensive long-distance exchange.

During their heyday, the Mississippian elite presided over breathtaking ceremonial centers, places today called Cahokia, Moundville, Spiro, and Etowah. The Mississippian aristocracy was invested with power by the thousands upon thousands of farming people who lived in smaller palisaded hamlets and farmsteads.

Much of eastern North America did not participate in full-blown Mississippian culture. But all were to some extent dependent upon

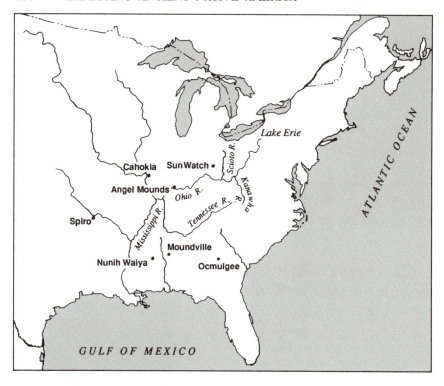

Map of the Eastern Woodlands, showing the location of several important Mississippian sites.

Mississippian-style economics. Descendents of the great American Indian confederacies of the American southland—including the so-called Five Civilized Tribes—are deeply rooted in their Mississippian ancestry.

CAHOKIA: MISSISSIPPIAN CITY OF THE SUN

One of the most revealing windows into the ancient Mississippian world is the storied site of **Cahokia**, the largest city in native North America. Built on the expansive flood plain that joins the Mississippi and Missouri rivers (near present-day St. Louis), Cahokia enjoyed rich soil and plentiful wildlife. About A.D. 700, late Woodlanders had established compact villages in this area, where they hunted, fished, gathered wild plant foods, and cultivated a variety of domesticates, including a little maize.

The more cosmopolitan Mississippian culture emerged later, between A.D. 850 and 900. Although the Mississippian lifeway differed markedly from that of the Woodland people, there is probably a genetic tie between the two. Mississippians simply had access to different ideas and technologies—not the least of which was a more intensified food-producing economy.

Between A.D. 800 and 1100, Mississippian people looked beyond traditional Woodland-era cultivation of native plants to focus instead on a single Mexican import—maize. Before long, maize-based agriculture engulfed eastern North America, responsible in part for the emergence of more complex sociopolitical structures. Ultimately, maize farming would support the evolving Iroquoian confederacy of the Northeast, the Fort Ancient polities along the middle Ohio River valley, and the diverse array of Mississippian chiefdoms that controlled the river valleys of the Southeast and Midwest. After European con-

Painting by William R. Iseminger showing downtown Cahokia about A.D. 1150 (looking northeast). At the center is Monks Mound connected by the Grand Plaza to the Twin Mounds. The central precinct is enclosed by the stockade wall, a defensive fortification that also served as a barrier between social classes in their society. The American Woodhenge can be seen to the left. The lakes formed in huge borrow pits dug for soil used for building the massive mounds. Behind Monks Mound runs Cahokia Creek, and agricultural fields surround the site for miles. (Courtesy of William R. Iseminger and the Cahokia Mounds State Historical Site.)

tact, it would be maize that sustained the Creek and Choctaw tribes of the Southeast, the Mandan and the Arikara of the Plains.

Maize had dominated southwestern diets from the time it arrived from Mexico. But in the eastern Woodlands, more than six centuries elapsed from initial introduction to the domination of maize as major crop of the East. Archaeologists are still attempting to explain this lag.

The emergence of maize-based agriculture at places like Cahokia was a watershed event in American history. Unlike their European counterparts, Mississippian people did not domesticate draft animals. Instead, Native American farmers tilled their land by hand and by hoe, their fields usually located along the fertile river valleys or abandoned levee meanders. Cahokia was deliberately sited near prime farmland and connected to the water and land routes tying the city to both neighboring and distant settlements.

This was also a time of social change. As Mississippians became increasingly agricultural, they relied more heavily on centralized authority and economic redistribution. In turn, as economic and social controls tightened, farmers were required to produce larger agricultural surpluses to support the infrastructure.

Cahokia became one of the most important regional centers in native North America, but the original name of this city is unknown. The modern term *Cahokia* derives from one of the subtribes of the Illini Indians, who apparently arrived after the fall of Cahokia. Some prefer the term City of the Sun to Cahokia because it refers to the sun symbolism so evident on certain artifacts, the use of sun calendars, and the inference that Cahokians worshipped the sun as a deity.

At its peak, Cahokia probably was home to 20,000 people (although some estimates run almost twice that number), and the major agricultural fields were located outside the city. The downtown area covered perhaps six square miles, subdivided by a series of open plazas and small gardens. By A.D. 1100, the city was protected by a massive wooden palisade that reached a height of twelve to fifteen feet. This two-mile-long encircling wall required 15,000 logs—the cutting of all those trees must have had a whopping environmental impact. Perhaps this palisade was built to separate Cahokia's sacred precinct from the rest of the city.

Mississippian people are often referred to as Moundbuilders, and at Cahokia, that's exactly what they did. The immediately adjacent area may have once contained 120 Mississippian mounds. A few mounds were used for burying the dead, but most were devoted to ceremonies of the living. In houses atop these temple mounds, Native American

Aerial view of Monks Mound, the largest precontact earthwork in the New World. It stands 100 feet high and covers over fourteen acres at the base, rising in four distinct terraces to the summit where the ruler's dwelling/temple once stood. (Courtesy of the Cahokia Mounds State Historical Site.)

aristocrats presided over the rituals that codified the Mississippian lifeway. Many of the Cahokia earthworks have been thoughtlessly destroyed, but sixty-five mounds still survive within the boundaries of the Cahokia Mounds State Historic Park.

Then as now, the Cahokian landscape was dominated by *Monks Mound*, the largest earthwork ever constructed in the Americas—and perhaps the largest in the world. Built in stages over a period of three centuries, Monks Mound covers fourteen acres, contains 22 million cubic feet of earth, and stands 100 feet tall. The summit once held a huge wooden building, measuring 105 by 48 feet, and perhaps 50 feet high. From this perch, the elite ruler manipulated both the ceremonial and secular lives of the Cahokian people. Monks Mound was not, incidentally, built by monks. The name recalls a group of early nineteenth-century Trappist monks who planted gardens and orchards on its expansive terraces.

Like all Mississippian societies, Cahokia was organized into ranked hierarchies. Monks Mound and the other temple mounds were designed, by their sheer size and spatial arrangement, to increase the social distance between classes. Sporting clothing and jewelry befitting their elevated status, the new nobility—maybe 5 percent of the total population—literally towered over everybody and everything. Townspeople supported their royalty, setting them apart from the population at large by social and political protocols.

Regional governments fused formerly autonomous groups into vast Mississippian empires. Warfare increased, directed largely toward territorial conquest. But unlike their European counterparts, Mississippian warlords allowed the vanquished to remain on their land.

Not far from Monks Mound, a remarkable triumph of Native Ameri-

Hypothetical reconstruction of how the sun circle at the American Woodhenge may have been erected by the workers at Cahokia. The figures at the left are shown excavating a post pit with a sloping ramp. The others are inserting a thirty-foot post into the hole; earth may have been heaped up around the base for additional support (after Warren L. Wittry, The American Woodhenge*).*

can science and engineering was accidentally discovered in the early 1960s. Anticipating the interstate highway scheduled to run through the heart of Cahokia, a team of professional archaeologists worked feverishly to keep ahead of the bulldozers. Looking over the results of the summer's excavation, archaeologist Warren Wittry noticed that several large oval-shaped pits seemed to have been arranged in arcs. Suppose, he thought, that each pit had held an upright post. If so, then perhaps the Mississippians at Cahokia had devised a kind of sun calendar. He called his find *the American Woodhenge*.

Wittry then predicted that—if his hunch was correct—other undiscovered pits should be buried along the rest of the arc. Follow-up excavations did indeed expose a series of post pits, exactly where Wittry had predicted. The new excavations also suggested that, over a two-century interval, several separate Woodhenges must have been built on this very spot. Some of the pits even contained remnants of the original cedar posts, stained with red paint.

Today, archaeologists recognize a number of sequential "woodhenges" at Cahokia, each having a center post, and up to 48 posts defining the precisely circular perimeter. These telephone pole-sized posts were set into deeply dug post pits, each the size of a modern bathtub.

Recent chronological refinements—based primarily on the radiocarbon-dated cedar posts and their relative superposition—show that the woodhenge does not span two centuries. It was built and used, at most, over a single century (between A.D. 1100-1200). Based on superposition, the earliest (and largest) of the woodhenges at Cahokia might have consisted of 60 posts.

Interpretations of Cahokia's woodhenge structures vary considerably. Wittry argued for a calendrical function, based on tracking of solar positions; for him, these were "sun circles" writ large. Robert Hall compared the woodhenges to Plains Indian "world center shrines," symbolizing an inherent cosmic order, related to annual fertility rites and, perhaps, calendrical reckoning. Others have challenged the calendrical hypothesis, suggesting that the woodhenges may have helped the Cahokia architects to lay out the basic site plan.

To be sure, if these Mississippian astronomers did follow a calendrical template, much of this knowledge has been lost, and today we cannot fully know how these Woodhenges operated. Perhaps a sun priest stood in the center of the circle, and "read" the calendar by observing where the sun rose. The simplest such calendars need only three points: one each marking the first days of winter and summer (the solstices), and one post halfway between to indicate the first days of spring and fall (the equinoxes).

The most spectacular sunrises occur at the equinoxes, when the sun comes up due east. Viewed from the Woodhenge at Cahokia, these sunrises take place directly over the top of Monks Mound. What a powerful sight: the elite ruler's residence giving birth to the sun.

Despite such impressive achievements, Cahokia was not to survive. The population began to trail off about A.D. 1300, and two centuries later, the City of the Sun lay in ruins. Nobody knows the exact cause of this decline. Over the centuries, the Cahokians must have seriously depleted the available natural resources, making this particular flood plain an increasingly difficult place to live. Significant climatic change was taking place about this time, with drier intervals cutting into the agricultural productivity upon which Cahokia depended. Some think that the forest lands were giving way to grasslands. Warfare, disease, and/or social discord could have taken their toll. Nobody knows where these Mississippian people went after they quit Cahokia.

Cahokia Mounds State Historic Site (East St. Louis, IL; 6 mi. E. off I-55/70 to SR 111 to Collinsville Rd.) covers 2,200 acres and preserves the 65 remaining Mississippian mounds. The interpretive center/museum tells the story of Cahokia through exhibits, murals, and dioramas. Large observation windows also permit viewing of Monks Mound and the plaza area from inside. Numerous site activities take place each year, including a Native American festival (September), craft and lecture series, archaeological field schools, and equinox and solstice sunrises (held at the reconstructed American Woodhenge). Guided tours are available. Phone (618) 346-5160.

THE ELITE AND COMMONERS OF MOUNDVILLE

Moundville, another intensively investigated Mississippian ceremonial center, overlooks the Black Warrior River, in Alabama. The site itself sprawls across about 300 acres and contains some two dozen earthen mounds, extraordinary reminders of past Native American achievements. This mound complex was a bustling ritual center between about A.D. 1000 and 1500. Like most Mississippian polities, this maize-based society engaged in extensive trade, their skilled artists worked in stone, ceramics, bone, and copper. The large earthworks were crowned by temples, council houses, and homes for the nobility. The site was protected by a stout palisade.

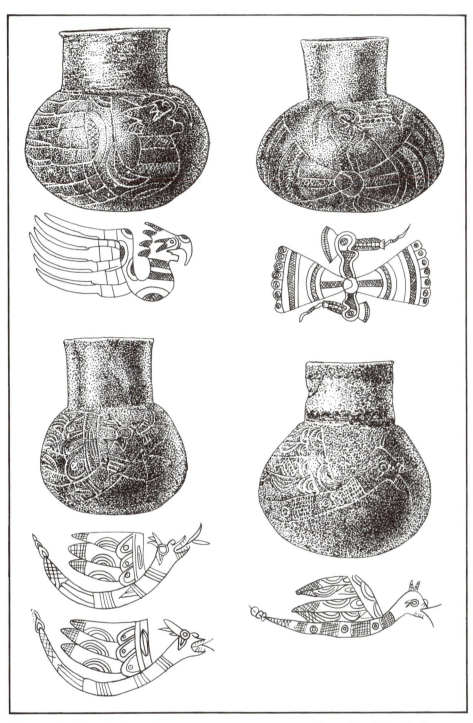

Various Southern Cult motifs evident on ceramics recovered by archaeologist C. B. Moore during his 1905–1906 excavations at Moundville, Alabama.

Three thousand people once lived at Moundville—an astonishing number. For five centuries, no city in the American Southeast would again reach that size. Smaller centers blossomed on other river systems, and satellite villages lined the streams for many miles around the major religious and market centers. Archaeologists have worked at Moundville for a century, excavating more than 3,000 individual human burials.

People often wonder why archaeologists spend so much time digging

△△△

LIFE AND DEATH IN MISSISSIPPIAN SOCIETY

The development of Mississippian society highlights a pervasive problem inherent in our conventional view of the past. Too often we view the past as a glorious succession of great technological revolutions that made the world a better place to live in. We have been taught that—through cultural ingenuity—our prehistoric ancestors whittled down the list of problems and dangers once faced by all humankind. The so-called Neolithic revolution (the domestication of plants and animals) is one of these transformations.

Farming supposedly solved an age-old problem by liberating human society from the restraints of nature. Implicit in this view is a celebration of progress, as measured by rising numbers and increasing power of human populations. We have been led to believe that the human workload became progressively lighter through time; that our nutrition improved and diseases diminished as we learned to produce our own food supply. We are tempted to believe that the quality of human life has improved along a steady, if irregular, upward trend. These assumptions about the progressive nature of the human past are today challenged by new research results which, taken together, suggest that the emergence of agriculture is more complex than we realize.

We now know that plant domestication—the genetic manipulation of crops—does not necessarily improve the nutrient value of plants; indeed, quite the reverse may be true. Moreover, storage can further decrease the nutritive value of crops. And as populations became sedentary and lived off stored staples, further nutritional problems arose.

New archaeological evidence suggests that the increased re-

△△△

up graves (do archaeologists have some kind of ghoulish fascination with the macabre?). Moundville is a good place to address that question. This unparalleled series of Mississippian burials have been studied to shed light upon two very different issues. For one thing, using new high-tech methods, archaeologists and physical anthropologists can now reconstruct, with some precision, the health, nutrition, and longevity of ancient people (see the sidebar **Life and Death in Mississippian Society**). In addition, the bones and grave goods at Moundville

———————————————— △△△ ————————————————

liance on domesticated plants was at best a mixed blessing for Mississippian people. At the **Dickson Mounds** in Illinois, for instance, the health, nutrition, and longevity of Mississippian people declined significantly from earlier times. There were higher rates of malnutrition and infectious disease (probably due to crowding), singularly high rates of trauma (suggesting increased interpersonal violence), high rates of anemia, greater incidence of dental disease, an elevated level of biological stress, and generally shorter life expectancy. Other evidence suggests that the percentage of individuals displaying signs of infection in Mississippian populations may have doubled in the transition from hunting and gathering to intensive maize agriculture.

Things were better in some places than others. The Mississippian communities at Moundville and Etowah were generally healthy and long-lived, but there was a substantial difference between classes. Although the high-status male adults—those buried in mounds—had a relatively advanced average age at death, those in surrounding village cemeteries (presumably a lower status area) had a much lower average age at death. Contemporary hunter-gatherers from an outlying satellite near Etowah were taller, more robust, and had lower rates of infection and arthritis than their farming neighbors.

Such recent studies not only highlight the potential downside of agriculture, but they point out the importance of setting aside ethnocentric notions of "progress" to consider alternative adaptive strategies practiced throughout the Americas and elsewhere. Surprisingly, these nonagricultural people may have lived healthier and longer lives than their agricultural counterparts.

———————————————— △△△ ————————————————

have also allowed archaeologists to reconstruct the social fabric of Mississippian society. This is possible because of the uniquely human way all people approach death and mortality.

Death is an inescapable period of transformation—for both the deceased and those left behind. As the dead are separated from the living, they must be properly integrated into the world of the departed. The social ties between the living and the once-living reflect, in microcosm, the larger social relations of an entire society. Burial rituals thus provide a measure of an individual's worth at death. "Last rites" provide the archaeologist with fossilized clues about the terminal status of an individual.

The Moundville social system provided for fewer positions of value than there were individuals capable of filling them. In such basically unequal or ranked societies, hard work was not enough to achieve a higher social status. At Moundville, one was assigned a cultural station at birth.

Social ranking at Moundville fell into a pyramid-shaped distribution. At the peak of the social pyramid was the chief of Moundville, a male of noble birth who was probably thought to be divine. This was the paramount individual on whom were lavished the most elevated emblems of status and rank available in Mississippian society. Slightly below the chief were those who enjoyed extraordinarily high status and considerable political authority. These individuals, also all males, were buried in the large truncated mounds of Moundville, often accompanied by infants and adult human skulls—ritual accompaniments, perhaps retainers and kinsmen sacrificed for the occasion. Each mound contained only a limited number of these very high-status adults, whose grave goods included copper axes, copper gorgets, stone discs, various paints, and assorted exotic minerals such as galena and mica. Many of the elite grave goods displayed symbols of the *Southern Cult*. The ceremonial axes and sheet copper plumes, for instance, depicted the "eagle being" and the "dancing priest."

The upper class or social elite were buried in a sacred area and accompanied by symbols of their exalted status. The Moundville elite apparently lived in larger, more complex dwellings than did the commoners.

Very high prestige items were buried with individuals of all ages and both sexes, and this is why we think that social status was assigned at birth. It looks like one's social position in Moundville was inherited and automatically assigned to all family members. This inference is reinforced by the fact that even infants and children—clearly too

Moundville Archaeological Park (Moundville, AL; ½ mi. W. of SR 69 at the edge of town), one of the country's best-preserved mound groups lies on the south bank of the Black Warrior River. The 320-acre park is arranged in a square design with a ceremonial plaza. Remnants of this early metropolis consist of twenty square and oval platform mounds varying in height from 3 to 58 feet. Graded paths climb to the mound summits, once topped by ceremonial houses and chiefs' lodges; a reconstructed temple dominates one mound.

The *Alabama Indian Resource Center* is also housed here, providing Alabama's teachers with up-to-date material on Native Americans and offering educational opportunities about Native Americans for both students and the general public.

A museum features exhibits illustrating the Mississippian lifeway, including lifesized figures and models of indigenous houses and earthworks. A new sixty-person theater has recently been opened, where several videos are available to illustrate the precontact and contact period archaeology of the Alabama/Moundville area. Phone (205) 371-2572.

young to have accomplished anything very noteworthy in life—were buried with lavish grave goods. They were important because of who they were, not what they did.

Each mound also contained some less well-accompanied (presumably lower-status) individuals, furnished for the afterlife with only a few ceramic vessels. These were probably second-order ritual or political officers who were buried in or near the truncated mounds.

At the base of the social order were adults and children buried in cemeteries near the mounds and in charnel houses near the main plaza. These villagers' graves also reflected their social position in life which was conditioned largely by sex and age distinctions rather than inheritance. Here less glamorous grave goods were distributed in a quite different manner. Graves contained pottery vessels, bone awls, flint projectile points, and stone pipes, which were distributed unevenly (mostly to older adults). These people had to achieve—rather than inherit—their social status. The prize artifacts in this social setting went to the "self-made individuals." Over half of the Moundville graves were for commoners who were buried without any grave goods at all.

THE SOUTHERN CULT

The *Southern Cult* was an iconographic network extending over much of the East during Mississippian times from about A.D. 1150 to 1350. Also called the *Southeastern Ceremonial Complex*, this huge network concentrated in three regional centers: **Moundville** (Alabama), **Etowah** (Georgia), and **Spiro** (Oklahoma).

The striking similarities in Southern Cult theme, motif, and medium imply more than simple trade networks; there was a higher degree of social interaction at work. The conch shell gorgets and cups, the copper plates, the ceremonial axes and batons, the effigy pipes and flint knives found at Spiro and elsewhere contain a distinctive set of Southern Cult symbols. The forked eye, the cross, the sun circle, the hand and eye, the bilobed arrow, among others, suggest a shared symbol system that extended beyond the limits of any single Mississippian empire,

The famed wooden feline, a six-inch high puma was excavated in 1884 at Key Marco, an island off Florida's western coast, about 15 miles south of Naples. Carved from a single piece of wood and saturated with a kind of varnish or animal fat, this image was probably crafted by Calusa Indians during the very late precontact period. It seems to represents a feline deity, replete with distinctive Southern Cult markings.

Miscellaneous Southern Cult artifacts. Repoussé copper profile of a man from Spiro, with familiar Southern Cult elements, including the forked symbol around the eye.

spreading from Mississippi to Minnesota, from the Great Plains to the Atlantic coast. In addition to small, "expensive" items, Southern Cult exchange may have involved critical subsistence resources such as food and salt.

Many of the representations of crosses, hand and eye, sun symbols, serpent, woodpecker, falcon, raccoon, and others, plus ceramics modeled on animal and human forms, can be traced to the belief systems of postcontact Native Americans of the Southeast, and to their folk tales, myths, and religious observances.

We can also place the ranked statuses at Moundville into a regional framework. The economy was probably redistributive, Moundville serving as a center of regional distribution of key goods. The twenty-plus sites of the Moundville social system were locked together into the same cultural system, joined by a common social organization and common ritual. This regional polity required and supported a number of specialized political and religious officers, most of whom were physically associated with the major Moundville site itself (although some were part of the minor ceremonial centers and villages in the hinterlands). Recruitment for these high offices was probably limited to members at the apex of the social organization. Nevertheless, bonds of clanship and genealogical relationship probably pervaded the whole of the society.

SPIRITUAL SYMBOLISM AT SPIRO

Then there is **Spiro,** that important Mississippian center in eastern Oklahoma. Named after the present-day community nearby, Spiro was situated on the first terrace and surrounding upland along the Arkansas River, where the temperate forest begins to trail off into vast expanses of the Great Plains. During Mississippian times, Spiro was one of the major trade centers in native North America, its leaders controlling exchange networks that expanded onto the plains and across the southeastern United States. Mississippian people began living at Spiro as early as A.D. 900, but the fame of Spiro dates to the later phase, between A.D. 1200 and 1350.

Like many Mississippians, people at Spiro practiced a religion that recognized the importance of the seasonal cycle, conducting special ceremonies to ensure successful planting, bountiful harvests, successful life, and reverence in death. The mounds at Spiro supported large temples, mortuaries, and houses for the priests/chiefs. People living at Spiro witnessed hundreds of esoteric religious rituals, apparently centered around the death and burial of the elite members of their society. Like many Native Americans, past and present, the people of Spiro also celebrated the various stages in the unfolding of the agricultural calendar, particularly celebrating the time of planting, harvesting, and changing of the seasons.

Today, Spiro is dominated by two large earthen mounds, one of them a reconstruction of Craig Mound, measuring 300 by 115 feet, and standing 35 feet at the highest point. Although it probably supported an enclosed and roofed structure, looters destroyed most of the evi-

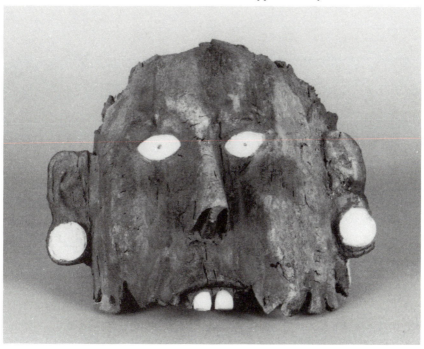

This extremely well-preserved cedar mask (ca. A.D. 1000) combines human and deer-like features with conch-shell eyes, earspools, and teeth. It was recovered from the Spiro Mounds in Oklahoma. (Courtesy of the Oklahoma Museum of Natural History.)

dence that could substantiate this suggestion. During the eight centuries of its use, more than 1,000 people were buried inside.

The artifacts from Craig Mound suggest that the dead buried there were persons of extraordinary import, probably the ruling elite that controlled the 200 to 300 ceremonial centers of the Arkansas River valley. Because of the great quantity of spectacularly crafted art objects found at this site, Spiro (like Moundville) was inextricably linked to the vast Southern Cult.

One of these original Spiro houses has been accurately reconstructed. The modern visitor can see how the walls were built of cedar posts set into the ground, with cane and grasses woven between. After clay was packed into and across the surface of the matting, a series of small fires ignited on either side of the wall hardened the clay walls in the way a kiln fires ceramic pots. The roof was thatched with grass tied to rafters and cedar center posts.

Mississippian houses such as this probably sheltered an extended

─── △△△ ───

VANDALIZING SPIRO'S ANCIENT PAST

The modern visitor can stroll around the mounds and village ruins at Spiro, reminded of the magnificent Mississippian trade expeditions that once originated here. But unfortunately, little remains of the splendor of **Spiro**.

Vandalism and looting of important archaeological sites is a problem everywhere. But Spiro was hit particularly hard. Mere mention of the name "Spiro" brings chills to many an archaeological spine. For here was played out one of North America's most ghastly acts of archaeological larceny.

It began in 1933, when a group calling themselves the "Pocola Mining Company" launched a commercial enterprise to loot and market the unusual artifacts buried in the mounds of Spiro. They leased the site, then began digging into Craig Mound, the largest of the Spiro earthworks—a splendid choice indeed, because this particular mound contained an unbelievable treasury of Southern Cult paraphernalia.

Inside Craig Mound, they found priceless stone effigy pipes, shell beads, ceramic vessels, copper plaques, axes, basketry, and cloth fragments. But particularly treasured were the spectacular

─── △△△ ───

family of five to fifteen people. During the winter, they provided welcome warmth, and many domestic activities took place inside. Then, during the summer, these tasks were moved outdoors, and the houses provided cover from the frequent summer thunderstorms. Smoky smudge fires helped keep summer insects at bay. This house is typical of the Mississippian settlements, hamlets, and villages associated with various ceremonial centers that characterized most of the eastern Oklahoma valleys between A.D. 1000 and 1450.

Mississippian life at Spiro, as elsewhere, was played out in long-term political cycles. Local communities—involving thousands of people—accepted the rule and leadership of a particularly effective chief. But upon his or her death, they fragmented once again into constituent communities. Competition for power and prestige became intense, both within local Mississippian communities and across regions, for control of key revenue-producing resources.

As political and social ranking proliferated, the Mississippian mind-

▲▲▲

marine shell cups and gorgets of Spiro. These finds enriched and energized the diggers of Pocola Mining Company, and they burrowed on relentlessly.

Literally thousands of the priceless Spiro artifacts were hawked to art dealers and private collectors of antiquities. And, of course, because of the way they dug, who knows how many more were destroyed in the recovery process? Once torn from their original setting, their scientific value diminished immeasurably. Even those artifacts that found their way into museum collections had been stripped of their all-important archaeological context.

The wanton destruction at Spiro continued unabated until 1935, when the Pocola Mining Company's lease expired. Thankfully, the Works Project Administration joined with local Oklahoma historical and archaeological societies to protect Spiro from further depredations, and to conduct limited scientific excavations there. Over a five-year period, detailed site maps were prepared, plotting locations of mounds, house foundations, trash deposits, and so forth.

But the damage had been done, and the destruction at Spiro reminds us all how fragile is our archaeological heritage. We should all work to protect it.

▲▲▲

set was increasingly reinforced by ceremony and sacrament. These beliefs expressed ancestral obligations, celebrated successful harvests, hunts, and warfare, and reinforced esteem for social leaders through elaborate mortuary ritual.

As at Moundville, the grave goods from Spiro have told archaeologists a great deal about ancient Mississippian lifeways. Ritual dress and ornamentation is vividly depicted on the engraved shell artifacts from Craig Mound and elsewhere at Spiro. Sometimes, even specific individuals can be recognized.

The falcon-impersonator, for instance, is known to have had a unique status in Spiro society. The falcon was considered to be a symbol of ferocious and courageous behavior, and the falcon-impersonator wore the forked eye motif to symbolize this valor. It is one of the most distinctive and widespread motifs across Mississippian America.

Like so many Mississippian ceremonial centers, Spiro experienced a gradual decline in population, and was abandoned about A.D. 1450.

The reasons for its demise are not entirely clear. Many scholars believe that the modern Caddo and/or Wichita tribes may be the modern descendants of the Mississippian people who once lived and worshipped at Spiro.

Spiro Mounds Archaeological Park (Spiro, OK; 2½ mi. E. of Spiro on SR 9, then 4¼ mi. N.) is Oklahoma's only archaeological park, covering 140 acres and containing a dozen Mississippian mounds. Craig Mound has been reconstructed, as has a Spiro period Mississippian house. The interpretive center presents an introductory slide program, interpretive murals, and exhibits with striking artifacts including effigy pipes, ornaments, and trade items. Phone (918) 962-2062.

THE OUTSIZED EAGLE OF OCMULGEE

Between A.D. 900 and 1100, a major Mississippian chiefdom was head-quartered at **Ocmulgee, Georgia.** During its heyday, it rivalled any place in North America for its distinctive achievements in architecture, crafts, commerce, and civic leadership.

Immense temple mounds dominate the landscape at Ocmulgee. Like other Mississippian chiefdoms, those of the Macon plateau erected a series of impressive earthen mounds for public ceremonies and key political events. These flat-topped pyramidal mounds were raised in layers, probably at distinct intervals. A stepped ramp ascended the front of the Great Temple Mound, which supported at least three separate wooden structures. Inside the Funeral Mound, archaeologists have encountered carefully built log tombs at the lowest level; other burials were placed in each of the mound's seven levels. Here lay the elite of Mississippian society.

But the most distinctive feature at Ocmulgee is an extraordinary subterranean earth lodge, painstakingly and accurately reconstructed in the center of the site atop the actual archaeological remains. The original clay floor has remained in place for a thousand years. Around the edge are remnants of a low clay wall, outlining a central circular area about forty-two feet in diameter. At the foot of the wall is the original clay bench that encircled the chamber. It is neatly divided into forty-seven individual seats, each with a shallow basin on its inside edge. Three of the seats are obviously special, set apart from the others on their own clay platform, facing the long entrance passage.

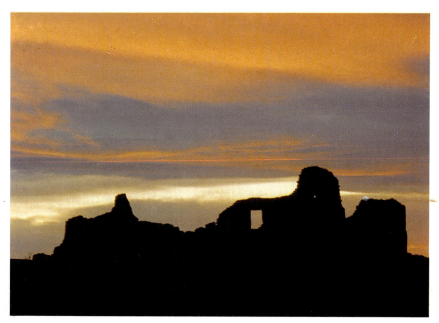

Sunset view of Pueblo del Arroyo, Chaco Canyon, New Mexico. (Courtesy of the American Museum of Natural History, photograph by Russ Finley.)

Detail of the excavated ruins at Tyuonyi, one of the most substantial pueblos in the Rio Grande area. According to the available tree-ring dates, these 400 rooms were built between A.D. 1383 and 1466. When the population was at its peak, the pueblo stood three stories high. (Courtesy of the American Museum of Natural History, photograph by Russ Finley.)

European glass trade beads worn by Native American people at Mission Santa Catalina de Guale, Georgia. Several beads have been wrapped with gold leaf. (Courtesy of the American Museum of Natural History photograph by William Ballenburg.)

Seventeenth-century ceramic vessel made by Native Americans living at Mission Santa Catalina de Guale, Georgia. The unusual form is thought to represent the shape of the mission bell used to summon mission Indians to Mass. (Courtesy of the American Museum of Natural History, photograph by William Ballenberg.)

European glass trade beads worn by Native American people at Mission Santa Catalina de Guale, Georgia. Several beads have been wrapped with gold leaf. (Courtesy of the American Museum of Natural History photograph by William Ballenburg.)

Seventeenth-century ceramic vessel made by Native Americans living at Mission Santa Catalina de Guale, Georgia. The unusual form is thought to represent the shape of the mission bell used to summon mission Indians to Mass. (Courtesy of the American Museum of Natural History, photograph by William Ballenberg.)

Mission San Xavier del Bac, on the Tohono O'Odham (Papago) Indian Reservation (south of Tucson, Arizona) is often called the "White Dove of the Desert." Many architectural historians consider San Xavier to be North America's most spectacular example of Spanish colonial architecture. (Photograph by the author.)

Map of Mission San Francisco Solano, located on the central plaza in downtown Sonoma, California. (Photograph by the author.)

Aerial view of the Emerald Mound, on the Natchez Trace Parkway, Mississippi. Covering nearly eight acres, this huge flat-topped platform mound is the second largest in North America—second only to Monks Mound at Cahokia. (Courtesy of the National Park Service.)

The stone "Rattler" pipe from the Spiro Mounds. (Courtesy of the Oklahoma Museum of Natural History.)

Woodpecker shell gorget from the Spiro Mounds, Oklahoma. According to modern interpretations the four woodpeckers symbolize both the sky and military power. Gorgets were common symbols throughout the American Southeast for chiefly power and authority. (Courtesy of the Oklahoma Museum of Natural History.)

A Hopewell platform pipe recovered from Mound City, Ohio. The bird effigy is hollowed out, to form the tobacco pipe bowl; the mouthpiece, with a narrow, drilled hole is to the left. (Courtesy of the National Park Service.)

Three views of a Hopewell platform pipe from Mound City, Ohio. (Courtesy of the National Park Service, photograph by Michael Bitsko.)

View across the central Hopewell mound group at Mound City, Ohio. (Courtesy of the National Park Service, photograph by Joe Murray.)

Desert bighorn effigies from the Hohokam site of Snaketown, Arizona. (Courtesy of the American Museum of Natural History.)

This classic Mimbres bowl depicts a stylized mountain lion motif. (Courtesy of the National Museum of the American Indian.)

Hohokam human effigies from Snaketown, Arizona. (Courtesy of the American Museum of Natural History.)

Petroglyphs on a sandstone boulder in the Petrified Forest National Park, Arizona. (Courtesy of the American Museum of Natural History, photograph by Josef Knull.)

Petroglyphs near Tucson, Arizona. The spiral is considered to be a hallmark for Hohokam rock art. The human dancers appear to be wearing tall headdresses. (Courtesy of the American Museum of Natural History, photograph by Evan J. Davis.)

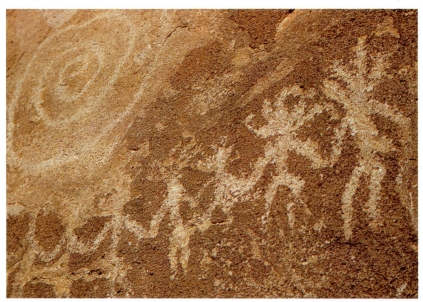

View of Montezuma Castle, near Camp Verde, Arizona. This remarkably well-preserved five-story, 20-room ruin was occupied between A.D. 1125 and 1400. Despite extensive vandalism, it contains original ceilings, doorways, floors, and a walled balcony. (Photograph by the author.)

Abstract and representational petroglyphs at "Newspaper Rock," located south of the Painted Desert Visitor Center, Petrified Forest National Park. (Courtesy of the American Museum of Natural History, photograph by Peter Goldberg.)

Sunset view of Pueblo del Arroyo, Chaco Canyon, New Mexico. (Courtesy of the American Museum of Natural History, photograph by Russ Finley.)

Detail of the excavated ruins at Tyuonyi, one of the most substantial pueblos in the Rio Grande area. According to the available tree-ring dates, these 400 rooms were built between A.D. 1383 and 1466. When the population was at its peak, the pueblo stood three stories high. (Courtesy of the American Museum of Natural History, photograph by Russ Finley.)

Extending from the wall almost to the sunken central fire pit is the most remarkable feature of all. Elevated slightly above the bench is the unmistakable larger-than-life effigy of an eagle, almost identical to Southern Cult images depicted on Mississippian copper plates. It has all the characteristic features, from the squarish shape of the body and wings, to the slight taper from the base toward the shoulder. At the eagle's head is a clear and obvious depiction of the forked eye, another distinctive characteristic of the Southern Cult.

Today's visitor can stoop inside the cool reconstructed earth lodge, and view firsthand this unique archaeological treasure. It requires little imagination to conjure up the fifty or so Mississippian dignitaries who, in this very space, conducted their sacred business and grappled with the complexities of their own time, slowly and deliberately arriving at the life-and-death decisions that determined the fate of their community. No doubt these deliberations were accompanied by the ceremonial consumption of the "black drink," another element of Southern Cult ceremonialism. The black drink was made from roasted leaves of the cassina (holly) shrub, boiled into a frothy brew. Drunk with great ceremony from shell cups emblazoned with Southern Cult motifs, the

---

Ocmulgee National Monument (Macon, GA; take US 80 E. from I-16 exit 4 and follow signs) contains some of the most impressive native American archaeology in the Southeast. Several different American Indian cultures inhabited this area over the past 10,000 years: Paleoindian and Archaic hunters and gatherers, Woodland hunters and gardeners, early and late Mississippian farmers, and historic Creeks.

Most impressive is the major Mississippian village and ceremonial center that once stood here. Six temple mounds, one burial mound, and a restored ceremonial earth lodge remain. A trading outpost operated here from 1690 to 1715.

The visitor center houses a major archaeological museum; a short film, *People of the Macon Plateau* is shown every half hour. The Discovery Lab provides numerous hands-on activities. Foot trails connect most of the park's features, and the Opelofa Nature Trail branches off the main walking trail and explores the lowlands of Walnut Creek. Temple Mound Drive permits visitors to tour the major mounds by car. Special events are held Feb.–Nov. Phone (912) 752-8257.

black drink conferred spiritual purification upon all who participated. The minds of village leaders were cleared for debate, the bodies of warriors cleansed and strengthened for battle.

More prosaic evidence was uncovered at nearby Cornfield Mound. When archaeologists excavated Cornfield Mound, originally about eight feet high, they found, to their amazement, preserved beneath it the remains of what one archaeologists called "rows of hilled-up dirt"—an unmistakable series of neatly cultivated rows from an ancient Mississippian agricultural field.

This old cornfield is particularly puzzling because of what we know about the spatial organization of most Mississippian elite centers. The crops are supposed to be growing in the rich bottom lands, not smack in the middle of a sacred Mississippian precinct. Clearly, this was no ordinary cornfield. Some archaeologists think it was a sacred seed patch, where the Mississippians grew their offerings to the gods, with a commemorative mound deliberately built on top.

ANGEL: MISSISSIPPIAN HAMLET IN THE OUTBACK

Not all Mississippians lived in powerful cities like Moundville and Cahokia. Our next stop takes us to a rather small, but also quite typical hamlet in the Mississippian hinterlands. **Angel Mounds State Historic Park**, Indiana, is one of the best-preserved precontact settlements in North America. Here, between about A.D. 900 and 1600, a Mississippian chiefdom flourished, numbering between 1,000 and 3,000 people.

The Angel townsite was probably chosen because of its proximity to the river, the rich soil, and the abundant wild food resource available nearby. The downtown area covered 103 acres, and served as a regional center for trade, religious, and political activities. At its peak, Angel boasted perhaps 200 dwellings, plus an impressive array of public buildings, gardens, and probably granaries for storing corn.

An imposing stockade protected the Angel site on three sides, the Ohio River providing the fourth boundary. Bastions were placed about every forty yards, protecting the homes of the citizenry inside. The cornfields outside were left undefended. To make this palisade, which has been partially reconstructed, the Angelinos first dug an encircling trench, into which they set upright posts. Twigs and cane were intertwined, and then the wall was covered with a mud-and-grass mixture called *daub*. Although this stockade provided adequate defense, the wattle-and-daub technique required considerable maintenance, and the stockade was rebuilt several times during the occupation of Angel.

Inside their palisaded town, the commoners lived in two kinds of houses. Winter houses were built of wattle-and-daub, like the stockade. The house interiors were painted for decoration, and a hole in the ceiling allowed smoke to escape from the central hearth. During the summertime, they erected open-sided huts that provided both shelter and ventilation for activities such as cooking.

Each house sheltered an entire family, and provided the focus for most domestic activities: sleeping, cooking meals, storing food (in below-ground pits), tool and pottery making, and so forth. In nearby household gardens, they grew corn, beans, squash, pumpkins, gourds, and sunflowers.

The people at Angel built earthen mounds, each used as an artificial platform on which to erect important structures. The largest, Mound A, covers four acres and towers forty-four feet above the settlement. These mounds were artificial mountains, designed to raise the temples—and the Angel elite—bringing them closer to the sun and the heavens. Less romantically, the temple mounds also kept royal feet dry from floodwaters when the nearby Ohio River annually overflowed its banks.

One of the temples has been reconstructed, using information gleaned during the archaeological excavations. This temple provided the religious focus of the community. And because the chiefdom at Angel relied heavily on maize-based agriculture, many of their rituals and ceremonies must have related directly to the planting, maintenance, and harvesting of the corn crop. Among other functions, the Mississippian elite reserved the right to predict the weather. They also used sophisticated calendars to monitor both lunar and solar events.

Although the Mississippian elite system disappeared at European contact, many of the Mississippian beliefs live on among southeastern Indian people. Vestiges of the Southern Cult survive in the *puskita* (or "green corn ceremony"), the most important ritual of Creek and many other historic period tribes in the Southeast. The Green Corn Ceremony was probably performed countless times at the Angel Mounds.

Toward the end of each summer's corn harvest, the Green Corn Ceremony, or *Busk*, was held to celebrate and give thanks. It was a time for renewing life. Men repaired the communal buildings. Old feuds and animosities were patched up. Women extinguished their hearth fires, cleansed their houses, and broke their cooking pots. All male-female contact was forbidden.

A handful of specially designated village chiefs—healers, tribal elders, and celebrated young warriors—gathered in the town square to fast and to purify themselves. Tribal elders occupied their own places of distinction, opposite the honored warriors, whose faces and torsos had been painted red. The high priest began the most critical part of the Green Corn ritual, ceremonially lighting the new sacred fire. To the sound of drumbeats and incantations, selected elders circled the flame. All wore white, the symbolic color of the Busk. Once the Green Corn dance was completed, coals from the ceremonial hearth rekindled the home fires. Village women prepared a sumptuous feast of celebration and thanksgiving. It only remained for the villagers to file to the nearby stream for a communal bath, purifying themselves for the new year to come and completing a sacrament handed down from ancient Mississippian times.

Angel was abandoned before the European explorers arrived. As we will see, archaeologists have great difficulty explaining the decline of the Mississippian culture, at Angel or anywhere else.

Angel Mounds State Historic Park (Evansville, IN; 7 mi. E. at 8215 Pollack Ave.) is a 103-acre Mississippian site containing reconstructed winter houses, a roundhouse, summer houses, a temple, and a portion of the stockade wall. The interpretive center, displaying artifacts found during excavations at Angel Mounds, shows films; a nature preserve offers bird walks and trails. Phone (812) 853-3956.

SUNWATCH: ARCHAEOLOGY IN ACTION

SunWatch Archaeological Park, near Dayton, Ohio, represents the remains of a community constructed by people of the Fort Ancient tradition, a Mississippian group living in the central Ohio Valley during the A.D. 1200s.

This once-thriving, carefully planned community covered about three acres on the well-drained first terrace of the Great Miami River, near the fertile soils in the river valley. These Fort Ancient people exploited three major life zones: the prairie, the woodland, and the river. The prairie environment during late prehistoric times was different from what we see today; it comprised big and little bluestem grasses, so-called Indian grass, and several other wild prairie plants used as dye, fiber, food, and medicine.

In the river bottoms, they grew corn, beans, squash, gourds, and sunflowers. They also grew tobacco for ceremonial and ritual purposes.

These fields were probably cleared by the age-old slash-and-burn method. Trees were first girdled to kill them, then the underbrush was fired. The loose, ashy soil around the dead trees was worked into the garden plots with digging sticks and shell hoes. Although men did the heavy clearing, the women and children were probably responsible for planting, weeding, and harvesting. Judging from more recent Native American groups, each family tended a four- or five-acre garden; Sun-Watch village had perhaps 150 acres under cultivation.

SunWatch was laid out with an open central plaza; in its middle stood a large pole around which an estimated twenty-five to thirty houses were built. It is thought that 250 people lived here for no more than fifteen to twenty years.

One of the Fort Ancient houses has been reconstructed using the original wattle-and-daub technique. Because the insides of these houses were dark and smoky, many household chores were done outside, in front of the houses. A wooden mortar was used to grind corn into flour. Women also made pottery, dressed skins, sewed, wove baskets and textiles, and made bone tools. Fortunately for the archaeologists, the tools and byproducts of these activities were often dropped on the ground or swept into nearby trash pits.

Along the western margin is the so-called Big House, perhaps the chief's dwelling, but more likely the communal council house that formed the center of the religious and political life at SunWatch. The fire hearth is not positioned in the center, but rather offset to the south, perhaps to line up with the sun calendar (discussed below). Judging from similar structures recorded by early explorers and missionaries, this council house was probably decorated with posts carved with human faces, turtles, and snakes. On the walls were brightly painted murals. Masks, pipes, sacred bundles, and costumes were stored in the rear room.

The main plaza, an oval area about 190 feet across was kept clean of trash and pits. A wolf burial was found here, accompanied by some wolf tooth ornaments; an effigy wolf-man pipe was also found, suggesting to some that the wolf was a clan symbol or legendary ancestor to the SunWatch village people.

The large pole in the center of the plaza was a red cedar trunk, nearly two feet in diameter and standing perhaps forty feet in height. A short distance to the northwest, four more posts were arranged in a line perpendicular to the center pole. Some archaeologists think that this arrangement functioned as a solar calendar, used to schedule events and rituals based on astronomical alignments.

If so, it may have worked like this: Twice each year—in late April and again in mid-August—the shadow of the center pole would line up with the hearth in the Big House, the largest structure known in SunWatch village. The spring date corresponds to the traditional time of planting, and late August signals the beginning of the harvest, traditionally observed in the Green Corn Ceremony throughout the eastern Woodlands. The central post also marked the winter solstice, the shortest day of the year.

SunWatch was initially located by avocational archaeologists in the 1960s. Because of threatened destruction (to make way for a sewage treatment plant), the Dayton Museum of Natural History conducted controlled excavations here, their work turning up evidence of such archaeological significance that the site was saved from destruction. Both professional and avocational archaeologists affiliated with Sun-Watch are conducting many useful experiments to reconstruct life during Fort Ancient times. SunWatch has several demonstration gardens that closely follow accounts by early trappers and traders and make use of data retrieved during the archaeological excavations.

The Dayton Society of Natural History reconstructed one wattle-and-daub house as a technological experiment, and also to show what the SunWatch houses must have looked like. Then, in 1982, the experimental building was burnt to the ground by vandals. Although the reconstructed house was no longer available for instructional purposes, the burning itself can provide archaeologists with important clues about what such structures look like in the archaeological record. The burnt ruins are still there, and may some day be excavated as another experiment.

Chris Turnbow, an archaeologist from the Dayton Museum of Natural History, has used this opportunity to conduct some modern experiments designed to flesh out what life must have been like at Mississippian SunWatch. In January 1992, Turnbow spent a week living in one of the remaining reconstructed SunWatch houses attempting to learn, among other things, how much firewood was required for cooking and warmth inside a Mississippian house. Once known, this figure could be extrapolated across the thirty such houses that once existed at Sun-Watch, allowing archaeologists to judge, quantitatively, the environmental impact of a village this size on the local forest.

How well did the wattle-and-daub structures shield the original inhabitants at SunWatch? Not very well, according to Turnbow's experiment. "The first three days we stayed there, the highs were in the 20s and the lows were about 10, with a 35 mph wind" he said. "We thought the thatched roof would be a good insulator, but the wind just whipped right through." During this cold snap, the SunWatch volunteers burned up to 200 pounds of wood a day. Later in the week, after temperatures settled into the 40s, wood consumption dropped to about 70 pounds per day.

Turnbow calculated that at this rate, roughly 180,000 pounds of firewood would be required for a single winter at SunWatch. "There just couldn't have been enough easily available firewood for that." Perhaps, as Turnbow believes, agricultural people such as those living at SunWatch moved to warmer places in the winter, or they established temporary winter camps deep in the woods where firewood was plentiful. Maybe they lived in wigwams, smaller and easier to heat. With the onset of spring weather, they may have moved back to SunWatch to prepare the fields for planting.

Other archaeologists, including David Brose of the Cleveland Museum of Natural History, question Turnbow's findings. Brose calls attention to early French accounts which note that Native American women from Ohio spent much of their time gathering firewood. Brose thinks that these Fort Ancient people were sedentary year-round; when the local resources such as firewood became overextended, they moved the entire village into a new area. If true, this may be why SunWatch was only occupied for three decades.

SunWatch Archaeological Park (Dayton, OH; is located S. on I-75 to exit 51, W. 1 mile on Edward C. Moses Blvd., then S. 1 mile on West River Rd.) is a twelfth-century Indian village, reconstructed on a partially excavated Fort Ancient settlement. Visitors can see a Woodhenge calendar for determining planting and harvesting times, plus artifacts on display and occasional ongoing excavations in the summer. Special events include craft and technology workshops, candlelight tours, summer classes, and Native American dancing. Phone (513) 268-8199.

MISSISSIPPIAN DEMISE AND SURVIVAL

Some of the great Mississippian centers were in decline by the time de Soto tramped through the American Southeast in 1540, but their ultimate collapse can be directly related to European incursions into their territory. The reasons are distressing even today.

Disease took a dreadful toll. A smallpox epidemic may have reached inland North American populations within a generation after Columbus stepped ashore in San Salvador. The largest Mississippian societies were hardest hit by disease. These towns attracted the unwelcome attention of the conquerors—Narváez, de Soto, and the like. They were searching for native wealth and local provisions to feed their hungry men. The de Soto diaries tell a story of deliberate Spanish cruelty and devastating military operations. Pitched battles killed hundreds. In at least one case, thousands of native people died.

Disease and disorder rapidly overtook the surviving Mississippian towns. As American Indian populations plummeted, most Mississippian societies simply imploded. Rarely could a group, such as the Natchez of Mississippi, continue to maintain their social and economic bureaucracies from Mississippi times into the historic period.

In the less populated hinterlands, epidemics wiped out agricultural and nonagricultural people alike. Some ancient tribes, like the Calusa of southwest Florida, survived and maintained their way of life for generations. But many smaller-scale societies were unable to maintain their numbers, and no remnant populations survived. By the first decades of the seventeenth century, the native population of Florida and coastal Georgia had become missionized Indians. They were soon to vanish as well.

Throughout the Southeast, survivors of this catastrophe struggled to create political and social solutions to the new, strange environment. More typical was the Mississippian province of Coosa, once preeminent over parts of Tennessee, northern Georgia, and Alabama. The complex political and social ties that had defined the Mississippian lifeway unraveled as epidemics decimated population numbers. People no longer constructed public works such as mounds and palisades. They no longer supported their royalty. They no longer hosted elaborate mortuary rituals for their ancestors. Like many other key sites, Coosa (northwestern Georgia) ceased to exist by about 1600. Depopulated, decentralized, and demoralized, Mississippian people became refugees in their own land. Facing alien invaders and slavers, the castaways and survivors tried to confederate.

In Georgia and Alabama, a confederation of many refugee groups came to be dominated by the Creeks (as the English called them). This confederacy comprised about fifty towns, divided into "red" (or war) towns and "white" (or peace) towns. From the red towns came the war leaders; the white towns, dedicated to the pursuit of peace, supplied civil leaders and the principal chiefs of the confederacy. They successfully adapted to the European presence, first Spanish, then English and French.

Other descendents of the mound-building Mississippians became the Chickasaws and the Choctaws. Their Mississippian heritage is evident in their symbolic attachment to the ancient temple mounds. While Indians of the contact period no longer constructed pyramids, the beliefs underlying the practice persevered in southeastern Indian language, folklore, and practice. The Mississippian mounds (often called earth islands) came to symbolize a oneness with the land. They became concrete manifestations of unbroken ritual traditions of fertility and purification, as carried on in the Green Corn ceremonialism of the displaced southeastern tribes.

In one Muskogee legend, warriors encounter and subsequently kill their enemies in a rival town. The survivors, mourning for their dead kinsmen, begin to build earthen mounds in which to bury their dead. These symbolic mounds provide supernatural support and sanctuary, creating a sanctified place for ritual purification. Another tradition describes a legendary attack by Cherokees upon the Muskogee, whose warriors were said to have hidden inside a ceremonial mound. The Muskogee surprise their attackers by "pouring up from the bowels of the earth" to defeat the invading Cherokees. Both cases are clear continuities linking ancient Mississippian people with historic southeastern tribes.

The huge platform mound at **Nanih Waiya** (in modern Winston County, Mississippi) is considered by the Choctaw to be the Great Mother in their creation tale. Legend holds that while wandering in search of a homeland, the Choctaw people finally reached the correct place, when the ancestors' bones were piled high on the ground and covered with cypress bark to create a great mound. Thereafter the mound at Nanih Waiya was planted with trees to symbolize the renewal and purification of their world. The Choctaws hold their Green Corn dances here.

Nanih Waiya Historical Site (Noxapater, MS; on SR 397) is believed to be the ancestral home of the Choctaw people. At the center of the site, erected about A.D. 400, is a large sacred ceremonial mound referred to by the Choctaw as "Mother." About 200 yards away is another large burial mound. Phone (601) 773-7988.

Still other refugees, the Cherokees, came to occupy the hill and mountain country of western North Carolina and eastern Tennessee. Survivors, they were to become the largest tribe in the Southeast, with some 20,000 people living in sixty towns. Today, many of their descendents live in the southern United States.

△△△

UNDERSTANDING THE MISSISSIPPIAN MOUND AT NANIH WAYA: A NATIVE AMERICAN PERSPECTIVE

Choctaw people tell a creation story that details how they wandered for forty-three years in search of a homeland, carrying with them the bones of their deceased relatives. Finally, upon reaching central Mississippi, the Choctaw *minko* (headman), called his people together and addressed them as follows:

"Let us call this place; this, Nunih Waya encampment, our home; and it shall be so, that when a man, at his hunting camp, in the distant forests, shall be asked for his home place, his answer will be, 'Nunih Waya.' And to establish Nunih Waya more especially as our permanent home, the place to which when we are far away, our thoughts may return with feelings of delight and respectful pleasure, I propose that we shall by general consent and mutual good feelings select an eligible location within the limits of the encampment and there, in the most respectful manner, bring together and pile up in beautiful and tasteful style the vast amount of bones we have packed so far and with which many of the people have been so grievously oppressed. Let each set of bones remain in its sack, and after the sacks are closely and neatly piled up, let them be thickly covered over with cypress bark. After this, to appease and satisfy the spirits of our deceased relatives, our blood kin, let all persons, old and young, great and small, manifest their respect for the dead, by their energy and industry in carrying dirt to cover them up, and let the work of carrying and piling earth upon them be continued until every heart is satisfied. These bones, as we all know, are of the same iska, the same kindred. They were all the same flesh and blood; and for us to pile their bones all in the same heap and securely cover them up will be more pleasing to the spirits, than it will be to let them remain amongst the people, to be scattered over the plains, when the sacks wear out in the hands of another generation who will know but little and care less about them. . . ."

Men were then appointed to select an appropriate place for the mound to be erected on, and to direct the work while in progress. They selected a level piece of sandy land, not far from the middle creek; laid it off in an oblong square and raised the foundation, by piling up earth which they dug up some distance to the north of the foundation. It was

△△△

△△△

raised and made level as high as a man's head and beat down very hard. It was then floored with cypress bark before the work of placing the sacks of bones commenced.

The people gladly brought forward and deposited their bones until there were none left. The bones, of themselves, had built up an immense mound. They brought the cypress bark, which was neatly placed on, till the bone sacks were all closely covered in, as dry as a tent. While the tool carriers were working with the bark, women and children and all the men, except the hunters, carried earth continually, until the bark was all covered from sight constituting a mound half as high as the tallest forest tree. . . .

At the Nunih Waya encampment, everything went well and there were no complaints. Their hunters made wide excursions, acquainted themselves with the geography of the country to the extent of many days' journey around. But, as yet, they had discovered no signs of the enemy, or of any other people. In this happy condition of health and plenty—for they had enlarged their fields and were harvesting abundant crops of corn—years rolled 'round; the work on the mound was regularly prosecuted; and at the eighth green corn dance celebrated at Nunih Waya, the committee who had been appointed at the commencement, reported to the assembled multitude that the work was completed and the mound planted with the seeds of the forest trees, in accordance with the plan and direction of the minko, at the beginning of the work.

The minko then instructed the good old Lopina, who had carried it so many years, to take the golden sun to the top of the great mound and plant it in the center of the level top.

When the people beheld the golden emblem of the sun glittering on the top of the great work, which by the united labor of their own hands, had just been accomplished, they were filled with joy and much gladness. And in their songs at the feast, which was then going on, they would sing:

"Behold the wonderful work of our hands; and let us be glad. Look upon the great mound; its top is above the trees, and its black shadow lies on the ground, a bowshot. It is surmounted by the golden emblem of the sun; its glitter (tohpakali) dazzles the eyes of the multitude. It inhumes the bones of fathers and relatives; they died on our sojourn in the wilderness. They died in a far off wild country; they rest at Nunih Waya. Our journey lasted many winters; it ends at Nunih Waya."

△△△

WHERE ELSE TO SEE MISSISSIPPIAN ARCHAEOLOGY

The following is a list of sites and museums that feature some of the artifacts and/or remains discussed in this chapter. Complete information on each is listed in the appendix by state at the end of the book.

Aztalan State Park and Museum (Lake Mills, WI)

Chickasaw Village Site (Natchez Trace Parkway, MI)

Chucalissa Indian Museum (Memphis, TN)

Dickson Mounds Museum (Springfield, IL)

Etowah Mounds State Historic Park (Cartersville, GA)

Field Museum of Natural History (Chicago, IL)

Florida Museum of Natural History (Gainesville, FL)

Illinois State Museum (Springfield, IL)

Indian Mound and Museum (Florence, AL)

Kansas Museum of History (Topeka, KS)

Kolomoki Mounds Historic Park (Blakely, GA)

Lake Jackson Mounds State Archaeological Site (Tallahassee, FL)

Frank H. McClung Museum (Knoxville, TN)

Oklahoma Museum of Natural History (University of Oklahoma, Norman, OK)

Parkin Archaeological State Park (Parkin, AK)

Shiloh National Military Park (Savannah, TN)

Toltec Mounds State Park (Scott, AR)

Town Creek Indian Mound State Historic Site (Mount Gilead, NC)

University of Iowa, Museum of Natural History (Iowa City, IA)

University Museum (Fayetteville, AR)

Wickliffe Mounds (Wickliffe, KY)

COLLIDING WORLDS:
OLD AND NEW?

Navajo pictograph of a Spanish cavalcade in Canyon del Muerto, Arizona. (Courtesy of the American Museum of Natural History.)

H O L L Y W O O D ' S simple-minded version of the American Indian–European encounter usually begins with a charming interlude between sensitive newcomer and Noble Savage, often ending with a bloody, one-sided denouement on a battlefield somewhere. Time after time, similar causes are seen as producing similar results.

Such views are suspect, of course, on a number of counts, not the least of which are the facts of geography, the long-standing patterns of Native American culture, and the specific motives of the European group involved—its size, composition, national and cultural origin, religious denomination, and economic orientation.

Too often, American Indian people are also assumed to share some kind of similar, if ill-fated, common strategy for dealing with the progressive waves of white invaders. The truth is that Native Americans were considerably more diverse than the Europeans who came to New World shores. American Indians were accustomed to dealing with those who looked different, spoke unintelligible languages, and whose motivations were suspect. The existence of Native American civilizations for thousands upon thousands of years had, in some way, pre-adapted Indian people for the arrival of the Europeans. In other ways, they were caught completely by surprise.

The truth is, the earliest European contacts in North America differed greatly in character, reflecting in part the differing ideologies and histories of the European powers involved. While not attempting

183

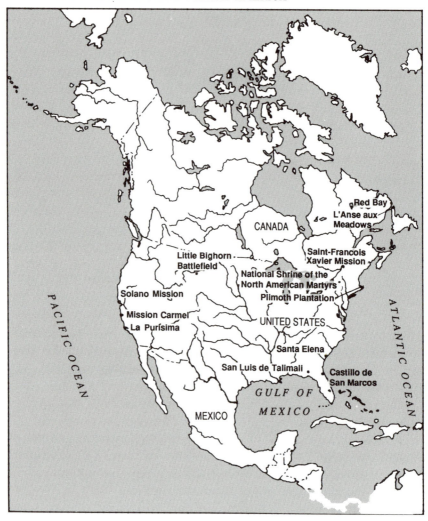

Some key sites of early European–Native American contact in North America.

to document the range of such interactions, I do wish to highlight some of the radically different circumstances under which native and European people were drawn together: in religious missions, commercial colonies, military establishments, and, inevitably, on blood-stained battlefields. Each encounter has its own human history and its own set of lessons.

MERCANTILE ENCOUNTERS

From Virginia northward, these early encounters were phrased in largely mercantile terms, initiated by privateers operating with crown permits or charters that granted rights to trade and exploit resources within a given territory. Here, European powers would exercise little control over day-to-day governance, and most European–Native American encounters were entrepreneurial and highly individualistic. Anglo-American colonists felt only a vague, after-the-fact sense of mission to "civilize" the Native American.

L'ANSE AUX MEADOWS: THE VIKING AND THE NATIVE AMERICAN

Who was the first European in Native America? Although most people automatically conjure up Columbus's 1492 exploits, we now know that Scandinavian Vikings actually beat Columbus by five centuries.

How do we know this? For one thing, the Norse sagas say so. Begun as oral narratives, the sagas were eventually written down a couple of hundred years later. Both *The Greenlanders' Saga* (probably written about 1200) and *The Saga of Erik the Red* (probably first copied down in the late thirteenth century) agree that in about 985, Erik the Red sailed from Iceland to settle in Greenland. That same year, Bjarni Herjolfsson tried to make the same trip, but poor weather drove him too far west, past Greenland, to a low, wooded coastline which he briefly explored before returning eastward.

In the early eleventh century, Erik's son Leif returned to the coast first seen by Bjarni Herjolfsson. After sighting this new territory several times himself, Leif finally came to a land with abundant salmon, fields of wild wheat, and "wineberries" that grew in profusion. He called this temperate land *Vinland*. After spending a frost-free winter constructing large houses, Leif and company sailed home to Greenland, where word of the discovery spread quickly. Others soon followed Leif's wake to Vinland, and the Norse sagas describe a number of encounters with native peoples. At times, the strangers engaged in peaceful trans-Atlantic trade. But these chance meetings were infrequent, and each side probably perceived more potential loss than assured gain.

By A.D. 1000 or so, the Vikings pulled back from their colonies west of Greenland, opting instead to concentrate on trade and lumbering. The sagas suggest that it was interruptions and outright opposition from native peoples that undermined the Vinland colonies. Native Americans had temporarily won out because of superior numbers and an unsurpassed knowledge of the American northland and how to survive in it.

But are the sagas to be trusted? Or were they simply Scandinavian folktales, forerunners of the ancient storytelling tradition of Hans

Christian Andersen. For more than a century, scholars and history buffs have debated when (and if) the Vikings made it to the Americas.

Today, we know that they did. In 1960, the century-long quest for Viking America successfully culminated on the remote tip of Newfoundland's Great Northern Peninsula, at a place called **L'Anse aux Meadows** (an English corruption of L'Anse aux Méduse, meaning Jellyfish Bay). The site had gone unrecognized for nine centuries, until Norwegian explorer and author Helge Ingstad rediscovered the unmistakable Viking presence here.

Ingstad's interest in the Vinland voyages began thirty years before, when he served as Norwegian governor of Erik the Red's country of eastern Greenland. Enthused with the idea of tracing the Norse voyages to America, Ingstad tried to think like a Viking. No armchair explorer, he launched a field expedition covering much of coastal eastern North America. His years of searching finally brought Ingstad to northern Newfoundland where he asked a local resident, Mr. George Decker, the same question he had posed dozens of times before: *Do you know of any ancient houses in this area?*

Intimately familiar with the landscape, Decker led him immediately to a rectangular group of overgrown bumps and ridges. This area, long known as L'Anse aux Meadows, looked promising indeed. Between 1961 and 1968, Ingstad and his wife, Anne Stine Ingstad—a trained archaeologist—conducted extensive excavations at L'Anse aux Meadows, uncovering a cluster of eight sod-walled structures, the unmistakable remains of an ancient Viking settlement.

The largest house at L'Anse aux Meadows contained six rooms arranged in three parallel rows. Its massive sod walls, seven feet thick in places, insulated the colonists from the cold, damp climate. Stone hearths were used for heat, light, and preparing food. Carefully constructed slate stone boxes were made for storing the late-night embers, ready to be rekindled into the morning's cooking fire. A radiocarbon date placed the occupation in the eleventh century—just the right time for a Viking settlement.

But the artifact inventory at L'Anse aux Meadows was sparse: all the diagnostic finds would fit into a single bread basket. One particularly important find, however, was a small soapstone spindle whorl—a women's spinning tool. Fitted to a wooden shaft, this small spinning ball was probably used for the hand spinning of wool. Not only did this diagnostic artifact definitely establish a Viking presence at L'Anse aux Meadows, but it also demonstrated that European women once lived in this remote American outpost.

The Ingstads also discovered an iron-processing smithy, across the brook from the major settlement. Bog iron occurs in abundance along the brook at L'Anse aux Meadows and while hardly a full-scale industrial smelting operation, the Norse smiths learned to produce the small rivets vitally necessary to repair their ships. This compelling evidence in hand, Helge and Anne Stine Ingstad confidently announced to the world that eleventh-century Vikings had indeed reached America.

The discovery of L'Anse aux Meadows shook the world. Many embraced these results as long-overdue proof of a pre-Columbian Viking presence in America. But others were unprepared to accept the Ingstads' claim at face value. From Newfoundland to New York, from Oslo to Montreal, newspapers and magazines featured the claims and counterclaims. The tone became downright ugly.

Today, there remains no reasonable doubt about the validity of L'Anse aux Meadows. The site was probably first occupied by a thirty-man Viking crew who put into the sheltered bay for a brief summertime visit. As they were plying up the small stream in their sturdy ship, they quickly found themselves surrounded by rich resources—streams abundantly stocked with salmon, timber aplenty, and a climate so temperate that the grass remained green throughout the winter. Entire families of settlers returned later.

But is L'Anse aux Meadows really Vinland? Probably not. L'Anse aux Meadows is more likely the entrance point to Vinland, a staging area from which explorers could range farther into Native America. Not having to return home in wintertime meant they could spend more time exploring and pulling together their cargo for resale in Greenland. As winter approached, they regrouped at L'Anse aux Meadows, gathered together to share tales and celebrated America's first Christmas.

L'Anse aux Meadows National Historic Park (St. Anthony, Newfoundland; from Corner Brook, take the Viking Trail 400 km N., then highway 430 N. to highway 436, follow it 30 km to the park) allows today's visitor to view the various artifacts recovered here, and a detailed model shows what the site might have looked like during its Norse heyday. Full-scale replicas of some buildings have been erected off-site, giving visitors the chance to see—and smell—what life was like here a thousand years ago. The structures themselves have been restored to look the way they did on the Ingstads' first visit. A film and audio program describe the discovery of L'Anse aux Meadows and reconstruct the lifeways of this unusual settlement. Phone (709) 623-2608 or 623-2601.

The finds at L'Anse aux Meadows confirm that Norse explorers voyaged to Newfoundland at least occasionally from the eleventh through perhaps the fourteenth centuries. The immediate vicinity also offered abundant seal, walrus, whale, codfish, salmon, fox, and caribou (now extinct). And, before the late Middle Age market was flooded with elephant ivory, Greenlanders provided much of Europe's ivory in the form of walrus tusks. Eventually, the Norse also discovered that dried codfish was a highly marketable item in Europe. They may have increased their fishing beyond immediate household needs.

What did the native people of Newfoundland think of all this? The sagas suggest that the Norse were willing to trade furs with the so-called Skraelings of Vinland, but otherwise they tell only of skirmishing attacks. And such contact probably took place even more frequently than noted in historical accounts.

There is also suggestive evidence from the United States, where an authentic Norse coin, minted between A.D. 1065 and 1080, was found near the mouth of Penobscot Bay. Today exhibited at the **Maine State Museum**, the coin had been perforated for suspension. Found in twelfth- or thirteenth-century Native American contexts, this distinctive coin was probably obtained from Norse sources far to the north, then worked its way southward through American Indian trade networks.

But apart from such small-scale acquisitions, few large-scale changes probably resulted from these early Norse–Native American encounters. There is also no evidence that disease was introduced, perhaps because of the low degree of face-to-face contact and the relative isolation of the Norse Greenland colonies from the European mainland. Nevertheless, such low-level, opportunistic trade and occasional discord are all important because they set in motion an interactive pattern that would persist in the eastern Arctic, with little modification, for the next 700 years.

RED BAY: AMERICA'S FIRST INDUSTRIAL SITE

Native American–Norse contacts probably persisted through the fourteenth and even fifteenth centuries, when the Greenland colonies declined and finally vanished altogether. The next wave of interaction was signaled by the arrival of John Cabot, and the installation of commercial enterprises north of the Gulf of St. Lawrence after A.D. 1500.

Basque fishermen had exploited whales in their European home port, the Bay of Biscay, since the eleventh or twelfth century. Ranging outward, they were among the first Europeans to exploit the vast cod fishery of Atlantic Canada. Recognizing the possibilities for a New World industry, they quickly adapted their traditional whaling technology to the New World waters, in part because overhunting was already destroying whaling in Europe.

Whaling was in full swing in Labrador by 1543, drawing several ships and a huge number of whaling boats from the Basque Provinces of southwestern France and northeastern Spain. These Basque whalers would spend six months each year here, pursuing bowhead and right whales off the coast of Newfoundland.

Dead whales were towed to one of the rendering stations along **Red Bay,** where flippers and flukes were removed; long strips of skin and blubber were cut into small chunks and boiled down in huge copper cauldrons in the "tryworks" which ringed Red Bay. The resulting whale oil was stored in wooden casks, newly made nearby by skilled coopers, then secured aboard the mother ships for transport back to Europe. The huge bones of whales dispatched by the Basques can still be found along the beaches of Red Bay Harbor. The whalers remained in the waters of Newfoundland and Labrador until mid-January when, just before freeze-up, they sailed home.

For almost four centuries, the Basque whaling headquarters lay abandoned, forgotten by history. Although fragments of red clay roofing tiles—used to roof over the sixteenth-century Basque buildings that once stood there—lay exposed on the beaches of Red Bay, few people gave them a second thought.

It was not until the mid-1970s that historical geographer Selma Barkham discovered thousands of documents in the obscure archives of the Spanish Basque region. Armed with stunning new information about the importance of the Red Bay whaling outpost, Barkham joined a team of archaeologists to search for these sites along the southern Labrador coast. Several whaling stations were quickly discovered, including the impressive remains at Red Bay.

The next year, Barkham joined with underwater archaeologists from Parks Canada in the search for the remains of the galleon *San Juan*, a Basque whaler that sank in Red Bay laden with 1,000 barrels of just-processed whale oil. Not only did the underwater team find the remarkably well-preserved *San Juan*, but they also excavated the remains of several other ships and boats beneath the frigid water of Red Bay Harbor.

A newly discovered cemetery contained the mass graves of seven sailors, apparently shipmates killed in pursuit of bowhead and right

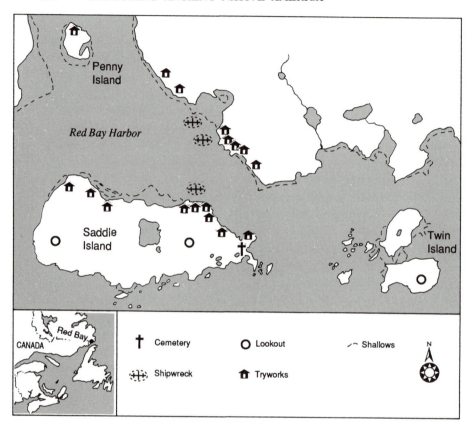

Distribution of sixteenth-century archaeological sites at Red Bay, Labrador. The terrestrial excavations have concentrated on sites located on Saddle Island. Underwater investigations have explored numerous well-preserved sunken whaling ships discovered throughout Red Bay waters.

whales. More than half of the Red Bay graves contained more than one sailor, mute testimony to the dangers of hunting the massive sea mammals.

Modern visitors to Red Bay can view plenty of archaeology and, if they are lucky, plenty of minke, humpback, giant blue, and even killer whales in the Strait of Belle Isle. But don't expect to see either right whales or bowhead whales—the Basque whalers took care of them. Today, bowhead whales are found only in arctic waters, and a small population of right whales now summer in the Gulf of Maine and the Bay of Fundy. Archaeologists working on whale bones recovered from Red Bay sites estimate that, during its eighty-year heyday, many thousands of whales were killed, severely straining the population sizes

Red Bay (Red Bay, LB; No phone) bills itself as the "World Whaling Capital, A.D. 1550–1600." It was the scene of a seasonal Basque whaling industry that had a major impact on both the sea mammal and Native American population here. Over the past several years, numerous terrestrial and underwater archaeological sites have been explored. An excellent visitor's center has been established to display and interpret the new finds.

required for survival. It is quite likely that the Basque predation started a global decline, from which right and bowhead whale populations may never recover. As in Europe a century before, overhunting did in the Basque whale fishery in Labrador.

The Basques had no grand designs on the native people: perhaps a little trade, but no year-round settlements, no missions, no deliberate modification of Native American culture. But regardless of their intent, these Basque whalers and the French fishermen after them, were to have a dramatic and irreversible effect all the same. American Indian and Inuit (Eskimo) people were quickly attracted by the possibilities of trade. But resourceful native people soon realized that whenever the Basques cleared out before freeze-up, the boats and iron implements left at the whaling stations were theirs for the taking.

Harvesting the spoils of Basque whaling rapidly created a new growth industry in Native America. Inuit people may have moved into Labrador specifically to exploit this new "natural resource." Each year, they could count on an annual replenishment of European implements, creating rapid culture change as these items were passed hand-to-hand. New trade routes sprang up, creating extensive down-the-line networks among the Inuit. These were significant contacts, with important ramifications for native cultures.

European goods became items of extraordinary prestige. Metal and hardwoods were refashioned into knife blades, drills, engraving tools, and axes—substitutes for locally available resources like stone, bone, and ivory. Although native people continued making traditional tools, they vastly preferred these new, exotic, and highly desirable materials, often going to incredible lengths to secure and control access to them.

These developments were to have far-reaching implications. Traditional Inuit social organization was well suited to circumstances defined by their natural environment. All families were inherently equal, with the proficient hunter or powerful shaman assuming positions of responsibility and authority. But beginning with the Basque presence, and continuing through the French exploitation of the rich fishery, Inuit life changed remarkably. Locations for settlement shifted to take full advantage of new sources for European prestige items. Hunting strategies shifted with the changing coastal ecology. And above all, a powerful class of native entrepreneurs arose, coming to dominate the political, social, and economic world of the Inuit.

In return, new European markets for baleen, oil, and skins were opened to them; later, the French were to add demand for feathers and ivory. Powerful Inuit individuals—perhaps those already empowered by hunting or shamanistic prowess—ignored their interregional relationships in their search for wealth, status, and power. In effect, these few wealthy individuals exploited traditional Inuit social and political forms, forging huge personal power bases at the expense of traditional family ties. Setting aside the traditional emphasis on stability, the new trade networks operated largely on bravado and an ability to manipulate people—all-important characteristics when dealing with European traders.

Because there were no traditional means of resolving conflict beyond the household level, blood feuds became alarmingly common. Reciprocal raiding, stealing, and stealth became the order of the day, as did captive-taking. In addition to heightened local competition for leverage and authority, the most assertive individuals found themselves highly rewarded in political and economic terms. In this way, the initial European contacts transfigured traditional Inuit society in a profound and irreversible way.

NATIVE AMERICANS AT PLIMOTH PLANTATION

Unlike Red Bay, New England was not a primary European target, at least not at first. But even prior to direct settlement, early explorers noted that natives in this region had widespread access to items of European dress and manufacture, perhaps having worked their way southward from the Maritimes. As among the Labrador Inuit, widespread changes were already taking place in response to the introduction of highly desirable European goods, with New England tribes adjusting to the new opportunities and hazards of European involvement.

Direct entrepreneurial commerce in New England did not commence until the seventeenth century. While still fundamentally mercantile in nature, the earliest encounters were different from those to the north. In New England, it was land, rather than the water, that held

△△△

INFECTIOUS ENCOUNTERS:
AN AMERICAN HOLOCAUST

It is almost impossible to fathom the massive loss of human life that took place when Europeans began to colonize Native America. The loss is inconceivable, for one thing, because nobody is sure how many people lived in pre-Columbian America. Estimates for the population of North America in 1492 range wildly. Fifty years ago, the distinguished anthropologist Alfred Kroeber estimated that only 900,000 people lived in North America on the eve of the conquest. At the other extreme, ethnohistorian Henry Dobyns has recently projected that population at 18 million. Cherokee sociologist Russell Thornton's estimate is about 7 million, and a recent assessment of the same data by Smithsonian Institution scientist Douglas Ubelaker weighs in at slightly less than 2 million.

But whatever figure one uses, it is clear that this population was devastated shortly after European contact. Native Americans started dying off in record numbers in 1493, and this trend continued throughout the centuries to follow. By 1900, the North American Indian population hit an all-time historical low of about 500,000 souls. Why all the death?

Although a complex mixture of cultural and historical factors was involved in the dramatic decline of Native American populations, the most telling (and least understood) was the impact of infectious disease. In the most elemental form of germ warfare, the European newcomers carried with them unseen agents that would decimate the indigenous population.

As Native American people began to have sustained interaction with European and African populations, they were subjected to a swift and violent series of epidemics, beginning as early as 1493. Spawned in the squalor of fourteenth-century European cities, diseases like smallpox, measles, typhus, and scarlet fever swept across Native America. Even before the introduction of smallpox, the native populations on many Caribbean islands simply vanished—perhaps from swine influenza introduced to America with pigs transported during Columbus's second voyage.

This is hardly to say that America before 1492 was a pristine,

△△△

disease-free paradise. It was not. Tuberculosis, venereal syphilis, amoebic dysentery, influenza, and pneumonia were all major health issues in pre-Columbian America. We also know that prior to European contact, Native North Americans suffered significantly from problems of local overpopulation, resource depletion, sporadic periods of starvation, chronic infectious disease, poor diet, and inadequate sanitation. These problems were particularly significant in areas that relied on intensive agricultural productivity.

But pestilence imported from Europe and Africa was radically different from anything previously seen in Native America. Because they had existed in virtual isolation since their ancestors had crossed the Bering Straits, the genetic makeup of American Indians made them highly vulnerable to everyday Old World diseases. These Old World diseases appear to have first spread throughout Native America as massive, hemisphere-wide epidemics—sometimes called *pandemics*—starting at initial points of contact with traders and explorers, then fanning out to engulf both continents.

Lacking immunity to diseases that thrive under crowded conditions, American Indians perished in droves—sometimes even before the first European explorers arrived in the area. The social cost of disease differed as well. Europeans had lived with these diseases for centuries. In Europe, most infections struck only the very young and those who survived became disease-immune as adults. Although mourned as individuals and family members, the deceased were economically unimportant. There was no threat to the social fabric.

But in America, European disease disrupted the core of Native American existence. As disease swept into a village, most of the population sickened because the adults lacked childhood immunity to it. As a result, few were well enough to care for the ill. And as more sickened, a sudden vacuum appeared in the labor force: nobody to hunt and fish, nobody to cultivate and harvest, nobody to govern, nobody even to bury the dead.

These new diseases did not just kill. They also disfigured survivors and led to despair, hostility, and dejection. Suicide became for some the only escape, entire families sometimes deliberately choosing to die together.

Introduced European diseases directly contributed to the downfall of many Mississippian societies. Diseases so decimated east Texas, that by 1680 the Caddoan-speaking peoples had completely abandoned large parts of their aboriginal territories. The native population of the southern Appalachian Mountains crashed dramatically in the wake of the 1539–1543 de Soto expedition.

Disease ripped through the densely populated Spanish missions of North America. Within a single generation, the California Indian population at Mission Santa Clara plunged 95 percent. The native population of California, estimated to have been about 300,000 when the first mission was built in 1769, had dropped by at least 50 percent by the time the missions were secularized in 1834. Mission records from the American Southwest indicate that two of every three native people perished between 1591 and 1638. Records at Mission Tumacacori (1773–1825), in southern Arizona, record that 93 percent of the children born there died before reaching the age of ten. Indian people living away from the missions usually fared better, at least for a while. But disease penetrated even the remote hinterlands, where entire tribes disappeared within a generation.

Traditional trade centers became the epicenters of sickness and disease. Eager to obtain the newly available European-manufactured goods, Native American traders now flocked to their traditional marketplaces. Many returned home with valuable hoards—gifts and guns, knives, and blankets. But the traders also unwittingly brought home with them the silent microbial killers. Even the booty was contaminated. The highly valued European horse and cattle introduced new diseases into Native American ecosystems, diseases that were to threaten indigenous species.

The devastation was more than numerical. In North America, along the rim of the earliest explorations, entire cultures were wiped out by disease before literate European witnesses could even record their presence. Lacking a conventional documentary

———— △△△ ————

record, we are left with only oral tradition and archaeology to learn of these vanished American cultures.

Our understanding of disease and human population in Native North America remains preliminary and incomplete. But one fact is beyond dispute: The American Indian population suffered a devastating reduction that began with initial Columbian contact and continued through the late nineteenth century. It is a shocking, ghastly story. Yet despite the biological and cultural disruptions, the remarkable fact is that American Indian populations survived. In fact, contemporary Native America is enjoying an unprecedented period of population recovery. By some counts, Native North American population figures have already surpassed the original numbers in 1492—and the numbers will grow in the foreseeable future. This demographic fact not only underscores the tenacity of Native American peoples but also provides a surprisingly upbeat postscript to this otherwise tragic chapter in American history.

———— △△△ ————

meaning for European settlers. European New Englanders came not to establish trading networks or exploit natural resources. They sought instead freedom of worship. These extreme Puritans, including the Pilgrims who came to the New World on the *Mayflower* in 1620, sought complete independence from the Anglican church.

Despite the hardships in founding Massachusetts—200 settlers died the first year—the progress was astonishing. In its first decade alone, the colony drew in 20,000 immigrants, many of them wealthy (a far cry from the impoverished idealists of the *Mayflower*). Like their Basque predecessors to the north, the New Englanders turned their eyes to the rich offshore codfish resources (later to become the symbol of the Commonwealth of Massachusetts). Massachusetts Bay Colony was to become an important commerce center that would seriously irritate London merchants before the end of the century.

These early settlers at Plimoth were heavily dependent upon peaceful relations with the local Wampanoag Indians, upon whose land the Pilgrims settled. Why, one might legitimately ask, were the Wampanoag so friendly to these aliens?

The answer is largely demographic. Immediately before the Pilgrims arrived, an epidemic left Wampanoag territory virtually depopulated and vulnerable to attack from traditional enemies to the west. The survivors welcomed the Plimoth settlers as potential allies, and Massasoit, the Pokanoket Wampanoag leader, willingly entered into a formal treaty of friendship in 1621. Remaining in power until the 1660s, Massasoit was clearly operating in the best interests of his people.

Life in early New England can be appreciated today at **Plimoth Plantation**, one of America's most successful museums of living history. The staff has painstakingly researched and learned seventeen regional European dialects from the seventeenth century. Tools and other possessions have been reproduced from antique specimens, true to the technology of the seventeenth century. But for years, Plimoth Plantation presented only a generic portrayal of seventeenth-century Wampanoag life and culture, lacking the specificity and detail re-created in the Pilgrim village. In 1989, the museum staff sought to improve its representation of Wampanoag life.

Although Native Americans are poorly represented in historical documents of early New England, more was known about an individual named Hobbamock than any other Wampanoag figure from the period. A Pokanoket Wampanoag who lived with his family adjacent to Plimoth Plantation, Hobbamock provided guidance and council to the Pilgrims about the ways of the land and its Native people. A large bark-covered dwelling now represents Hobbamock's house, outfitted with the tools and artifacts from the domestic environment of the Wampanoag culture. Little else is known about Hobbamock's family (he had more than one wife and the entire household consisted of "above ten persons"), the staff at Hobbamock's Homesite do not attempt to portray him in character, in large part because the Wampanoag language is extinct.

Still, a visit to Hobbamock's village reminds the visitor how individual Native Americans lived in the seventeenth century. Contrary to generalized stereotypes, Hobbamock and the other Wampanoags had never seen a tipi, and they did not know what horses or buffalo were. Among other topics, the living museum staff demonstrations emphasize planting, food preparation, and toolmaking; presentations by Native Americans deal with topics as diverse as traditional healing practices, ancient trade networks, and the use of wampum.

The Mashpee-Wampanoag Tribe, including the descendents of tribal leader Massasoit, has lived along the central part of Cape Cod for centuries. The survival and participation of Wampanoag people at Plimoth Plantation are living testimony to the resilience and strength of their own cultural tradition.

Plimoth Plantation (Plymouth, MA; 20 minutes N. of Cape Cod on SR 3 and take Plimoth Plantation Highway exit) is a nonprofit living history museum, largely supported by admission, sales, contributions, and memberships. Plimoth Plantation is divided into the *1627 Pilgrim Village*, *Hobbamock's Homesite*, the *Carriage House Crafts Center*, and the *Mayflower II*. Phone (508) 746-1622. The *Mashpee-Wampanoag Museum* (Mashpee, MA; SR 30) has a collection focusing on the Mashpee-Wampanoag people. The *Mashpee Tribal Meetinghouse* can also be visited, but permission must be obtained from the tribal office. Phone (508) 477-1536 or 477-0208.

SPIRITUAL ENCOUNTERS

Today, the conspicuous ruins of Spanish missions punctuate the landscape of the American West. Each year, thousands of visitors tour ruins at national monuments such as Pecos, Quarai, Abo, Gran Quivira, and Tumacacori. Still-operating mission churches are highly visible at Taos, Zuni, Laguna, and Acoma pueblos. The "Mission Trail" connects the Alamo (itself a former Spanish mission) to three other eighteenth-century missions within the city limits of San Antonio and another just over the city line. All twenty-one California missions are open to the public, and even the long-lost missions of Spanish Florida are being resurrected.

The widespread Spanish mission complex demonstrates a radically different mode of European–Native American interaction. Whereas the mercantile ethic pervaded the northeastern seaboard, the southland was conquered by Spain, where Catholicism exhibited a uniquely sacred aspect as well. Unlike their European competitors to the north, the Spaniards colonizing the Americas made no pretense of separating Church from State.

Spanish-Indian contact in native North America was governed by formal policies designed both to apply Christian principles of governance and to reap economic benefits from the colonies. Spanish policy was grounded in a sense of duty to change the Indians from heathen barbarians into good Christians. The Spanish sphere of influence was settled not by private individuals acting in their own interests, but rather by the priest, the soldier, and the bureaucrat—each of whom answered to a higher authority.

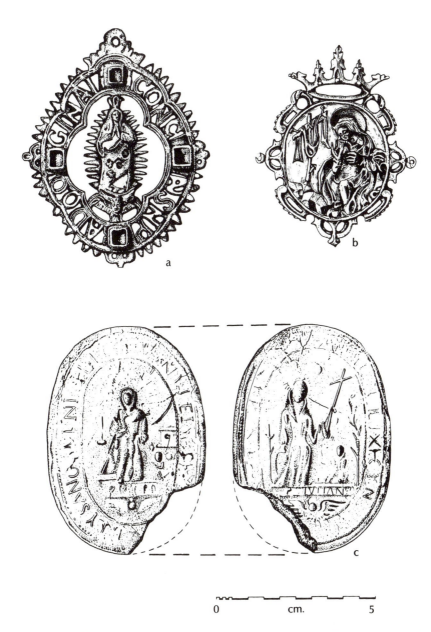

Religious medallions recovered during excavations at Mission Santa Catalina de Guale, Georgia. Top-left: This image of Our Lady of Guadeloupe was sacred to both Franciscan and Native American neophytes; the inscription translates "Hail, Mary, conceived without original sin." Top-right: This silver venera shows the "Sorrowing Mother" of Jesus, seated in grief on the rocks at Golgotha. Bottom: This fired clay medallion may have been used to impress wax seals; both scenes commemorate Franciscan and Jesuit missionaries being martyred during the sixteenth century while evangelizing in Asia. (Courtesy of the American Museum of Natural History.)

— ᐱᐱᐱ —

KATERI TEKAKWITHA: THE FIRST
NATIVE AMERICAN SAINT?

Today there is a tendency, when discussing missionization of the American Indian, to emphasize only the downside—the forced labor, sexual assaults, enforced separation of families, malnutrition, and even outright cruelty that at times crept into the missionary experience. Exclusive adherence to this view, however, overlooks the thousands upon thousands of cases in which the missionary gospel was wholeheartedly embraced and accepted by willing neophytes. The story of Kateri Tekakwitha reveals the more benevolent side of mission life in native America.

Kateri Tekakwitha was born in 1656. Her mother, a Christian Algonquin, having been captured by Mohawk warriors near Quebec, married a Mohawk man. But both parents died of smallpox, leaving their four-year-old daughter Tekakwitha, the lone survivor of the epidemic, in the care of her father's brother, a Mohawk village chief. Her eyesight was permanently damaged and her skin badly pockmarked for life.

After fleeing from French forces, Tekakwitha and her adopting family eventually joined other refugee Iroquois in Caughnawaga, near Montreal. After peace was declared, Jesuit missionaries arrived in 1667, staying for three days in the longhouse of Tekakwitha's uncle. As soon as nearby St. Peter's Chapel was finished, Tekakwitha, now nineteen years old, asked the Jesuits to instruct her in their faith. On Easter Day, 1676, she was baptized *Katherine* in English, *Kateri* in Mohawk.

Many of the Mohawk people living in her village retained their more traditional beliefs and harassed those who shared with Kateri her Catholic faith. On one occasion, she was stoned for refusing to work in the tribal cornfields on Sundays. Distraught at such persecution, Kateri eventually traveled with other Christian Indians to the St. Francis mission, south of the St. Lawrence River. She soon took the vows of the Society of the Holy Family, including a promise never to marry. Here, despite her devotion to

— ᐱᐱᐱ —

△△△

the Christian faith and her physical disabilities, she did her best to carry out her traditional Indian work obligations, so long as they did not interfere with her religious observances.

In poor health since childhood, Kateri Tekakwitha died at the age of twenty-four years. The priest administering last rites was astonished when, upon her death, Tekakwitha's face was miraculously cleared of pox, becoming clear and beautiful. The word of this miracle quickly spread to other members of the Roman Catholic community, who began praying and revering Kateri. Her grave became the object of visitation by those with personal prayers. These devotions were often rewarded and by the early twentieth century, the followers of Tekakwitha successfully convinced the Vatican to begin the lengthy process of recognizing her with sainthood.

Saints are an integral part of the Roman Catholic church, then as now. Practicing Catholics pray to saints and honor them, they treasure their relics, and name their children after them. The Catholic church maintains a formal and continuous process for "making" saints, including a board of professionals who investigate and at times validate the miracles thought to have been performed. The purpose of this methodical process is to determine whether a given holy man or woman has achieved "the level of Christian perfection that, in Catholic reckoning, constitutes sainthood."

Three hundred years after her death, on June 22, 1980, Vatican investigators determined that Kateri Tekakwitha was blessed, the final step prior to canonization. She is the first lay woman in North America to be so honored. Should Kateri Tekakwitha achieve the final step of canonization, she will become the first American Indian saint.

Her advocates still visit the **National Shrine of the North American Martyrs** (Auriesville, New York), near the village where Kateri was born and where she spent most of her life. Others visit the **Saint Francis Xavier Mission** (in Caughnawaga) and *Sault St. Louis* (near Montreal), where she died.

△△△

National Shrine of North American Martyrs (Auriesville, NY; E. on SR 5S between exits 27 and 28) commemorates the site of the Mohawk Indian village of Ossernenon, where Father Isaac Jogues and his companions (later canonized as martyrs) were killed in the 1640s. It is also the birthplace of the Blessed Kateri Tekakwitha. The National Shrine has been called by Pope Pius XII "nature's own reliquary—the verdant hill that slopes up from the quiet, easy-flowing river of the Mohawk." Phone (518) 853-3033.

The National Shrine of Blessed Kateri Tekakwitha and Native American Exhibit (Fonda, NY; ½ mi. W. on SR 5), 4 miles from the National Shrine of North American Martyrs, this site commemorates the place where the Indian girl was baptized and lived almost half her life. This is also the site of the Caughnawaga Mohawk village (occupied between 1666 and 1693), a completely excavated and interpreted Iroquois village. Phone (518) 853-3646.

Saint Francis Xavier Mission and Shrine of Kateri Tekakwitha (Kahnawake, PQ; at the center of the reservation) contains the tomb of Kateri Tekakwitha. A small museum is on site. Phone (514) 632-6030.

FLORIDA'S INVISIBLE SPANISH MISSIONS

The Spanish crown initially employed the term *La Florida* to denote an extensive, if ill-defined territory covering practically all of the eastern half of the present United States. During the subsequent mission period, La Florida consisted of about 70,000 square miles—an area roughly the size of New England—embracing the state of Florida, the Georgia coast, and the southeastern coast of South Carolina (up to Port Royal Sound).

Men of the cloth accompanied the conquistadors from the earliest European penetration of Spanish Florida. Some priests were needed to administer to the religious needs of the explorers, but others were enlisted specifically to scout out possibilities for ecclesiastical outreach among the native populations. The first of these explorations took place here in 1513, when Juan Ponce de Leon made a landfall somewhere in northeastern Florida. But don't be fooled by the "Fountain of Youth" tourist park in modern St. Augustine—in fact, nobody knows exactly where the explorer landed.

In 1565, Spanish King Philip II assigned Pedro Menéndez de Avilés the task of colonizing La Florida and later that year, Menéndez established his beachhead at St. Augustine, which remained a Spanish colony until 1763. Today, more than 750,000 visitors arrive here annually, to see firsthand the acclaimed St. Augustine architecture and ambiance. Unlike any other city in the United States, St. Augustine retains its Old World flavor. The original Hispanic grid plan is still evident and the state-operated restoration area and living-history museum continues the tradition of narrow streets and colonial buildings, each with its one well-tended garden.

The north end of St. Augustine is dominated by the massive **Castillo de San Marcos**, built of local coquina shell stone between 1672 and 1695. The oldest masonry fort in the United States, the Castillo protected St. Augustine and helped defend the Florida coast route of the treasure fleets. The symmetrical fort has four bastions and the massive walls—twelve feet thick at the base—are skirted by a moat on three sides. A stairway leads to the gun deck overlooking the Old City Gate, quaint old streets, and Matanzas Bay.

Castillo de San Marcos National Monument (St. Augustine, FL; at Castillo Dr. and Ave. Menéndez, US 1 business route and SR A1A) defended St. Augustine from many attacks. The English acquired the fort in 1763, when Florida was ceded to them. Spain regained possession by treaty in 1784 and returned to the fort. Upon acquisition of Florida by the United States in 1821, the fortress became part of the nation's coastal defense system. It was also used as a military prison. The Indian leader Osceola was confined here with others of his nation during the Seminole War of the 1830s. Exhibits trace its history, and cannon firings take place during the summer. Phone (904) 829-6506.

St. Augustine safely established, Menéndez sailed northward to found the city of **Santa Elena,** on present-day Parris Island (South Carolina). More than 400 settlers were sent to Santa Elena, and by 1569 it had become the capital of Spanish Florida. From here, Juan Pardo led expeditions into the interior of the Carolinas, and a mission was established in the Chesapeake Bay area. Although three forts were erected to guard Santa Elena, Indian hostilities caused it to be permanently abandoned in 1587 after Sir Francis Drake burned St. Augustine. Archaeologist Stanley South has discovered the ruins of Santa Elena beneath the U. S. Marine Corps golf course on Parris Island.

Santa Elena (Parris Island, SC; ask for directions at the entrance to the Marine base), the early Spanish settlement dating from 1565 has been discovered beneath the U. S. Marine Corps golf course. Excavations continue at this important site, and arrangements can be made for visitation. Phone (803) 525-2951.

The early Jesuit missions failed because of lukewarm support from their own hierarchy, intransigent attitudes on the part of the missionaries themselves, dissension between religious and secular officials in Florida, and the wretched conditions in the colonies and missions themselves. The Jesuits thoroughly alienated native populations by their association with the Spanish garrison, which demanded heavy payments by the Indians in cultivated foodstuffs.

Thinking that another religious order might be more effective, Pedro Menéndez turned for help to the Franciscan Fathers. These early Franciscan undertakings seemed as ill-fated as the Jesuit attempts, the Indians of La Florida particularly resenting the continual ecclesiastical meddling in political matters. But these missions were ultimately successful (at least in their own terms) and during the middle of the seventeenth century—the pinnacle of the so-called Golden Age—the Franciscans boasted that 26,000 Christianized Indians lived in La Florida, with seventy friars operating nearly forty principal missions.

Although these figures are probably optimistic exaggerations produced by church officials, it is clear that the mission system of Spanish Florida was fully comparable to its better-known counterparts in California, Texas, and the American Southwest. The Franciscan mission remains a highly visible feature on America's western landscape. But despite their former importance, the missions of Spanish Florida barely exist in America's perception of its own past.

Part of this relative invisibility can be ascribed to the so-called Black Legend, a systematic and undeserved bias that has belittled Spanish achievements for centuries. Spanish Florida also lacks the historical continuity of the American West. Although substantial populations of Spanish-speaking Native Americans still live west of the Mississippi, and many of them still practice Catholicism, hispanicized Native Americans disappeared long ago from Spanish Florida. By the 1750s, only two small villages of Christianized Indians remained outside St. Augustine. When the Spaniards turned over rule to the British in 1763, the 83 surviving Native American converts fled from Florida as well.

The physical elements also conspired against Spanish Florida. Viewing St. Augustine in the 1620s, one eyewitness remarked that the walls of the fort were so dry that firing one of the guns would have set them aflame and, indeed, St. Augustine was burned down several times, most notably by Sir Francis Drake in 1586 and Carolinian Governor James Moore in 1702. The combination of flimsy construction methods, periodic fires and hurricanes, and British military superiority effectively erased sixteenth- and seventeenth-century La Florida from the landscape. Not a single mission structure in Georgia survived the rebellion of 1597, and British attacks from 1702 to 1704 totally leveled mission churches throughout Florida.

Except for the sturdy coquina walls of Castillo de San Marcos in St. Augustine, not a single building—mission or secular—survives from the mission period. The absence of structural reminders is responsible, in part, for allowing La Florida to slip from the historical consciousness. Fortunately, the Spanish missions of the Deep South are being rescued from obscurity by archaeologists and historians. In the last decade, several important mission excavations have taken place in Georgia and Florida, and the mission history of this area is being rewritten. The results of some of this important research can be seen at *San Luis de Talimali*, a seventeenth-century Spanish and Apalachee Indian settlement located in downtown Tallahassee, Florida. **San Luis** was established in 1656, part of a network of mission and townsites that extended westward from St. Augustine, Florida. This was the homeland of the powerful Apalachee Indians, living in a region endowed with abundant wildlife and fertile soils, where their farms prospered.

At its peak, San Luis was home to the provincial deputy governor, and 1,400 Apalachee Indians, Spanish settlers, soldiers, and Franciscan friars. San Luis was overrun in 1702 by British and Creek Indian forces, who swept through the Province of Florida, burning all but two of the mission villages here.

In September 1983, the state of Florida acquired San Luis, setting aside this fifty-acre site as a preserve for archaeological and historical research. Visitors are welcome to learn about (and participate in) the

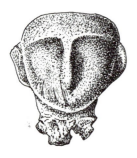

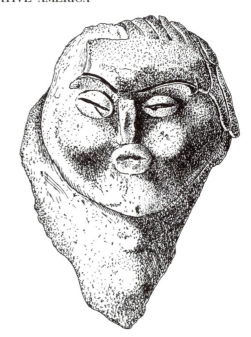

These baked clay Native American faces once decorated the inside walls of the seventeenth-century Mission Santa Catalina de Guale, Georgia. (Courtesy of the American Museum of Natural History.)

important ongoing research at San Luis. One of the most significant features located at San Luis is the Apalachee Council House, a truly remarkable circular structure located on the main plaza. For years, historians doubted the veracity of Spanish accounts that described circular buildings, the scene of feasting and dancing, capable of sheltering 2,000 to 3,000 people. Then, here at San Luis, archaeologists unearthed the well-preserved remains of one such structure, measuring

San Luis Archaeological and Historic Site (Tallahassee, FL; on Mission Rd. ¼ mi. NW off US 90) was the site of an important Apalachee Indian village and Franciscan mission. This active dig has trails with interpretive displays describing the excavations. Excavations are conducted periodically, and tours are available daily. A permanent exhibit hall is being planned for the park. Phone (904) 487-3711.

nearly 120 feet in diameter. Around the interior were two rows of benches and a central hearth, where a great bonfire would be set, illuminating an indoor dance ground 75 feet across. The Council House at San Luis conforms in all respects to the documentary portrayals of the astonishing council houses throughout Spanish Florida.

Visitors to San Luis can also see the remains of the church complex, across the central plaza from the Council House, and the Spanish village, where military personnel and civilians lived and worked.

THE SPANISH MISSIONS OF CALIFORNIA

Nowhere is the North American mission system more visible than in California, where each of the twenty-one historic Franciscan missions can be visited today: fourteen are parish churches, three have become museums, one houses a seminary, another is a university chapel, and two are state historical parks. Religious services are regularly held in all but two.

My favorite is **Mission La Purísima Concepción**, located east of Lompoc, California. At first, La Purísima might seem an unlikely candidate because after secularization, the mission buildings were quickly plundered of tiles and timber, leaving the unprotected walls to wash away. Before long, only the monastery at La Purísima was left standing. After considerable abuse as a private residence and sheep ranch, it too collapsed. By 1934, only wall stubs and a few solitary pillars were left standing.

Because the ruins at La Purísima were wholly unsuitable for church-related purposes, they became fair game for the preservation community. Beginning in 1934, an important series of archaeological investigations were begun. Year after year, the team unearthed new finds and, because the archaeologists dug extensively beyond the central mission compound, they could highlight the Native American presence by excavating large parts of the Chumash dwelling areas and barracks. The La Purísima excavations were truly exceptional for their time.

Then, working with these professional archaeologists, some of the most knowledgeable authorities collaborated to restore Mission La Purísima. Because the 1930s archaeologists and restorers worked hand-in-hand, unexcavated archaeological deposits were sufficiently protected so that subsequent excavations are still possible. The same could hardly be said of the overly aggressive and ultimately destructive restorations at some of the other California missions (see **California's Simulated Mission Reality**).

△△△

INDIANS AND THE CALIFORNIA MISSIONS: A NATIVE AMERICAN PERSPECTIVE

Edward D. Castillo (A Cahuilla Man)

Today's descendants of Mission Indians, as well as many others, find the public perceptions of those colonial institutions to be seriously distorted. This is due in large measure to the fact that of the twenty-three original missions built in Alta California, today all but three are owned and controlled by the Catholic Church. In fact the two mission/pueblos established among the Quechan Indians on the Colorado River, La Purísima Concepción (1780) and San Pedro y San Pablo de Bicuner, were utterly destroyed by the militant Quechan, who found the colonists insufferably arrogant and abusive. Curiously, this has been forgotten by most California historians who would have us remember only the twenty-one missions established along the coast.

Around the turn of the century, historic preservationist groups were buying up the coastal missions and deeding them to the Church. About the same time, Franciscan historian Zephyrin Englehardt began publishing voluminous polemic tomes to counter the mild criticism of the Franciscan missions and missionaries offered by secular historians like Hubert H. Bancroft and others. Fortunately, a few testimonies of mission Indians were recorded in the nineteenth century. Furthermore, a handful of mission Indian descendents who survived into the twentieth century occasionally commented on their parents' and elders' oral reminiscences of life under Franciscan authority, in the course of linguistic and ethnographic interviews with anthropologists. These sources and the growing body of archaeological data developed over the last twenty years have provided ethno-historians with a body of data that challenges the simplistic and paternalistic nature of popular church-inspired literature about the missions and Indians of Hispanic California.

In California, state history is introduced in the fourth-grade curriculum. Consequently, visits by millions of school children to local missions have become annual rituals. But the reconstruc-

△△△

tions and interpretations at these missions continue to perpetuate and glorify the colonial enterprise, and almost completely ignore or seriously distort the role of the Indians in mission history.

Children and adult visitors alike are told the Spanish padres "built" the missions to evangelize the "poor, backward, and primitive" Indians. Nothing could be further from the truth. The Indians of California built the missions. The majority of missions seen today are in fact simply the church building itself, and as such hardly provide visitors with a true picture of the enormous colonial enterprise fully functioning missions represented at their height. More than curious, these tourist meccas are missing the instruments of coercion, the stocks, hobbles, iron restraints, and horsewhips, used to control and punish the unpaid laborers, Indian men, women, and children.

Usually absent from these reconstructions are the military barracks for the *escolta* (soldiers) stationed to protect the padres at each mission. Such buildings might serve to remind visitors of the military support essential to prevent the Indians from ejecting or assassinating the Franciscans and their supporters. Perhaps with a reconstruction of the always-present hospitals found at each mission, visitors would begin to understand the terror that epidemic and later endemic diseases engendered in the short lives of Indians living under the filthy and disease-ridden conditions characteristic of those institutions. At Mission San Gabriel, for instance, the hospital was larger than the main church building. So deadly was the place that a special chapel was built inside the hospital so that the padre's last rites could be performed there, avoiding further demoralization of the terrified survivors by an endless stream of dead Indians passing through the main church.

More significant still is the lack of reconstructed *monjerios*, and with good reason. These were special dormitories for female children and unmarried female adults. Following baptism, the padres dismantled Indian families by requiring the incarceration of all unmarried females, supposedly to protect their virtue—an interesting idea conceived by the Spanish/European male elite that made up the Franciscan padres. Of course it had the added benefit of keeping males from fleeing with their families back to the

△△△

homeland they had been required to abandon. Once baptized, Spanish law and Franciscan practice permitted the padres to compel the Indians to relocate to the missions to better manage their labor and otherwise control them. A tragic consequence of these policies was a disproportionate death rate among the females brought about by the filthy conditions of the *monjerios* often described by contemporary military officials and foreign visitors.

The singular exception to this trend is found at the state-owned Mission La Purísima, near Lompoc, California. Here nearly the entire mission has been reconstructed, and thoughtful visitors often leave with the disturbing realization that these places, far from being ecclesiastical boarding schools, more closely resembled plantations of the antebellum South. Yet, even here the interpretive program concerning mission Indians and their great revolt of 1824 is weakly developed.

Present throughout the missions of California are numerous native artistic motifs discovered by historic archaeologists. They reveal that many of the Indian laborers who constructed those institutions secretly engraved pagan symbols on fired floor tiles, walls, and other construction materials. These actions are consistent with other cultural expressions by the neophytes (baptized Indian laborers) who continued to demonstrate allegiance to the old pagan deities, despite the padres' draconian measures to prevent such activities. An extremely rare example of neophyte art is a series of paintings of the stations of the cross found at Mission San Gabriel executed by a Tongva neophyte, Juan Antonio. These paintings reveal a cleverly disguised artistic protest against the oppression suffered by mission Indians at the hands of the padres and soldiers. More important still are at least two murals painted by Tongva neophytes at Mission San Fernando that depict a hunting scene and other decidedly non-Christian themes. Interestingly, these murals were plastered over sometime after completion and rediscovered during a W.P.A. restoration about 1936. When church officials saw the restored murals, they again had them obliterated, and the murals remain hidden under plaster to this day.

Perhaps the most revealing aspect of the omission of Indians in the historic reconstructions, both interpretively and physically, is

△△△

▲▲▲

the absence of any burial monuments honoring the thousands of California Indians buried all around the mission sites. Many of these are mass burials. Both church and state reconstructions lack any form of proper acknowledgement of the very people who built the missions and labored there until death. A staggering number of these burials were Indian children.

Today my people still sing this mournful lament about the children locked up in the *monjerio* at Mission San Luis Rey.

Cham'chapaa'chum amayom Chi Kwiskwi Cham
Cham'chapaa'chum amayom Chi Kwiskwi Cham
Yam-ya-pa Yam-ya-pa Ya'ani—Amayom
Ya'ani—Amayom

[Translation] *Three of us children are suffering . . . in this building (place). We want to escape, us children.*

Contemporary California Indians have recently witnessed an 8-million-dollar effort by church officials to canonize Junípero Serra, the Franciscan founder of the California missions. Knowledgeable Indians protested the honoring of a man whose colonial enterprise caused the loss of Indian land, resources, and freedom and provoked catastrophic and massive suffering, slavery, and death of our ancestors. In response church activists have carried on an abusive campaign that denigrates California's aboriginal peoples and their culture.

If historic preservation efforts truly seek to reveal the story of our collective past, then accurate and balanced interpretive programs and suitable monuments ought to be established at each mission in California with the names of all Indians who erected those buildings and labored to make the enterprise productive. With one exception, historic records naming each baptized California Indian exist for the California missions. A Vietnam-type memorial would best achieve a reconciliation between a living people, their dead ancestors, and the church and state authorities whose present efforts to Eurocentrically define our understanding of the mission's past is no longer good enough.

▲▲▲

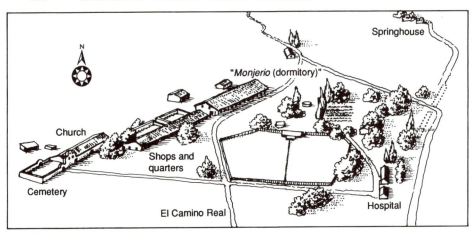

Map of reconstructed structures and grounds at Mission La Purísima Concepción, unusual because of its emphasis on mission life beyond the mission church proper.

Today, Mission La Purísima is the largest and most complete restoration in the American West. Eighteen major buildings and features were investigated and restored, including the church, *convento*, workshops, a water system with fountain and cistern, neophyte residence, blacksmith shop, warehouse, tallow and soap works, and cemetery. Original materials and techniques were employed wherever possible. Even though virtually no above-ground architecture remains from the original mission complex, the modern visitor is confronted not only with Hispanic mission lifeways, but also with the active involvement of Native Americans living there. Their hide processing, candle-making, carpentry, cooking, irrigation, and other craft work are all in evidence.

La Purísima Mission State Historic Park (Lompoc, CA; 4 mi. NE of Lompoc) is actually the second site of this mission. The original mission, founded in 1787 was demolished by an earthquake in 1812; this site has recently been acquired by the City of Lompoc. Between 1813 and 1822, the Franciscans moved the mission a few miles from the original site. Extensively restored, it provides the best picture of what life was like for both Native American and Franciscan. Rooms are furnished as they would have been in the 1820s. The grounds comprise more than 900 acres and have 13 miles of hiking and riding trails. Phone (805) 733-3713.

CALIFORNIA'S SIMULATED MISSION REALITY

Beyond its spiritual roots, the physical mission presence in California has long been a tremendous economic boon, inspiring a significant architectural "revival." In the late nineteenth century, when an expanding middle class drifted away from Victorian excess to embrace more properly "American" forms, many turned to the homes of early American colonists for inspiration. Countless seventeenth and eighteenth century (mostly British- and Dutch-derived) dwellings survived along the eastern seaboard, providing architectural roots that ultimately fostered the widespread Dutch and Colonial Revival styles.

Post-Victorian architecture evolved along a very different pathway in California, where colonial precedents were largely Spanish. Although eighteenth century mission structures were falling into disrepair, public-spirited citizens had begun to clamor for their restoration by 1880. Hundreds of tourists were already undertaking California mission pilgrimages by the turn of the century.

A distinctive Mission Revival architectural style was legitimized by architect A. Page Brown's design for the California State Pavilion at the World Columbian Exposition in Chicago in 1893: "At the fair that brought America the triumphs of French classical architecture . . . California told the story of its founding by reassembling the missions and their forms in an eclectic pile of porous architecture which reminded visitors of the climate and the open-ended possibilities of the new state."

Virtually overnight, house facades in America's West began to look like church fronts, with prominent scalloped ornamentation, reddish-brown tiled roofs, round-headed window openings, and clearly recognizable parapets.

The evolution of Mission Revival architecture and the restoration of Franciscan prototypes proceeded hand in hand, defining the romantic mission style that has become a lasting cultural tradition in California. One simply does not overlook the mission heritage in the West.

No visit to the California missions is complete without a stop-

The California Building at the 1893 Columbian Exposition in Chicago. This eclectic assemblage of mission elements single-handedly kicked off the explosion of Mission Revival architecture throughout the American West. The Roman-style facade of Mission Santa Barbara appears at the left; the main entrance is a heavily modified version of that of Mission San Carlos Borromeo, as are the quatrefoil windows along the long axis. Yet a third stylized mission facade appears at the far end. (Courtesy of Raymond Fogelson.)

over at **San Carlos Borromeo**. Most visitors will want to see the personal bedroom (the "cell") of the venerable Father Junípero Serra, patriarch of California's mission chain. In this very room, on Saturday, August 28, 1784, a devoted Father Francisco Palóu brought the weary Serra a cup of broth. As he later recorded in his diary, Father Palóu heard Serra whisper: "Now, let us go to rest." It was *siesta* time and when Palóu returned, he found Serra "asleep in the Lord . . . his body showing no other sign of death than the cessation of breathing."

Each day, dozens of weary tourists pause for a few moments in Serra's cell, reflecting perhaps upon kinder, gentler mission days.

But how many visitors realize that Serra's cell is a simulated reality—it was completely reconstructed during the Depression! The floor tiles were scavenged from elsewhere at Carmel, the replica bed and table constructed from original mission timbers. Serra practiced private self-mortification in this room, and hanging on a nail, is his iron and braided-wire "discipline" (his penitential scourge). His eighteenth-century bible lies on the reconstructed bench. Serra's cell looks just like the real thing, yet virtually everything you see is fake.

Retrofitting the past can also take place through omission. As so commonly happens with tourism-directed restorations around the globe, only the more spectacular, elite archaeological sectors are restored—the temples, the pyramids, the king's tomb. In California, "mission" was commonly equated with "church," and early restorers universally emphasized the latest colonial construction, to the exclusion of earlier forms and attendant structures. Only rarely is the restoration extended to other important structures around the quadrangle—the *convento*, the *monjerio* (women's quarters), the workshops, and storerooms. Today's visitor to most mission reconstructions cannot escape the feeling that these were feudal Mediterranean villages practicing European technologies.

Such restorations inflate the white, Catholic, European aspects of mission life. The surrounding, "lower status" structures of the Indian *ranchería* are usually ignored. Although Franciscan graves are carefully marked and venerated, the mission reconstructions do not identify individual Indian graves. Most Indians were apparently interred in mass graves; some, such as those at San Juan Bautista, are not marked at all. This progressive Europeanization of California's missions denigrates, if not eliminates, Indians in the mission context.

Considerable damage has been done to California's missions by

Today's history-minded tourist can visit Father Junípero Serra's cell, the bed-room where he died at Mission San Carlos Borromeo on August 28, 1784. Hanging on a nail is Serra's authentic iron-and-braided wire "discipline," his penitential scourge. Few have any inkling that this legendary locale is but a simulated reality, reconstructed in 1937 from total ruins. (Courtesy of Bell Magazine Agency, Monterey, California.)

overzealous restorers and revisionists. Not only has such mis-guided over-restoration resulted in the unwarranted destruction of archaeological deposits, but the simulated realities of lush gardens and romanticized architecture have contributed nu-merous misinterpretations of history. The importance of high-quality historical and archaeological research has never been fully realized, and mission exhibitions still contribute to the near invis-ibility of Native Americans in California's past. Too often, con-temporary mission exhibits attempt to present themselves as bona fide heirlooms of the past—and many succeed in giving just that false impression. **Mission San Francisco Solano,** located on the central plaza of downtown Sonoma, is a gratifying exception, a textbook example of how restorations *should* be presented to the public. Like so many missions, Solano passed through a series of hands after secularization, serving variously as a barn and a blacksmith shop. The Historic Landmarks League finally came to the rescue, purchasing the property in 1903. Badly damaged by the 1906 earthquake, the church was initially restored in 1911–1912, and title was handed over to the California State Parks Commission in 1927. More extensive restoration took place in 1943–1944 and significant state-sponsored archaeological excavations took place in the 1950s, followed by more renovation. By the late 1960s, only a portion of the padre's quarters remained as original construction. *The Guide to Architecture in San Francisco and Northern California* says it all: today's Mission Solano is, a "Mission Revival version of what a California Mission should be."

But what sets this mission above its contemporaries is that

This is what Father Serra's cell and the rest of the convento *wing of Mission San Carlos Borromeo actually looked like in the 1920s, before extensive reconstruction; the cross marks the approximate location of Serra's cell. (Courtesy of the California Section, California State Library.)*

————————————— ∆∆∆ —————————————

Mission Solano explicitly owns up to what it is—a heavily reconstructed interpretation of the past. This disclaimer is not subtle;
immediately after entering the *convento*, all visitors run squarely
into an impossible-to-overlook sign, warning in boldface:

> Reconstruction of this mission and many others throughout
> the state was done around the first years of this century.
> Often accomplished without the benefit of historical or ar-
> chaeological research, these reconstructions were based on
> romanticized paintings and accounts of the 19th century.
> Occasionally walls appeared or disappeared in these paint-
> ings and sketches. The reconstructions would reflect this
> misinformation.

> Nearby are a dozen photographs and period sketches of various
> attempts at reconstructing Mission Solano. Other prominent ex-
> hibit cases show how archaeology was conducted here, and how
> archaeologists interpreted what they found. Another caption,
> highly visible as one enters the chapel explains the extent of
> restoration, and discusses the evidence leading to the specific
> reconstructions.
> The state of California has done a first-rate job presenting this
> reconstructed mission to the public. Only the most obtuse visitor
> could leave **Sonoma State Historic Park** thinking they had ob-
> served the authentic, unrestored nineteenth-century Mission
> Solano—although I am certain that some still do.

————————————— ∆∆∆ —————————————

In other words, we see at La Purísima that a *mission* comprised an
entire settlement—not just the religious edifices—in which indigenous people were reorganized (including introduction of new crops and
European methods of cultivation). Because scattered Native American
groups were commonly absorbed into new settlements for instruction,
missions also had an explicit cultural function. Although their primary
task was to effect religious conversion, the friars also tried to raise the
natives from their perceived primitive state to that of civilized and
responsible citizens of the Spanish empire. Because colonists were in
short supply, the Spanish crown employed the missions as an agency to

occupy, hold, and settle its frontier. As a pioneering "frontier" institution, the mission theoretically would vanish with the advance of civilization.

These energetic Franciscans built some of the first Christian churches in what is now the United States, mastered numerous native languages, and wrote the first dictionaries based on the Indian dialects. Friars provided instruction not only in the catechism, but also in music, reading, and writing. To some degree, they influenced not only religious and social conduct within the Spanish colonies, but also acted as primary agents in placing new settlements, determining the nature of defensive installations, and deciding the primary emphasis of policy within the Hispanic sphere. In the words of one early friar, "we are the ones who are conquering and subduing the land." (For another view, see **Indians and the California Missions: A Native American Perspective.**)

Mission San Carlos Borromeo Del Rio Carmelo (Carmel, CA; 3080 Rio Rd.), more commonly known simply as Mission Carmel, was initially founded by Father Junípero Serra at Monterey in 1770, then moved to Carmel the following year. Mission Carmel became Serra's residence and headquarters until his death in 1784. He is interred beneath the church floor in front of the altar. The architecture of this mission is world famous, and served as a model for the reconfiguration of thousands of train stations, post offices, schools, and other public buildings in California as a result of the Mission Revival architectural movement. Although visitors are warned to distinguish carefully between original mission buildings and the extensive restorations that have taken place since the 1930s, the effect is charming, particularly the courtyard gardens, the quatrefoil window over the church entrance, and Moorish bell tower. Phone (408) 624-3600.

Sonoma State Historic Park (Sonoma, CA) includes the Tosca and Sonoma barracks on the plaza, Mission San Francisco Solano and the home of Sonoma's founder, General Mariano Guadalupe Vallejo. Although heavily restored, the excellent museum explains the process and interprets the mission period. Phone (707) 938-1519.

MILITARY ENCOUNTERS

Concocting a moral basis for the American appropriation of native lands has been almost as difficult and divisive as defending slavery. Just as slavery divided North and South, so the Indian wars of the nineteenth century divided East and West. But an occasional massacre—indeed, any unfortunate skirmish that might be passed off as a massacre—could at least temporarily unify Americans in their essential contempt for the moral condition of native peoples, buttress their belief in their own cultural superiority, and obscure their own atrocities with the fire and brimstone of their vengeance.

— A N D R E W   W A R D
T H E   L I T T L E   B I G H O R N

According to the Norse sagas, the first recorded conflict between European colonizer and Native American took place in the eleventh century. While this tale may be more apocryphal than factual, it does serve to anchor the conventional wisdom regarding white-Indian military interaction. Spanning the millennium between the Norse sagas and *Dances with Wolves*, the white-Indian conflict has been characterized as an unfortunate but inevitable armed confrontation between predestined adversaries.

European explorers are commonly depicted as an extraordinarily nasty and aggressive breed, eager to establish their military "beachhead." From there, they expand into hostile hinterlands, progressively advancing their "front" against an unrelenting "enemy." In this view, the Native American is commonly depicted as the hapless and ill-starred stooge, incapable of understanding why the pale-faced intruders are so heartless, but willing to defend his homeland at all costs.

As historian Wilcomb Washburn points out, this whole battlefield paradigm is specious. As we have seen, the early Europeans in North America were often seeking commercial allies or religious converts; during the early days especially, overtures of peace far outnumbered declarations of war. White colonists were far more hostile toward their fellow European opponents than toward the American natives. And while the European intrusions without question destroyed much of the native North American lifeway, it distorts history to suggest that the earliest European settlers waged a deliberate and coordinated military campaign.

Both the European newcomers and the Native Americans they encountered reflected a broad range of objectives and concerns. Indian people had lived in this land for a thousand generations, and they were themselves engaged in their own long-standing rivalries and disagreements. Although the occasional Indian leader would urge native people to unite, tribal self-interest and perennial animosities throttled virtually all attempts at a united resistance. Again and again, some tribes would see it in their own best interest to align themselves with whites against their traditional native antagonists.

Surely enough has been written, filmed, dramatized, and reenacted about these storied military confrontations between Indian and white. While not wishing to gloss over the military aspects, I think a single example will suffice to illustrate the complexities behind the stereotypes regarding Indian-white warfare in early America.

THE BATTLE OF THE LITTLE BIGHORN: THEN AND NOW

The United States of America was in the midst of celebrating its centennial when shattering news arrived from the western frontier. The July 6, 1876, edition of the *New York Herald* blared the news:

A BLOODY BATTLE.

An Attack on Sitting Bull on the Little Horn River.

GENERAL CUSTER KILLED.

An Entire Detachment Under His Command Slaughtered.

SEVENTEEN OFFICERS SLAIN.

Narrow Escape of Colonel Reno's Command.

A HORRIBLE SLAUGHTER PEN.

Over Three Hundred of the Troops Killed.

Incredibly, half of Lieutenant George Armstrong Custer's invincible Seventh U. S. Cavalry had been decimated by a combined force of Sioux (Lakota) and Cheyenne Indians. Custer had fallen victim to one of the largest fighting forces ever seen on the Plains. Forget that it was the United States government that had violated its treaties with Native Americans. There was gold in them thar (Black) Hills; the railroad must be built, and savages could not be allowed to impede the path of progress.

Custer's Last Stand, by Edgar S. Paxson (1899). *This fanciful nineteenth-century depiction of Custer's Last Stand encapsulates the anti-Indian perspective that has traditionally surrounded this historical battle. (Courtesy of the Buffalo Bill Historical Center, Cody, Wyoming.)*

Nationwide reaction was no different in 1876 than it is today upon receipt of bad news: bewilderment, followed by incredulity, rage, and a craving for instantaneous revenge. America became galvanized, as quick-tempered volunteers offered their services from all corners of the land. Salt Lake City wanted to send 1,200 troops. Austin's *Daily State Gazette* lobbied that "Texas deserves the honor of attempting to wipe out the Sioux." Not to be outdone, the *Daily Herald* in Dallas countered that "Killing a mess of Indians is the only recreation our frontier rangers want."

The gunsmoke had barely lifted at the **Little Bighorn** before moral outrage was tempered by morbid curiosity. Hundreds of volumes have been written about the Battle of the Little Bighorn, and hundreds of thousands of people flock each summer to that windy, grassy field, where patient National Park Service guides struggle with still-unanswered questions. How, exactly, did Custer die? How could this disaster have taken place? How could such a great soldier meet such an unworthy end?

Others probe more deeply for Custer's motivations. Some think he wanted to surprise the Sioux enemy; others claim that he was scrambling to resurrect a foundering military career by stealing the glory from his commanders. Some skeptics view his headlong push to the Little Bighorn as a campaign ploy to gain the presidential nomination from the Democratic National Convention assembling on June 27 in St. Louis—two days after his death.

Whatever the answer to these (and hundreds of other) questions, the commonly accepted view tells only a fraction of the Little Bighorn story.

SOME LAKOTA PERSPECTIVES

Shortly after the battle, an editorial in the taciturn London *Times* struck a different tone, suggesting that Custer's defeat should more properly be viewed as an insult rather than an injury. After all, "The conduct of the American Government towards the Indians of the Plains has been neither very kindly nor very wise . . . ." To understand the battle behind the battle, it is necessary to look beyond the well-chronicled saga of Custer and his Seventh Cavalry at the broader context.

The Indian coalition that faced Custer consisted mostly of Cheyenne and Hunkapapa Sioux (Lakota) people, the latter led by chief Sitting Bull. These participants saw the events of June 25, 1876, in a very different manner.

Warfare was nothing new to the Hunkapapa Sioux, who had battled their enemies alone and in concert with allied tribes such as the Northern Cheyenne and the Northern Arapaho. They fought to control their hunting grounds. They fought to defend themselves against the incursions of other Indian tribes. They fought for booty, particularly the horses by which they computed their wealth. They fought for retribution, for respect, and to obtain the war honors that defined and expedited leadership.

Traditional enemies of the Hunkapapa Sioux were legion. The Sioux had migrated onto the upper Plains states from the headwaters of the Mississippi River in the sixteenth century because of warfare with the Cree, who themselves were being pressured from the east. By the mid-nineteenth century, the sedentary farming tribes along the Missouri— the Arikara, Mandan, and Hidatsa—had been so shattered by smallpox that they could no longer forestall the advances of their traditional Sioux enemies. But as the Hunkapapa moved westward into Crow territory, they were vigorously resisted by those who had been there first. Sioux and Crow hunting territories now overlapped, creating a deadly zone of conflict on the Powder River. Sioux war parties also ventured northward, engaging the Assiniboine, each raiding far into the other's territory. It was such intertribal warfare and skirmishing that eventually allowed a young Sitting Bull to solidify his position of leadership. Throughout much of his life, he wore a single eagle feather, symbolic of bravery in battle, not against the hated whites, but against the long-standing enemy, the Crow.

When the Fort Laramie Treaty of 1851 set out to establish peace between the United States and all the Plains tribes, it also required that the tribes make peace with one another. As various tribal representatives signed, smug American onlookers naively assumed that the signatories understood and agreed to these conditions. In truth, even the Sioux delegates could agree on few issues among themselves, and sometimes they violently split into factions. Few Americans understood the depth of these long-standing hostilities and the degree to which intertribal warfare was ingrained.

The Hunkapapa had only recently wrenched the land around the Yellowstone and its tributaries from the Crows, at the cost of considerable Lakota blood. This land had now come to define the Lakota homeland, and they had no intention of stopping the fight with their Indian enemies. Bloody attacks and counterattacks continued, often ending only after hand-to-hand fighting had dispatched the last warrior. Even on that warm June evening in 1876, as they camped in the valley of the Greasy Grass, Hunkapapa leaders worried less about a confrontation with American soldiers than about their traditional Indian enemies.

Some Crow Perspectives

The Lakota's greatest enemy, the Crow, were descended from the settled Plains farming villages discussed earlier. At some point, farming Hidatsa people from the Knife River area had begun to overwinter on the Plains, tracking elk, antelope, and buffalo. The Crow trace their ancestry to one of these farming groups, who eventually gave up their settled village life to hunt full time on the Plains. One tribal elder, Medicine Crow, tells the story this way:

> The people of this tribe, still without a name, referred to themselves as "Our Side." One day, the leaders called a council. The consensus of opinion was, "The place is too harsh; the winters are long and cold. We must move and find a better place to live." Once again, they packed their dogs and wolves and headed south through the valleys and passes of the mountains.

Oral traditions and archaeological evidence shows that the Crow arrived on the Plains during the 1500s, or perhaps earlier. Before too long, outsiders began encroaching on Crow territory from everywhere. The Oregon Trail opened in 1847, and the gold rush of 1849 unleashed a flood of Euro-Americans westward. Along their eastern flank, Indian people—particularly Sioux and Cheyenne—were being forced out of their own territories by non-Indian settlers. Whites in northwestern Montana forced the Blackfeet southward, further encroaching upon the western reaches of Crow territory. Nineteenth-century Crow people became understandably protective of their hunting territories. According to historian Fred Hoxie, "A century earlier they might have allowed a visit from a Sioux or Blackfoot band, [but] in 1850, the appearance of strangers meant war."

Faced with the prospect of increased warfare and the quickening pace of American migration across the Plains, the Crow readily joined leaders of other Plains tribes at Fort Laramie in the summer of 1851, to clarify their boundaries and establish the safety of white travelers. Thousands of Crow, Sioux, Blackfeet, Shoshone, Cheyenne, and others—the largest gathering of Plains Indians ever recorded—sat down to iron out differences.

When it was over, the Crow homeland had been precisely—and artificially—delineated on official government maps. It was bounded on the east by the Powder River, on the west by the headwaters of the Yellowstone River, on the north by the Missouri and the Musselshell rivers, and on the south by the Wind River Mountains. Although huge—38 million acres—the Crow country, so defined, excluded many places they traditionally considered their own.

Warfare had always been an integral part of Crow life, and they now chose to side with the United States, following this difficult course because they perceived that it would best serve their own tribal interests. The Crow well understood that most of the Indian tribes menacing them had themselves been pushed out of their homes by white settlers elsewhere in the United States; the Crow looked to their U.S. allies to live up to the treaties, and deliver them from the Indian newcomers.

Although suspicious of white incursions, the Crow never went to war with the United States. Many Crow deliberately chose neutrality, withdrawing into the Bighorn Mountains to avoid hostilities. Other tribal members elected to serve actively with their U.S. allies, mostly as army scouts and couriers. As the hostilities at the Little Bighorn remind us, the "Indian Wars" in the 1860s and 1870s were not simply battles between whites and Indians. The Crow were trying to protect their territory from all manner of land-hungry enemies—not just white miners, settlers, and soldiers, but their Indian enemies as well.

Crow scouts rode with Custer's jinxed Seventh Cavalry into the valley of the Little Bighorn. But, following the custom of the time, Custer discharged them before the fighting began. Two Crow warriors did remain, however, to serve and fight with Major Marcus Reno's detachment.

Following the battle, Sioux were pursued by U. S. forces, and eventually forced to return to Dakota Territory. The Crow quickly reoccupied that portion of their lands that the Sioux had forcibly encroached upon for two decades.

Harassed on all sides by powerful enemies, the Crow leadership maintained a steady course. Although some sided with the United States and others vowed neutrality, their unswerving goal was always to maintain their homeland. Pursuing their own brand of statesmanship, the Crow suffered less than most Plains tribes during this violent era in American history.

AN ARCHAEOLOGICAL PERSPECTIVE

Though Native American eyewitness accounts have been available since the battle at Little Bighorn took place, American history has traditionally dismissed such narratives. After all, when Indian contestants were first interviewed, many battlefield recollections were tempered by a fear of retribution for Custer's defeat (and given the tenor of the country at the time, their fears were clearly warranted). And because of the freestyle conduct of Indian warfare—"unencumbered by American Victorian standards of military obedience and duty"— Native American warriors saw little of the overall picture of the battle.

Particularly disturbing to Custer fanatics were the Indian accounts that attributed cowardly behavior to soldiers from the Seventh Cavalry: breakdowns in military discipline, widespread panic, attempted desertions, and even suicide. Many Indian eyewitnesses spoke in disgust of the troopers' hysteria, suggesting unbecoming cowardice that tarnished the image of a brave adversary. Yet even today, many American historians discredit Indian testimony as suspect, garbled, and overly partisan.

Support for the Native American viewpoint has come recently from an unexpected quarter. In 1983, a grassfire spread across the national monument, clearing the terrain of brush and grass, and making possible an unprecedented view of the battlefield. For the next two years, professional and avocational archaeologists and historians scoured the

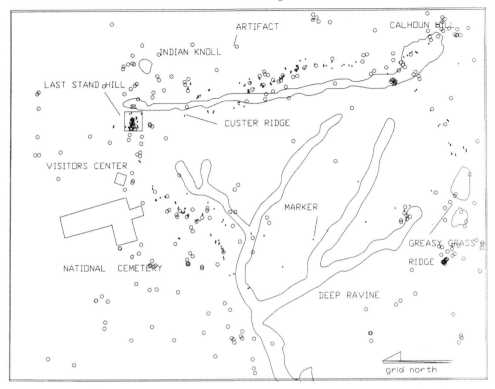

Computer-generated plot showing the distribution of archaeologically recovered artifacts relative to grave markers, major topographic features, and modern cultural features at the Little Bighorn Battlefield (after Douglas G. Scott and others, Archaeological Perspectives on the Battle of the Little Bighorn, fig. 37).

area, locating previously unknown finds and mapping the battle site in great detail.

Archaeological teams recovered more than 2,200 artifacts, and 300 human bones. Using modern techniques of ballistic and forensic science, spent shells found on one part of the battlefield could be matched with slugs found elsewhere. Investigators not only could establish various lines of fire but they also could chart the progression of specific firearms as weapons changed hands during the battle.

The physical evidence from archaeology suggests that the Indian testimony was basically correct. For the first time, archaeologists could demonstrate exactly what weapons were used by both sides, precisely where soldiers fought, and what happened to their bodies after they fell. We now know where the ill-starred troopers were deployed, what kind of clothing they wore, and how they fought.

Richard Fox, archaeologist in charge of the Little Bighorn research, concludes: "What the archaeology and the Indian accounts told me, is that there was *no gallant defense* on Custer Hill . . . the troopers put up no substantial resistance. It was a complete rout."

STILL BATTLING AT THE LITTLE BIGHORN

Regardless of such evidence, Americans will always love their martyrs, from the doomed Texans defending the Alamo to the star-crossed troopers on Last Stand Hill. Reenactments of such watershed historical events have become an important way for mainstream Americans to keep their own history alive. Each year over the past three decades, a re-creation of the Battle of Little Bighorn has been sponsored by the Hardin chamber of commerce. Striving for authenticity and historical accuracy, the participants portray the events that culminated in Custer's colossal defeat.

Crow people are understandably ambivalent about the Little Bighorn. The battle took place on *their* land, and while some of their ancestors scouted for Custer's cavalry, many Crow wonder if they should have thrown in with Sitting Bull instead.

Similar feelings bubbled to the surface when Barbara Booher, herself a Native American and now Park Superintendent at Little Bighorn, first visited the battlefield in 1988. Although entranced by the aura of the place, she also noted that the dozens of white marble grave markers were mostly for American soldiers. Estimates of the Indian dead range between about 40 and 150 killed that day, and yet only one was commemorated with a grave marker. "It looked like a NO PARKING

Little Bighorn Battlefield National Monument (Hardin, MT; main entrance is 15 mi. SE via exit 510 off I-90, then a half mi. E. via US 212) not only commemorates the dramatic Indian victory of June 1876 but it also embraces a national cemetery established in 1879. Just inside the entrance is a visitor center and museum. Phone (406) 638-2621.

Volunteers interested in participating in the summer reenactments of the battle should contact *Hardin chamber of commerce.* Phone (406) 665-1672.

Those wishing to document the reenactment process should contact *Smithsonian Research Expeditions, U.S. and International Events.* Phone (202) 287-3210.

sign," she commented dryly. Two years later, when Booher took charge, she vowed that "This will all change."

Some things have changed already. On December 9, 1991, President George Bush signed into law a bill declaring that the former "Custer Battlefield National Monument" will henceforth officially be known as the **Little Bighorn Battlefield National Monument**. A monument to honor the Cheyenne, Sioux, and other Native Americans who perished defending their families, their lifestyle, their culture, and their lands will be erected, near the existing monument honoring the cavalry.

The reenactment of the battle has also changed. In 1992, Henry Real Bird, a member of the Crow tribe, introduced a Native American version of the conflict. Today, the reenactments sponsored by both the chamber of commerce and the Crow are carefully observed and recorded—not only the battle itself but also the elaborate preparations for the event. Horses, weaponry, and costumes are carefully documented and photographed, and participants from both sides and all ranks are interviewed by volunteers.

WHERE ELSE TO SEE THE ARCHAEOLOGY OF THE ENCOUNTER

The following is a list of sites and museums that feature some of the artifacts and/or remains discussed in this chapter. Complete information on each is listed in the appendix by state at the end of the book.

Abenakis Museum (Odanak, PQ)

Buffalo Museum of Science (Buffalo, NY)

Canadian Museum of Civilization (Ottawa, ON)

Cherokee Heritage Center (Tahlequah, OK)

Colville Confederated Tribes Museum (Coulee Dam, WA)

Coronado-Quivira Museum (Lyons, KS)

Creek Council House Museum (Okmulgee, OK)

The Five Civilized Tribes Museum (Muskogee, OK)

Fort Ross State Historical Park (Jenner, CA)

Thomas Gilcrease Museum (Tulsa, OK)

Huronia Museum (Midland, ON)

Indian Pueblo Cultural Center (Albuquerque, NM)

Iowa, Sac and Fox Indian Mission State Historic Site (Highland, KS)

Iroquois Indian Museum (Schoharie, NY)

Marquette Mission Park and Museum of Ojibwa Culture (St. Ignace, MI)

Manitoba Museum of Man and Nature (Winnipeg, MB)

Mescalero Apache Cultural Center (Mescalero, NM)

Mission Nombre de Dios (St. Augustine, FL)

Mission San Juan Capistrano (San Juan Capistrano, CA)

Mission Santa Barbara (Santa Barbara, CA)

Mission San Xavier del Bac (Tucson, AZ)

Museum of the Cherokee Indian (Cherokee, NC)

Museum of the Plains Indians (Bozeman, MT)

New York State Museum (Albany, NY)

Old Mission State Park (Kellogg, ID)

Oneida Nation Museum (Green Bay, WI)

Rochester Museum & Science Center (Rochester, NY)

Royal Ontario Museum (Toronto, ON)

Salinas Pueblo Missions National Monument (near Mountainair, NM)

Saskatchewan Museum of Natural History (Regina, SK)

Schiele Museum of Natural History and Planetarium (Gastonia, NC)

Seneca-Iroquois National Museum (Salamanca, NY)

Sequoyah Birthplace Museum (Vonore, TN)

Sioux Indian Museum & Craft Center (Rapid City, SD)

Sternberg Memorial Museum (Fort Hayes State University, Hays, KS)

The Turtle: Native American Center for the Living Arts (Niagara Falls, NY)

Tumacacori National Historical Park (Nogales, AZ)

Yakima Nation Museum and Cultural Center (Toppenish, WA)

EPILOGUE: AN ENDURING ENCOUNTER

Not long ago, I went into a bookstore and asked the salesclerk for help in finding a particular book about American Indians. Believe it or not, he referred me to the Nature section! *It's as if we Native Americans were considered to be something less than human—something apart from the family of man.* By the same token, it was not unusual when I was a child to walk into a museum and find Indians displayed next to dinosaurs and mammoths—as if we too were extinct.

— W. RICHARD WEST, JR. (CHEYENNE; DIRECTOR,
NATIONAL MUSEUM OF THE AMERICAN INDIAN)

To this point, we have spoken only in the past tense. This tone has been entirely appropriate, since we have been considering the long-term history of native North America. It is an important and distinguished history, too often clouded by non-Indian ethnocentrism. Even on the eve of the twenty-first century, many continue to overlook and belittle the achievements so evident throughout ancient Native America. We hope that these pages can, in some small way, help erase these images by shedding light on a largely ignored chapter of American history.

But it is equally important to erase the image of the Native Americans as a *dying race*. Fortunately for us all, American Indian people are still here. In fact, as mentioned in the last chapter, more Indians may live in America today than when Columbus arrived more than five centuries ago.

△△△

WHAT'S APPROPRIATE WHEN YOU'RE VISITING INDIAN COUNTRY?

Before heading out, you must remind yourself that a destination in Indian Country is different from anywhere else in North America. Relations between Indian and non-Indian people have varied radically over the past centuries, and the legacy of these historical interactions unquestionably remains. Many non-Indians are reluctant visitors to Indian Country; others barge right in. The best path is somewhere toward the middle.

On the "reservations" of the United States and the "reserves" of Canada, you are effectively entering another country. Keep in mind that tribal authorities have the legal right to control their own natural resources. Don't stray from public areas. Tribal management should be consulted regarding special regulations and/or permits required for hunting, fishing, hiking, or picnicking.

Various tribes in Indian Country sponsor numerous social, cultural, and religious events. Many tribal events—powwows, hand games, seasonal dance celebrations, rodeos—are open to the public, Indian and non-Indian alike. Museums, churches, and tribal facilities can also be visited, but keep in mind that you are a guest.

Local customs vary considerably, and it is your responsibility, as a visitor, to determine what is considered appropriate. Some cultural and religious ceremonies require special permission to attend, and you should be certain to obtain such authorizations. In some places in Indian Country, host families customarily extend their personal invitation to non-Indian guests, and they will usually inform their visitors of the appropriate protocol. At times, non-Indian callers are simply not allowed. Sacred sites are particularly sensitive and due to their very nature, few outsiders are welcome there. You should inquire about and respect all local protocols.

On the other hand, powwows are festive occasions, and visitors are almost always welcome. They commonly feature traditional drumming and dancing, native dress and food. Guests might be allowed to participate in communal events such as a "Round

△△△

Dance," but wait for an invitation from the emcee. "Indian time" may not necessarily be your time. Events often proceed according to an internal clock that can disconcert the unsuspecting visitor. Don't plan split-second connections when attending Native American events.

Pay attention to the rules, which are often posted. Sometimes, you will be asked to leave your camera, video equipment, and tape recorder behind. There may also be prohibitions on smoking, drinking alcoholic beverages, sketching, or taking notes. Photography is always a potential point of conflict. Using a flash is often discouraged at dance ceremonies and contests. It is always best to ask dancers and singers before taking pictures. Sometimes, a small gratuity will be requested: if you don't want to pay, don't shoot.

It's better to be overly formal than the reverse. Try to be invisible, keeping questions and interruptions at a minimum. Behave as you would when visiting any other religious service. Respect is often best shown by being unobtrusive. Dress casually, but conservatively. Clothing is a form of communication in all cultures. When visiting Indian County, leave the shorts, halter tops, and other skimpy clothing in the trunk.

Above all, keep your sense of cultural sensitivity close at hand. Forget the racist terms and Indian jokes. Leave the Washington Redskins and Atlanta Braves hats at home. Indian people almost universally detest being somebody else's mascot.

But the key question is this: *Am I welcome in Indian Country?* The answer is almost always "Yes." Indian people in general are increasingly interested in overturning their image as the "invisible Americans." Many reservations have constructed facilities to encourage your visits: hotels, resorts, historical attractions, camping areas, golf courses, recreational facilities, and casinos. Part of the motivation is clearly financial. But many want to show off their heritage and to educate you about their past—both the good and the bad parts.

If you feel uncomfortable visiting Indian Country, that's good. Some Indian people feel just as uncomfortable about your being there. But if you're on your best behavior, chances are that your Native American hosts will be too.

Native Americans still retain some of their land. Some live on reservations; many do not. Indian people often run their own businesses. They create jobs. They protect their environment. They pay their taxes. And, more often than not, they welcome you to visit Indian Country.

ENCOUNTERING NATIVE AMERICA: THE MUSEUM AT WARM SPRINGS

To our children, those of this lifetime and those of many generations to follow, we leave this legacy: preservation of the past, the birthright of your heritage; and the inheritance of our hopes and dreams for the future

—ADMONITION AT THE MUSEUM
AT WARM SPRINGS

Native Americans also build museums. One of the best is the **Museum at Warm Spring**, on the Warm Springs Reservation in central Oregon. Visitors entering the Museum at Warm Springs may be surprised when they read these words. Although envisioned, created, and managed by Native Americans, this Museum contains little that says "Indian" to most non-Indians. There is none of the grinding poverty that too many Americans associate with "their" reservations. There is none of the shrill activism of the 1960s—no calls to storm Alcatraz. There is none of the bellicose greener-than-thou aggressive conservationism of the 1980s. Instead, the visitor to Warm Springs is welcomed and the privilege of education extended.

The initial exhibit does not denounce the Bering Strait theory of Indian origins. Instead, the exhibit begins with a deceptively simple declaration "We are here . . . people have lived here from time immemorial." Time being a relative commodity, this unembellished, yet elegant statement is unarguable. The exhibit cases that follow (labeled "Stories: Legends that Live") trace in general terms the remote past of the Wasco, the Paiute, and the Warm Springs—the three tribes whose history this museum recounts.

In museum terms, the presentation is decidedly high-tech, drawing upon the profession's newest ways to present important ideas. Many visitors, even those who frequent museums with some regularity, may be surprised at the sophistication of the displays. There are frequent alcoves, spatial sidebars where those seeking more can wander through the detail that keeps a museum alive. In the gently lit "Songs of Our People" chamber, for instance, one is enveloped by the lyrics and rhythms of traditional Native American music.

Members of the Museum's accession committee, all enrolled members of the Confederated Tribes, have attempted to assemble an outstanding tribal collection, complete with life-history documentation for the pieces, and their place within traditional family contexts. As a result, the museum's acclaimed collection contains many prized heirlooms, protected for generations by their tribal families and placed on public view for the first time in this grass-roots showcase of pride and community.

The historical exhibits bring out the spiritual meaning behind the artifacts, the Indian side of material culture, whether it's the amazing beadwork, the hand-crafted basketry, or the story-telling parfleches. Many adults and most kids take the rare opportunity to touch fur pelts used in traditional powwows and pick up the audio headset to hear the spoken native languages of the people whose museum this is.

Impressive full-scale reconstructions show how these three very different tribes made and lived in their traditional houses: the simple Paiute wickiup, the Wasco plank house, the Warm Springs tule mat lodge. Neither an architectural flaunting or a "first ecologist" declaration, these long-used houses are eloquent "we are here" statements, offered without value judgment about whose ancestors were richer or more clever. Considerable space is also devoted to the time of treaties, the time spent on reservations, and the optimistic tones of today and the future.

The Museum at Warm Springs (Warm Springs, OR; SR 26 on the Warm Springs Reservation) is an outstanding tribal museum opened to the public in early 1993. It was created by the Confederated Tribes of the Warm Springs Reservation to present and preserve the traditions of the Confederation, the Wasco, the Paiute, and the Warm Springs people. Phone (503) 553-3331.

The attitudes personified in tribal museums still vary considerably. A few remain sullen and surly, dingy reminders of the antagonisms and intrusions that have bedeviled Indian/non-Indian relations for decades. But at many others, such as the Museum at Warm Springs, there is an awareness of the timely importance and huge payoffs in educating an increasingly interested non-Indian audience. They stress the new role of tribal members and leaders as guardians and conservators of the considerable land and resources owned by Indian people.

THE MEDICINE WHEEL: ARCHAEOLOGICAL ENIGMA
OR CONSECRATED GROUND?

From time immemorial, Indian tribal Holy Men have gone into the high places, lakes, and isolated sanctuaries to pray, receive guidance from the Spirits, and train younger people in the ceremonies that constitute the spiritual life of the tribal community. In these ceremonies, medicine men represented the whole web of cosmic life in the continuing search for balance and harmony . . .

When the tribes were forcibly removed from their aboriginal homelands and forced to live on restricted, smaller reservations, many of the ceremonies were prohibited by the Bureau of Indian Affairs, and the people were forced to adopt various subterfuges so that the ceremonial life could continue. Some tribes conducted their most important ceremonies on national holidays and Christian feast days, explaining to curious whites that they were simply honoring George Washington and celebrating Christmas and Easter . . .

Every society needs these kinds of sacred places. They help to instill a sense of social cohesion in the people and remind them of the passage of the generations that have brought them to the present.

— VINE DELORIA, JR. (STANDING ROCK SIOUX)

This panorama of the Medicine Wheel was taken in 1926. Since then, the protective stone wall has been removed and replaced with a chain-link fence. (Courtesy of the American Heritage Center, University of Wyoming.)

On one such high place—on a windswept peak in Wyoming's Bighorn Mountains—lies the celebrated Medicine Wheel, an ancient stone configuration that figures prominently in both high-tech approaches to archaeology and long-term indigenous theology. Here at the **Medicine Wheel** one finds played out in dramatic fashion the sometimes conflicting aims of modern science and traditional religion. Like so many elements of the human past, the Medicine Wheel means many different things to many different people.

Standing there looking at it, today's visitor is confronted by simplicity itself: a stone circle (or "wheel") nearly 90 feet in diameter, built atop an isolated peak 9,640 feet above sea level. Inside are 28 unevenly spaced "spokes," each radiating out from the central "hub," a central stone cairn about 15 feet across. Five smaller cairns dot the periphery.

For nearly a century, scientists have puzzled over why anybody would build this high-altitude rock alignment. The Medicine Wheel was first reported in *Forest and Stream* magazine in 1903, the author pointing out certain similarities with Mexico's celebrated calendar stone. Soon thereafter, the Field Museum of Natural History in Chicago launched an expedition to study the enigmatic rock alignment. Several subsequent teams of archaeologists have also trekked into the Bighorns, discovering that the Medicine Wheel was apparently constructed in more than one stage, with some parts older than others. Cultural materials recovered in association with the Medicine Wheel date to the late precontact and historic periods. On this point, there is little controversy.

Medicine Wheel (Lovell, WY; 25 mi. E. of Lovell, off US14A, follow signs) is one of the most compelling Native American religious sites, past and present. The Forest Service has recently closed the last segment of the road leading to the Medicine Wheel, so visitors should be prepared for a three-mile round trip hike. The road is usually free of snow from late June through September. Phone (307) 672-0751.

But consensus vanishes when it comes to precisely who built it—and why. Numerous hypotheses have been advanced, each enjoying varying degrees of acceptance and derision. Some have suggested that the rock cairns were constructed as memorials, grave markers to mark locations where particularly powerful people died. The lines of rocks

─────────── ◬◬◬ ───────────

ARCHAEOLOGICAL SITES OR SACRED PLACES? A NATIVE AMERICAN PERSPECTIVE

William Tallbull (Elder, Northern Cheyenne Tribe)

To the Indigenous Peoples of North America, the archaeological sites found on North American soil are not "archaeological" sites. They are sites where our relatives lived and carried out their lives.

Sacred Sites such as the Medicine Wheel and Medicine Mountain are no different. To Native Americans they are living cultural sites from which help comes when "The People" needed or need help. They were/are places where tribal peoples went in times of famine and sickness, in periods of long drought when animals would leave, or in more current times when tribes are being torn apart by politics, alcohol, or other abuses.

The men make a pledge to go and vision quest at these places, seeking help. As we leave to go to these sites, our every breath is a prayer. We follow the path to the sites; observing a protocol that has been in place for thousands of years. The Native American approaching these sites must stop four times from the beginning of

─────────── ◬◬◬ ───────────

show the different directions in which they ranged "on the warpath," recording in effect the dead chief's war deeds. The rock piles at the end of the rock lines have been attributed to enemies killed in battle.

Others have related the alignment to the Plains Indian vision quest. One Crow legend tells the story of the Bighorn Medicine Wheel this way:

Red Plume, a famous Crow chief of the period of Lewis and Clark, obtained his inspiration and received his medicine and the token which resulted in the application of that name by him at the Medicine Wheel. As a young man, Red Plume visited the wheel in the hope of receiving a strong medicine which would make of him a great warrior and chief. Without food, water or clothing, he remained for four days and nights awaiting recognition from the spirits. On the fourth night he was approached by the three little men and one woman who inhabited the underground passage to the wheel and was conducted by them to the

△△△

his or her journey to arrival at the site. A trip to a Sacred Site was/ is not done just for curiosity, but only after much preparation and seeking.

Many blessings have come to "The Peoples" in this way. Many tribes have received covenants (bundles) from these sites. Some Tribes still carry the bundles that were received from a certain mountain or site. These are considered no different than the covenants given Moses or the traditional law that went with it.

When Native Peoples have been blessed by a site or area, they go back to give thanks and leave offerings whenever they get a chance. These should be left undisturbed and not handled or tampered with.

Today many of our people are reconnecting with these sites after many years of being denied the privilege of practicing our own religion at these very sacred areas. In the past, trips were made in secret and hidden from curious eyes.

If you go to see a Sacred Site, remember you are walking on "holy ground," and we ask that you respect our culture and traditions. If you come to a site that is being used for a religious purpose, we hope you will understand.

△△△

underground chamber. He remained there for three days and three nights and was instructed in the arts of warfare and in leading his people. He was told that the Red Eagle would be his powerful medicine and would guide him and be his protector through life. He was told to wear always upon his person as an emblem of his medicine, the soft little feather which grows upon the back above the tail of the eagle. This little red plume gave him his name. Upon his death, after many years of successful warfare and leadership, he instructed his people that his spirit would occupy the shrine at the medicine wheel which is not connected with the rim, except by an extended spoke, and that they might at all times communicate with him there.

An alternative name for Red Plume is Long Hair, a Crow leader known to have died in 1836. His possible association with the Bighorn Medicine Wheel could have taken place during the late 1700s.

The site is certainly well suited for such a vision quest. Built on its

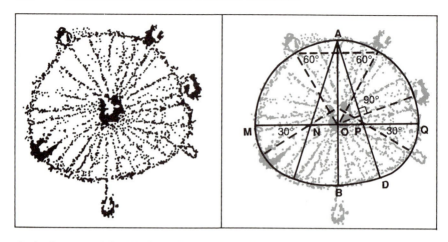

Scale drawing of the Medicine Wheel, located at an elevation of 9,640 feet, just above timberline in the Bighorn Mountains of northern Wyoming. The spoked wheel is roughly 90 feet across, and the five cairns stand about four feet high. At the right, a series of geometrical projections have been superimposed over the Medicine Wheel, demonstrating how the overall shape closely approximates a ring made up of four precise geometric arcs, each of which could be readily laid out on the ground by use of stakes and ropes (after Michael W. Ovenden and David A. Rodger, Megaliths to Medicine Wheels).

lofty perch, the Medicine Wheel commands a spectacular view of the Bighorn Basin to the west. Upslope winds whistle through countless crevices, creating a babel of moaning and shrieking voices when velocities are high. During the early historic period, the rock cairns were apparently protected by small enclosures, perhaps to provide some modicum of shelter during a vision quest.

Perhaps the most publicized hypothesis was offered two decades ago by astronomer John A. Eddy, who suggested that the Medicine Wheel was a Native American astronomical observatory. Noting that selected stone cairns might once have held wooden poles, Eddy argued that these posts could have served as foresight and backsight, defining the azimuth of the rising and setting of some important celestial object (probably the sun). Predicting significant celestial events such as the summer and winter solstices, would have been powerful knowledge, prized for its calendrical, ritual, or even agricultural purposes. The Hopi horizon calendar did this by charting the progression of the sun's rise over the nearby mountains, thus enabling the "sun watcher," a religious official to forewarn people of important agricultural and ritual dates.

Because of its elevation—the Medicine Wheel is buried beneath deep snow drifts throughout the winter—Eddy focused on the summer solstice. On the morning of June 20, 1972, Eddy laid out imaginary sighting poles using a surveyor's transit, steel tape, and compass. At dawn, he found that the sun rose exactly where it was supposed to. His conclusion: Simply by observing the sunrise over the cairns at the Medicine Wheel, aboriginal astronomers would have been able to predict the timing of the summer solstice "with a precision of several days." After further experimentation, Eddy suggested that the additional cairns may have marked rising spots of the brightest stars in the summer dawn, stars which themselves further enhanced predicting of the coming solstice.

Skeptics have pointed out several flaws in Eddy's argument. Unlike the American Woodhenge at Cahokia (see page 157), the Medicine Wheel lacks convincing evidence for such sighting poles. The cairns are so large that precise sighting (even with a pole) would not be possible. And even allowing for poles and precision, Eddy's astronomical argument still leaves one cairn unaccounted for.

Other investigators have suggested instead that the Medicine Wheel was built to aid navigation, the rock piles left as directional aids to newcomers. Still others believe that the floor plan of the Medicine Wheel was a two-dimensional imitation of the 28-raftered lodge built as part of the Sun Dance ceremony. Other hypotheses hold that the Medicine Wheel may have been a boundary marker, a depiction of a stone turtle, and an enduring stone marker demonstrating geometrical expertise. The point is this: After a century of probing and digging, mapping and sighting, the Medicine Wheel is still, as one investigator puts it, "a well-known archaeological structure whose origin and purpose remain unexplained."

But the Medicine Wheel is much more than an archaeological site. To many contemporary Indian people, it is also a holy place, one of many sacred sites where important ceremonies are performed to this day. Sacred lands are considered to be vital to individual and tribal harmony (see **Archaeological Sites or Sacred Places?: A Native American Perspective**).

And yet many of the most important sacred sites—places like the Bighorn Medicine Wheel—are being overrun each year by thousands of non-Indians: well-meaning tourists, scientific teams, and New Agers looking for a spiritual experience. In the worldview of many tribes, the birds, animals, and plants are part of their religious traditions. There is great concern in Indian Country that the plants, paths, shrines, rocks,

— ⟁⟁⟁ —

SACRED GROUND

Suzan Shown Harjo (Cheyenne/Hodulgee Muscogee)

eagles disappear into the sun
   surrounded by light from the face of Creation
   then scream their way home
      with burning messages of mystery and power

some are given to snake doctors and ants and turtles and salmon
   to heal the world
      with order and patience

some are given to cardinals and butterflies and yellow medicine
flowers
   to heal the world
      with joy

some are given to bears and buffalo and human peoples
   to heal the world
      with courage and prayer

messages for holy places
   in the heart of Mother Earth
   deep inside the Old Stone Woman
      whose wrinkles are canyons
   in the roaring waters and clear blue streams
   and bottomless lakes
      who take what they need
   in the forests of grandfather cedars
   and mountains of grandmother sentinel rocks
      who counsel 'til dawn

messages for holy places
   where snow thunder warns
   and summer winds whisper
      this is Sacred Ground

— ⟁⟁⟁ —

Sacred Ground at Spirit Falls
    where the small round stones have secrets
        that clear-cutters can never discover

Sacred Ground at Mount Graham
    where Apaches pray for a peaceful world
        invisible through the vatican telescope
Sacred Ground at Bear Butte
    where Cheyennes and Lakotas hide from tourists
    to dress the trees in ermine tails and red-tail hawk feathers
        and ribbons of prayers to the life-givers

Sacred Ground at the San Francisco Peaks
    where Navajos and Hopis dodge ski-bums and bottles
    to settle the spirits
        where they walk

Sacred Ground at Badger Two Medicine and Red Butte and Crazy
Mountain
    where miners have drills for arms
        and gold in their eyes

Sacred Ground at Chota
    where even Tellico's dam engineers hear Tsulagee voices
        through the burial waters

Sacred Ground at Medicine Wheel
    and all the doors to the passages of time
    to Sacred Ground of other worlds
        where suns light the way
        for eagles to carry messages
        for fires on
            Sacred Ground

and other aspects of their sacred sites are being destroyed by the curious and the insensitive.

A coalition representing varied interests—tribal, scientific, ecological, and government—are cooperating to be certain that the Medicine Wheel is protected, preserved, and respected. The last 1.5 miles of road have been closed to vehicular traffic, the Forest Service requiring visitors to travel the remaining distance on foot. In this way, the negative impact of tourism is minimized, the religious freedom of native people respected, and this powerful place is still kept accessible to the many people who wish to visit, who wish to understand the strength of the place that has drawn people to this isolated mountain-top for centuries. In the words of Northern Cheyenne elder and religious leader, William Tallbull, "remember you are walking on 'holy ground,' . . . we ask that you respect our culture and traditions."

APPENDIX

MAJOR SITES, MUSEUMS, AND PROGRAMS THAT FEATURE NATIVE NORTH AMERICAN HISTORY AND ARCHAEOLOGY

Many of the following sites and museums are discussed in the text, some in great detail, as they relate to the chronological development of successive Native American cultures. However, for the convenience of those who may be traveling to a particular area, they are listed here alphabetically by state. Where much additional information can be found about the historical context of these sites, the reader is referred to the text by page number.

This Mississippian mask from Key Marco, Florida, combines human and deer-like features.

ALABAMA

INDIAN MOUND AND MUSEUM (Florence, AL; S. Court St.; Phone 205/760-6427) contains one of the largest Mississippian mounds in the Tennessee Valley, measuring 43 feet high, with a summit 145 feet by 94 feet. The visitor's center displays several artifacts from the area.

MOUNDVILLE ARCHAEOLOGICAL PARK (Moundville, AL; ½ mi. W of SR 69; Phone 205/371-2572) is one of the country's most well-preserved prehistoric mound groups. (See pages 158–66.)

RUSSELL CAVE NATIONAL MONUMENT (Bridgeport, AL; 8 mi. NW via CRs 91 and 75; Phone 205/495-2672) contains a large cavern system that extends about 7 miles into a limestone mountain. (See page 78.)

STATE ARCHIVES AND HISTORY MUSEUM (Montgomery, AL; in the Alabama Department of Archives and History, 624 Washington Ave.; Phone 205/242-4363) have numerous artifacts from local Native American groups, particularly the Choctaw, Chickasaw, and Seminole.

ALASKA

ALASKA STATE MUSEUM (Juneau, AK; ½ blk. W. of Egan Dr. on Whittier St.; Phone 907/465-2901), called "Alaska's Attic" exhibits the material culture of native Alaskan people, including Aleut, Athapascan, Haida, Inuit (Eskimo), Tlingit, and Tshimsian. Continuity between past and present is stressed through an extensive program of traveling exhibitions.

ANCHORAGE MUSEUM OF HISTORY AND FINE ARTS (Anchorage, AK; 121 W. 7th Ave.; Phone 907/343-4326) exhibits the art, history, and cultures of Alaska, from pre-Columbian times to the present; features Aleut, Inuit (Eskimo) and other native American peoples.

SHELDON JACKSON MUSEUM (Sitka, AK; 104 College Dr. on the Sheldon Jackson College campus; Phone 907/747-8981) is Alaska's oldest museum, containing displays of native Alaskan artifacts.

SHELDON MUSEUM AND CULTURAL CENTER (Haines, AK; Main St. near the boat harbor; Phone 907/766-2366) contains native American materials from the Chilkat Valley, with an emphasis on Tlingit culture.

UNIVERSITY OF ALASKA MUSEUM (Fairbanks, AK; on the West Ridge of the University of Alaska campus; Phone 907/474-7505) displays artifacts obtained from their long-term archaeological research program, including St. Lawrence Island, Point Hope Peninsula, and Cape Denbigh. Also contains various Alaska native arts and natural history exhibits, including the carcass of a steppe bison killed by a lion 36,000 years ago and preserved in the permafrost.

WRANGELL MUSEUM (Wrangell, AK; 2 blks. from the ferry terminal and city dock at 2nd and Bevier sts.; Phone 907/874-3770) exhibits local native rock art and a large collection of Tlingit Indian artifacts.

ALBERTA

GLENBOW-ALBERTA INSTITUTE (Calgary, AB; part of the Convention Centre at 9th Ave. and 1st St., S.E.; Phone 403/264-8300) is a museum dedicated to documenting the long-range history of western Canada, with particular emphasis on native artifacts and the settlement of the West. A new third-floor exhibit explores the lives of the Inuit (Eskimo) people, and displays past and present artifacts.

HEAD-SMASHED IN BUFFALO JUMP INTERPRETIVE CENTRE (Ft. McLeod, AB; 18 km. NW on Hwy. 785, off Hwy. 2; Phone 403/553-2731) is one of the best-preserved buffalo-hunting sites in America. (See pages 74–76.)

MEDICINE HAT MUSEUM & ART GALLERY (Medicine Hat, AB; 1302 Bomford Crescent at jct. Hwys. 1 and 3; Phone 403/527-6266) presents the region's native American cultural heritage.

PROVINCIAL MUSEUM OF ALBERTA (Edmonton, AB; 12845 102nd Ave.; Phone 403/427-1786 or 403/453-9100) documents the early arrival of native people in Alberta and traces their heritage through the eighteenth- and nineteenth-century fur trade into the present day. Their relationship to nature is brought out through several exhibits and dioramas—the use of plants for curing, of hide and bark for dwellings, and of quills for decorating clothing.

WRITING-ON-STONE PROVINCIAL PARK (Milk River, AB; 32 km E. and 10 km S. on secondary Hwy. 501 to jct. Hwy. 500 following signs; Phone 403/647-2364), on the Milk River, is one of North America's largest concentrations of pictographs and petroglyphs, inscribed on massive sandstone outcrops by nomadic Shoshoni and Blackfeet Indians. Access to the archaeological preserve is permitted only on 1½-hour guided tours.

ARIZONA

APACHE CULTURAL CENTER (Fort Apache, AZ; SR 73 on the loop road through the White Mountain reservation; 21 mi. SE of US 60 from Carrizo; Phone 602/338-4625) is an Indian-operated institution that tells the history of the Apache people who live on the White Mountain reserve.

ARIZONA STATE MUSEUM (Tucson, AZ; University of Arizona campus at Park Ave., and University Blvd.; Phone 602/621-6302), also discussed in chapter 6, contains permanent exhibits in the South gallery interpreting the lifestyles of contemporary and prehistoric Indians of Arizona.

CANYON DE CHELLY NATIONAL MONUMENT (Chinle, AZ; 3 mi. E of Chinle; Phone 602/674-5436) is located on the Navajo Indian Reservation. Canyon de Chelly, 26 mi. long, joins Canyon del Muerto, 25 mi. long, each bounded by red sandstone walls rising up to 1,000 feet above the valley floor. Archaeological ruins span several periods of Native American culture, from early Basketmaker pithouses to the apartment-style Pueblo homes in caves or rock shelters above the canyon floor.

The principal area archaeological sites are White House, Antelope House, Standing Cow, and Mummy Cave. Scenic drives, on both sides of the canyon, afford spectacular views of most of the major sites.

CASA GRANDE RUINS NATIONAL MONUMENT (Coolidge, AZ; 1 mi. N. SR 87; Phone 602/723-3172) is an impressive group of remains from the Hohokam culture. More than 600 years old. (See page 116.)

CASA MALPAIS (Springerville, AZ; less than 1 mi. W off US 60; Phone 602/333-5375). This elaborate Mogollon village complex dates from between 1250 and 1400.

COLORADO RIVER TRIBES MUSEUM (Parker, AZ; off SR 95 at Mohave and 2nd streets; Phone 602/669-9211) is an Indian-operated institution located at tribal headquarters. It displays traditional crafts and history of the Chemehuevi and Mojave people, with particular emphasis on the impressive basketry.

FORT YUMA QUECHAN MUSEUM (Yuma, AZ; Fort Yuma Indian Hill; Phone 619/572-0661) displays local Indian culture and early European contact materials. Nearby are the old Methodist Indian Mission and St. Thomas Mission buildings.

HEARD MUSEUM (Phoenix, AZ; 22 E. Monte Vista Rd.; Phone 602/252-8848) is a world-class museum introducing the lifeways and art of Native American people. The collection contains more than 75,000 artifacts. Authentic house types include a Navajo hogan, an Apache wickiup, and a Hopi corn-grinding room.

HOPI CULTURAL CENTER MUSEUM (Second Mesa, AZ; 5 mi. W. of SR 87 on SR 264; Phone 602/734-6650), an Indian-operated institution, displays basketry, Kachina dolls, weaving, jewelry, and other Hopi materials.

MISSION SAN XAVIER DEL BAC (Tucson, AZ; 9 mi. SW on San Xavier Rd. on the Tohono O'Odham [Papago] Indian Reservation; Phone 602/294-2624), often called the "White Dove of the Desert," is North America's most spectacular example of Spanish colonial architecture. Founded by Jesuit Father Kino before 1700, the present structure was built from 1783–97 by the

Franciscans. This mission is still active. An extensive restoration and conservation training program for Tohono O'Odham people makes it an extraordinarily interesting place to visit.

MOHAVE MUSEUM OF HISTORY AND ARTS (Mohave, AZ; 400 W. Beale St., ¼ mi. E. of US 93, exit off I-40; Phone 602/753-3195) depicts the history of northwestern Arizona, with re-created Mohave and Hualapai Indian dwellings.

MONTEZUMA CASTLE NATIONAL MONUMENT (near Camp Verde, AZ; from Flagstaff, 50 mi. S. on I-17, 2.5 mi. E.; Phone 602/567-3322) contains a remarkably well-preserved five-story, 20-room ruin. Built and occupied by Sinaguan people between A.D. 1125 and 1400. Despite extensive vandalism, it contains original ceilings, doorways, floors, and a walled balcony.

MONUMENT VALLEY NAVAJO TRIBAL PARK (Utah/Arizona border; from Kayenta, 24 mi. N. on US 163, 5 mi. E. on local road; Phone 602/871-6436, 6466) lies within the Navajo Reservation in Arizona and Utah. Human occupation in the area is documented by more than 100 Anasazi sites occupied prior to A.D. 1300. Self-guiding and guided tours from the visitor center are offered daily. Restrictions apply.

MUSEUM OF NORTHERN ARIZONA (Flagstaff, AZ; 3 mi. N. on US 180, Fort Valley Rd.; Phone 602/774-5211) is a noteworthy facility presenting the archaeology and ethnology of the American Southwest. Displays present both contemporary Native American materials, and also show artifacts from precontact past beginning in Paleoindian times.

NAVAJO NATIONAL MONUMENT (Navajo Indian Reservation, AZ; a 9-mi. paved road [SR 564] leads from US 160 to the monument headquarters; Phone 602/672-2366) contains several excellent archaeological sites. The visitor center exhibits Anasazi artifacts, presents a slide program, and a 25-minute film program.

NAVAJO TRIBAL MUSEUM (Window Rock, AZ; in the Navajo Arts and Crafts Enterprises building on SR 264; Phone 602/871-6673 or 602/871-4941, ext. 1457 or ext. 1459) is an Indian-operated institution, presenting Navajo culture and history, as well as Anasazi archaeology. A re-created trading post of the 1870–1930 period and changing exhibits by Navajo craftspeople and artists are also featured.

PETRIFIED FOREST NATIONAL PARK (from Gallup, NM; 69 mi. SW into AZ on I-40; Phone: 602/524-6228) contains numerous Anasazi sites, including *Puerco Ruins*, a 150-room site constructed six centuries ago. *Newspaper Rock* bears petroglyphs that can be viewed from an overlook. *Agate House* ruin has been partially reconstructed.

PUEBLO GRANDE MUSEUM (Phoenix, AZ; 4619 E. Washington St.; Phone 602/495-0900) is one of the largest of the Hohokam mound sites and includes two ballcourts. (See pages 114–16.)

SMOKI MUSEUM (Prescott, AZ; Arizona Ave., N. of Gurley St.; Phone 602/445-1230) displays artifacts of the native American Southwest, housed in a reproduction of pueblo architecture.

TONTO NATIONAL MONUMENT (Globe, AZ; 4 mi. W. on US 60, then 28 mi. NW on SR 88; Phone 602/467-2241) contains two Salado Province cliff dwellings, constructed about A.D. 1300–1450. These two-storied pueblos were built in large caves, and the original ceilings are still preserved. The lower dwelling of 19 rooms is better preserved than the large 40-room upper pueblo. A visitor center and museum presents archaeological background.

TUMACACORI NATIONAL HISTORICAL PARK (Nogales, AZ; 19 mi. north on I-19; Phone 602/398-2341) preserves the abandoned Mission San Jose de Tumacacori. Formerly a large Pima Indian village, it was visited by Spanish missionaries as early as 1691, but the massive adobe church was not begun until 1802. The heavily restored mission now houses a visitor's center that tells the story of the Sonora missions.

TUSAYAN RUIN AND MUSEUM (Grand Canyon National Park, AZ; 22 mi. E. of Grand Canyon Village on a short spur leading off East Rim Dr.; Phone 602/638-2305) highlights a small pueblo site, a hamlet of perhaps thirty people who lived here for two decades in the late twelfth century.

TUZIGOOT NATIONAL MONUMENT (Clarkdale, AZ; 2 mi. E. of Clarkdale; Phone 602/634-5564) contains the ruins of a hilltop pueblo, occupied between about A.D. 1125 and 1400/1450 by Sinagua people. The visitor center displays numerous artifacts recovered from excavations at this important site.

WALNUT CANYON NATIONAL MONUMENT (Flagstaff, AZ; 7.5 mi. E. on I-40, then 3 mi. SE; Phone 602/526-3367) preserves a series of masonry cliff dwellings built into overhangs along the canyon rim. Farmers built check dams that held water and soil for crops.

WUPATKI NATIONAL MONUMENT (Flagstaff, AZ; 32 mi. N. on US 89 to entrance; Phone 602/556-7040) consists of the Wupatki site as well as hundreds of others. Wupatki is one of the largest sites, and one of the few that has been extensively excavated. This three-story structure originally contained about 100 rooms, an amphitheater, and ball court. The soil of this area was enriched by volcanic ash with the eruption of Sunset Crater in A.D. 1065. So productive was the farming that this region became one of the most densely populated sections of northern Arizona.

ARKANSAS

HAMPSON STATE MUSEUM (Wilson, AR; ¼ mi. N. on US 61; Phone 501/655-8622) displays artifacts from the late Mississippian Nodena site, located nearby. Numerous artifacts are on display from this 15-acre palisaded Mississippian village (A.D. 1400–1650).

PARKIN ARCHEOLOGICAL STATE PARK (Parkin, AR; north edge at the junction of SR 64 and 184; Phone 501/682-1191) features a 17-acre Indian town occupied from A.D. 1350–1550, surrounded by a ditch and log palisade. The Parkin site, capital of the Casqui Province, is unique because it has been protected from careless digging and modern agricultural practices. The visitor's center includes an exhibit area and archaeological research station.

TOLTEC MOUNDS STATE PARK (Scott, AR; 4 mi. SE off US 165; Phone 501/961-9442) contains one of the largest and most complex sites in the lower Mississippi Valley. Prehistoric earthworks date from about A.D. 400 through 1400; mound construction began A.D. 750. Despite the name, these were constructed by native North Americans, *not* the Toltecs of central Mexico. The visitor center has interpretive exhibits, audiovisual programs, and an archaeological laboratory.

UNIVERSITY MUSEUM (Fayetteville, AR; Garland Ave. on the University of Arkansas campus; Phone 501/575-3555) exhibits prehistoric, historical, and ethnographic materials. Particularly good are displays of Ozark bluff-dweller collections (derived from Woodland-Mississippian peoples ca. A.D. 700–1700), artifacts from the nearby Spiro Mounds in Oklahoma, and Paleoindian artifacts.

BRITISH COLUMBIA

KWAGIULTH MUSEUM AND CULTURE CENTRE (Quathiaski Cove, BC; 3 km. S. of Quathiaski Cove; Phone 604/285-3733) is an Indian-operated institution that presents native cultural heritage and guided tours of nearby rock art sites.

MUSEUM OF ANTHROPOLOGY (University of British Columbia, Vancouver, BC; on the Point Grey Cliffs; Phone 604/822-3825) houses major collections from the First Nations of British Columbia. Several artifacts are "touchables," and visitors are invited to gently feel the finely adzed surface on Haida artist Bill Reid's Bear in the Ramp. Other touchables are so labeled. Another highlight is the "visible storage" program, where all visitors can catch a rare glimpse at research collections, those not normally available to the nonprofessional.

ROYAL BRITISH COLUMBIA MUSEUM (Victoria, BC; next to the Parliament Buildings at 675 Belleville St.; Phone 604/387-3701) has numerous innovative displays dealing with the ancient cultural history of British Columbia.

U'MISTA CULTURAL CENTRE (Alert Bay, BC; on Cormorant Island via ferry from Vancouver Island; Phone 604/974-5403) is an Indian-operated institution, with an excellent collection of Native American masks, cedar baskets, copper items, and other artifacts from local potlatch ceremonies.

CALIFORNIA

ANDERSON MARSH STATE HISTORIC PARK (Kelseyville, CA; off SR 53, between Lower Lake and Clearlake; Phone 707/279-2267 or 707/279-4294) contains extremely ancient archaeological sites. Park docents lead tours explaining the ancient history of the area, especially the park's petroglyphs. The local Pomo community has recently reconstructed a dancehouse in the park, which is used for spring ceremonials.

CALICO EARLY MAN ARCHAEOLOGICAL SITE (Yermo, CA; 7 mi. NE via I-15 and Minneola Rd; Phone 909/798-8570) provides a good look at how archaeologists work. Excavations have been conducted at this site since the 1940s in search of evidence of early human occupation. (See pages 43–46.)

CALIFORNIA STATE INDIAN MUSEUM (Sacramento, CA; 2618 K St.; Phone 916/445-4209) is located at old Sutter's Fort. Exhibits depict the extensive range of native Californian culture. This excellent collection has been recently reinstalled, incorporating considerable Native American input, and demonstrating the continuities between past and present.

CHAW'SE: INDIAN GRINDING ROCKS STATE PARK (Jackson, CA; 10 mi. NE of Jackson on SR 88 to Pine Grove, then 1 mi. NW on Pine Grove-Volcano Rd.; Phone 209/296-7488) displays native Californian artifacts and a reconstructed Miwok Indian village. (See pages 60–63.)

CHUMASH PAINTED CAVE STATE HISTORIC PARK (near Santa Barbara, CA; drive on SR 154 to Painted Cave Road, then 4 mi. to marker; Phone 805/968-3294) is a spectacularly decorated overhang in the Santa Ynez Mountains, one of dozens known to contain ancient multicolored paintings and carvings. Painted Cave, the only of these sites available for visitation, contains numerous pictographs, painted in red, yellow, white, and black.

COYOTE HILLS REGIONAL PARK (Fremont, CA; off SR 84 to Thorton Ave., N. on Paseo Padre Freeway, left onto Patterson Ranch Road, which ends in park; Phone 510/795-9385) displays Ohlone culture, one of the densest populations in native North America. This site, partially excavated, dates between about 400 B.C. and A.D. 1800.

EASTERN CALIFORNIA MUSEUM (Independence, CA; 3 blks. W. of the courthouse at 155 Grant St.; Phone 619/878-2411, ext. 2258) has a small, but very interesting collection of local archaeological and ethnographic artifacts.

FORT ROSS STATE HISTORIC PARK (Jenner, CA; 12 mi. N. of Jenner on SR1) was the site of the former Russian fort and trading center, established in 1812. Extensive excavations have taken place in the past decade, with an emphasis on the Native American participation in this unusual enterprise. The visitor center interprets Native American, Native Alaskan, and Russian interaction between 1812 and 1841.

PHOEBE HEARST MUSEUM OF ANTHROPOLOGY (Berkeley, CA; on the University of California Campus, in 103 Kroeber Hall; Phone 510/642-3681) is one of the premier research museums in the country. Formerly the Lowie Museum, the Hearst Museum maintains a rich collection of native Californian materials, and rotating exhibits display various parts of this important collection.

HOOPA TRIBAL MUSEUM (Hoopa, CA; from US 101, take SR 299 E. to SR 96 N.; Phone 916/625-4211), an Indian-operated institution, is a "living" museum, displaying excellent collections of Hoopa, Karok, and Yurok artifacts, including baskets, jewelry, tools, hats, and ceremonial clothing, and a redwood dugout canoe. Most of the items on display are on loan by tribal members, and are removed annually to be used in traditional ceremonies.

KERN COUNTY MUSEUM (Bakersfield, CA; 3801 Chester Ave., Phone 805/861-2132) displays numerous local archaeological artifacts, with an emphasis on Yurok culture.

LA PURÍSIMA MISSION STATE HISTORIC PARK (Lompoc, CA; 4 mi. NE of Lompoc; Phone 805/733-3713) is the second site of the Mission La Purísima Concepción. Although extensively restored, it provides a good interpretation of what life was like for Native American and Franciscan alike. (See pages 207–18.)

MALKI MUSEUM (Banning, CA; N. of I-10 from the Fields Road Exit; Phone 909/849-4697), an Indian-operated institution, is part of the Morongo Reservation, home of the Cahuilla and Serrano people. The museum was organized to help retain elements of tribal heritage and to display traditional crafts and clothing.

MISSION BASILICA SAN DIEGO DE ALCALÁ (Mission Valley, CA; 10818 Mission Rd.; reached via Mission Gorge Rd. off I-8 and Twain Ave.; Phone 619/281-8449) was first established by Fr. Serra in 1769 at Presidio Hill. Mission San Diego was moved to its present site in 1774, destroyed by earthquakes in 1803 and 1812 and subsequently rebuilt. The new church was constructed 1931, behind a facade that is probably original.

MISSION NUESTRA SEÑORA DE LA SOLEDAD (Soledad, CA; 3 mi. S. of Soledad on Fort Romie Rd.; Phone 408/678-2586) was founded in 1791. It collapsed in 1831. The replacement chapel has been restored and a museum built on site.

MISSION SAN ANTONIO DE PADUA (King City, CA; is 20 mi. SW of King City in Fort Hunter Liggett; Phone 408/385-4478) has been heavily restored, although the site still features the original well, gristmill, tannery, and parts of the aqueduct system. A small museum has been established, and archaeological excavations have been conducted there for several years during summer.

MISSION SAN ANTONIO DE PALA (Pala, CA; N. of SR 76 on Pala Mission Rd.; Phone 619/742-3317) was originally a *visita* (outpost) of Mission San Luis Rey de Francia. It has since been restored and contains a museum.

MISSION SAN BUENA VENTURA (Ventura, CA; is at 225 E. Main St.; Phone 805/648-4496) was founded in 1782 and completed in 1809. The original mission location has been excavated and is effectively interpreted, alongside a restored church and a small museum.

MISSION SAN CARLOS BORROMEO DEL RIO CARMELO (Carmel, CA; 3080 Rio Rd.; Phone 408/624-3600), more commonly known simply as Mission Carmel, was initially founded by Father Junípero Serra at Monterey in 1770, then moved to Carmel the following year. (See pages 214–19.)

MISSION SAN FERNANDO REY DE ESPAÑA (Mission Hills, CA; midway between I-5 and I-405 at 15151 San Fernando Mission Blvd.; Phone 818/361-0186) has several restored mission buildings. Special features are the old gardens, which contain plants from all 21 California missions. A small museum and an Indian craft room are featured.

MISSION SAN FRANCISCO DE ASÍS (San Francisco, CA; 16th and Dolores Sts.; No phone), one of San Francisco's oldest buildings, was founded in 1776. Mission Dolores, as it is usually called, has been heavily restored, but visitors can see the original redwood roof timbers still lashed together with rawhide. Original books and decorations are displayed in a small but interesting museum.

MISSION SAN GABRIEL ARCÁNGEL (San Gabriel, CA; Mission and Junipero Serra Drs.; Phone 818/282-5191) was badly damaged by the 1987 earthquake and remains closed for repairs. The bell tower still contains the original 200-year-old bell.

MISSION SAN JOSE CHAPEL AND MUSEUM (Fremont, CA; 43300 Mission Blvd.; Phone 415/657-1797) consists of a recently reconstructed church, complete with crystal chandeliers, murals, religious paintings, and a goldleaf altar. The small museum is excellent, displaying mission vestments and other artifacts, as well as period paintings, photos, pioneer artifacts, exhibits on the local Ohlone Indians, and how the mission was restored.

MISSION SAN JUAN BAUTISTA (San Juan Bautista, CA; on the plaza; Phone 408/623-4528.) was one of the largest mission churches. In recognition of its importance, a set of nine bells once graced the chapel area; now only three remain. It is the only mission with a three-aisle entrance to the altar. The heavily restored mission has period furnishings.

MISSION SAN JUAN CAPISTRANO (San Juan Capistrano, CA; 2 blks. W. of the SR 74/I-5 jct.; Phone 714/493-1424) was founded by Fr. Serra in 1776. Three churches are here: the splendid ruins of the Great Stone Church, the new seven-domed parish church (a likeness of the Great Stone Church, thoughtfully created without destroying the original), and the so-called restored adobe structure called Padre Serra's Church, dedicated in 1778 and still in use. The ten-acre site has a quadrangle, soldiers' barracks, padres' living quarters, tallow-processing areas, and a museum wing.

MISSION SAN LUIS OBISPO DE TOLOSA (San Luis Obispo, CA; Chorro and Monterey Sts.; Phone 805/543-6850) was established in 1772 and burned three times. Although for a time it was reconstructed in New England style, the original Hispanic configuration has been reconstructed and, since 1934, it has been used as a parish church. The museum contains Chumash Indian artifacts.

MISSION SAN LUIS REY DE FRANCIA (Oceanside, CA; 4 mi. E. on SR 76 at 4050 Mission Ave.; Phone 619/757-3651) was founded in 1797 or 1798 by Fr. de Lasuén, named for Louis IX, King of France. The present church, finished in 1815, has lofty beamed ceilings, with original Native American decorations. It is now a Franciscan college, and a museum displays mission period artifacts.

MISSION SAN MIGUEL ARCÁNGEL (San Miguel, CA; 801 Mission St. on the S. edge of US 101; Phone 805/467-3256) was established in 1797 and remains one of the most original of the California missions. Still used as a parish church, it retains many of its original decorations, frescoes, and paintings.

MISSION SAN RAFAEL ARCÁNGEL (San Rafael, CA; 1104 5th Ave. at A St.; Phone 415/454-8141) is a replica built in 1949 approximately atop the archaeological remains of the original ruin on the approximate site of the original mission.

MISSION SANTA BARBARA (Santa Barbara, CA; E. Los Olivos and Laguna Sts.; Phone 805/682-4149) was founded in 1786 and is the best preserved of the California missions.

MISSION SANTA CLARA DE ASIS (Santa Clara, CA; Santa Clara University campus; Phone 408/554-4023) was founded in 1777, and the present building is a replica of the third mission (built in 1825). The original garden is still here.

MISSION SANTA INÉS (Solvang, CA; 1760 Mission Dr.; Phone 805/688-4815) was founded in 1804. This captivating mission, now restored with a small convent, also contains a museum.

MUSEUM OF MAN (San Diego, CA; on the California Quadrangle in Balboa Park; Phone 619/239-2001) contains numerous Native American exhibits from North, Middle, and South America.

NATURAL HISTORY MUSEUM OF LOS ANGELES COUNTY (Los Angeles, CA; 900 Exposition Boulevard; Phone 213/744-3414) has recently (mid-1993) opened the Times Mirror Hall of Native American Cultures, a large series of galleries that attempts to impress upon the visitor the diversity of Native American lifeways. The exhibits begin, appropriately enough, by emphasizing the California homelands. One complete bank of exhibit cases, for instance, describes in detail how to harvest and prepare acorns—the staple of native California. On view are some of the original Hugo Reid letters, the earliest published records of Gabrielino Indian oral traditions about life in precontact and mission times.

PATRICK'S POINT STATE PARK (Trinidad, CA; off US 101 on the Patrick's Point Dr. exit; Phone 707/677-3570) contains the recently reconstructed Coast Yurok village of *Sumig*, erected by an all-Yurok crew under the supervision of community elders. The village is open to the public, and used by the Yurok for dances and other ceremonies.

PROVIDENCE MOUNTAINS STATE PARK (near Blythe, CA; off US 95, 15.3 mi N. of I-10/US95 intersection; No phone) preserves giant desert figures, also called *intaglios*, huge (100 to 150 feet in length) sculptures laid out onto the desert pavement. Because the figures are stylized hunters and game animals, many think they relate to some form of shamanistic hunting practice. These extremely fragile sites were once badly damaged by off-road vehicles, but have now been protected.

RANCHO LA BREA TAR PITS (Los Angeles, CA; Wilshire Blvd. and Curson Ave.; Phone 213/936-2230) provides a dramatic look at ice age fauna. The adjacent **George C. Page Museum of La Brea Discoveries** (213/936-2230, or 213/857-6311) exhibits many reconstructed fossils. (See pages 38–39.)

ROCK MAIZE (Fort Mojave Reservation, near Needles, CA; E. of Needles, take Park Moabi Exit off I-40, at mi. 1.7, keep left and at mi. 1.9 [Road Closed sign] find parking lot; Phone 619/326-4591) is an Indian-operated institution. Here, about two acres of a field that appears to have once been plowed or furrowed in mazelike fashion. Some Mohave people believe this site was created to confuse evil spirits that float down the river, and until recently, they have used this place for mortuary purposes. Further information can be obtained from the Ft. Mojave Tribe.

JUNIPERO SERRA MUSEUM (Old Town San Diego, California; 2727 Presidio Dr.; Phone 619/297-3258) concentrates on this city's Hispanic heritage, with some Native American artifacts also included. The museum and surrounding Presidio Park mark the site of the eighteenth-century presidio and the first mission in Alta California.

SIERRA MONO MUSEUM (North Fork, CA; jct. of CRs 225, 228, and 274; Phone 209/877-2155) is an Indian-operated institution, highlighting the material culture of the Mono Indians, featuring an extensive collection of the world-famous Mono basketry.

SONOMA STATE HISTORIC PARK (Sonoma, CA; Phone 707/938-1519) includes Mission San Francisco Solano. The museum explains the process and interprets the mission period. (See page 219.)

SOUTHWEST MUSEUM (Los Angeles, CA; 234 Museum Dr., Highland Park; Phone 213/221-2163) has long been a leader in presenting Native American art and culture to the southern California audience. Major collections include basketry, ceramics, textiles, and decorative arts.

TULE RIVER RESERVATION (Porterville, CA; 21 mi. E. of Porterville, take SR 190 to Reservation Road; Phone 209/781-4271), an Indian-operated institution, encourages visitors to register with the tribal office Natural Resources section to arrange a tour to Painted Rocks cave, which contains superb examples of Southern Sierra rock art, pictographs painted in white, yellow, red, and black pigments. Other archaeological sites can be visited with tribal permission.

COLORADO

ANASAZI HERITAGE CENTER (Dolores, CO; on SR 184; Phone 303/882-4811) is maintained by the U.S. Bureau of Land Management as a lasting legacy of the Dolores Archaeological project, a long-term salvage program conducted in conjunction with McPhee Dam and Reservoir, completed in 1984. The Discovery Area allows visitors to grind corn, weave on a loom, identify seeds, and hold artifacts.

DENVER ART MUSEUM (Denver, CO; 100 W. 14th Ave. Parkway; Phone 303/575-2793) exhibits Native American materials from the Southwest and Southeast culture areas.

DENVER MUSEUM OF NATURAL HISTORY (Denver, CO; in City Park, Between 17th and 23rd aves. and York St. and Colorado Blvd.; Phone 303/322-7009), one of the country's major museums of natural history, is famous in archaeological circles for pioneering work at the Folsom site in the 1920s (see chapter 1).

FORT COLLINS MUSEUM (Fort Collins, CO; 6 blks. W. of SR 14 on Mulberry, then 2½ blks. N. at 200 Mathews St.; Phone 303/221-6738) specializes in the cultural history of northern Colorado. Exhibits include Folsom artifacts.

LOWRY RUINS (Cortez, CO; 9 mi. W. of Pleasant View; Phone 303/247-4082) consist of eleventh-century Anasazi ruins, superimposed upon an eighth-century archaeological component. Visitors can see one of the largest Great Kivas known in the area.

MESA VERDE NATIONAL PARK (Mesa Verde, CO; midway between Mancos and Cortez, turn south on US 160 to Park entrance, then drive 21 miles to museum; Phone 303/529-4465) is one of the most important archaeological sites in North America, including several Anasazi villages and more than forty cliff dwellings. (See pages 96–99.)

SOUTHERN UTE CULTURAL CENTER AND GALLERY (Ignacio, CO; 24 mi. SE of Durango, via SR 172, S. from US 160) is an Indian-operated institution featuring a multimedia production depicting the early history of the Ute people. Exhibits feature examples of excellent beadwork and leather.

UNIVERSITY OF COLORADO MUSEUM (Boulder, CO; in the Henderson Building off Broadway between 15th and 16th sts.; Phone 303/492-6892) boasts a newly renovated display of archaeological materials illustrating the natural history of Colorado and the Southwestern United States. A section on the early phases of archaeology emphasizes the work of Earl Morris.

UTE MOUNTAIN TRIBAL PARK (Towaoc, CO; 15 mi. S. of Cortez on the Navajo Trail; US 160/666 runs through the reservation; Phone 303/565-3751, ext. 282, or 565-8548), an Indian-operated institution, includes 125,000 acres set aside on the Ute Mountain Reservation to preserve the precontact sites of the Anasazi culture. Guided tours are scheduled daily, leaving from the Ute Mountain Pottery Plant in Towaoc.

CONNECTICUT

INSTITUTE FOR AMERICAN INDIAN STUDIES (Washington, CT; 1½ mi. S. on Curtis Rd. off SR 199; Phone 203/868-0518) documents the past 12,000 years of the area's Native Americans. A replica of a Northeastern Indian village, a nature trail, a simulated archaeological site, and changing exhibits highlight different aspects of American Indian lifeways, including contemporary themes.

PEABODY MUSEUM OF NATURAL HISTORY (Yale University, New Haven, CT), 170 Whitney Ave. at Sachem St.; Phone 203/432-5050) has numerous exhibits on the ethnography and archaeology of native North America.

TANTAQUIDGEON LODGE MUSEUM (Uncasville, CT; 1819 Norwich–New London Turnpike, SR 32; Phone 203/849-9145) is an Indian-operated institution that displays objects of the Mohegan and other New England cultures.

DISTRICT OF COLUMBIA

SMITHSONIAN INSTITUTION (Washington, DC; Phone 202/357-2700) contains two museums that present very different views of Native American culture. See also The National Museum of the American Indian listing under New York State.

The National Museum of Natural History (facing the Mall, 10th St. and Constitution Ave. NW; Phone 202/357-2020) has extensive permanent and temporary exhibits, drawing upon the first-rate collection of archaeological and ethnographic artifacts.

The National Museum of the American Indian (under construction on the Mall, between The National Air and Space Museum and the Capital Building; Phone 202/357-1680) was created by an Act of Congress in 1989. Based on the collections from New York's Heye Foundation, this new museum, when completed in the 1990s, will be the most important museum in the United States dealing with the Native American past and present. A facility will also be constructed in New York City's Custom House.

FLORIDA

CASTILLO DE SAN MARCOS NATIONAL MONUMENT (St. Augustine, FL, at Castillo Dr. and Ave. Menéndez, US 1 business route and SR A1A; Phone 904/829-6506) defended Spanish St. Augustine until the English acquired the fort in 1763. Spain regained possession by treaty in 1784; then, upon acquisition of Florida by the United States in 1821, the fort became part of the nation's coastal defense system. Exhibits trace its history; and cannon firings take place during the summer. (See page 203.)

CRYSTAL RIVER STATE ARCHAEOLOGICAL SITE (Crystal River, FL; 2½ mi. W. off US 19 North on North Museum Pt.; Phone 904/795-3817) preserves the multicomponent mound site just inland from the Gulf beach. It includes two burials mounds, two ramped mounds, plazas, shell mounds, and refuse middens.

FLORIDA MUSEUM OF NATURAL HISTORY (Gainesville, FL; Museum Rd. and Newell Dr. on the University of Florida campus; Phone 904/392-1721) exhibits numerous aspects of Florida's archaeological past, much of the material recovered from the Museum's research program.

INDIAN TEMPLE MOUND MUSEUM (Ft. Walton Beach, FL; 139 Miracle Strip Pkwy.; Phone 904/243-6521), the first municipally owned museum in Florida, illustrates 10,000 years of Indian occupation on the northwest Florida coast. The temple mound—billed as "the largest earthwork on salt water"—was initially erected around A.D. 1400. The mound has been restored, complete with a replica temple atop the mound; this was the political and ceremonial epicenter for a powerful Mississippian chiefdom.

LAKE JACKSON MOUNDS STATE ARCHAEOLOGICAL SITE (Tallahassee, FL; 2 mi. N. of I-10 at the southern tip of Lake Jackson; Phone 904/562-0042) is a major mound and village complex, dating A.D. 1250–1500. The area contains seven mounds, a plaza, and village middens. Southern cult paraphernalia have been recovered from high-status burials in one of the mounds.

MICCOSUKEE CULTURAL CENTER AND MUSEUM (Miami, FL; 25 mi. W. of Miami on US 41, the Tamiami Trail; 305/223-8380) is an Indian-operated institution where the Miccosukees hold public activities including annual Green Corn ceremonies (call for exact dates). The museum displays traditional *chickees*, open-sided cypress houses built on stilts and thatched with palmetto fronds.

MISSION OF NOMBRE DE DIOS (St. Augustine, FL; 5 blks. N. of the city gate on San Marco Ave.; Phone 904/824-2809) and *Shrine of Our Lady of La Leche* stand near the site of where Menéndez originally landed in 1565. A 208-foot stainless-steel cross marks the site of the founding of St. Augustine.

MUSEUM OF FLORIDA HISTORY (Tallahassee, FL; in the R.A. Gray Building at Bronough and Pensacola Sts.; Phone 904/488-1484) has archaeological and historical artifacts depicting the state's history, from prehistoric times through the historical period.

MUSEUM OF SCIENCE AND HISTORY (Jacksonville, FL; 1025 Gulf Life Dr.; Phone 904/396-7061) has exhibits on the Native American history of this area.

SAN LUIS ARCHAEOLOGICAL AND HISTORIC SITE (Tallahassee, FL; on Mission Rd., ¼ mi. NW off US 90; Phone 904/487-3711) was once an important Apalachee Indian village and Franciscan mission. This ongoing archaeological excavation can be visited; there are interpretive displays describing the dig. A permanent exhibit hall is being planned for the grounds. (See pages 205–207.)

SEMINOLE TRIBAL MUSEUM (also called the *Ah-Tha-Thi-Ki Museum*; Hollywood, FL; 3240 North 64th Ave.; Phone 305/964-4882) is an Indian-operated institution, founded in 1989 to preserve and interpret Seminole culture. Seven buildings house exhibits and study areas. Water and land trails also connect a village site and various camps.

GEORGIA

ETOWAH INDIAN MOUND STATE HISTORIC PARK (Cartersville, GA; 6 mi. S. of I-75 on SR 61/113; Phone 404/387-3747) preserves the site of a major Mississippian ceremonial center. The earliest published description of the mounds dates from 1817, when a clergyman was guided to the site by a group of Cherokee chiefs who presumably were unaware of the long-abandoned area's significance. A museum displays artifacts excavated from the mounds.

KOLOMOKI MOUNDS HISTORIC PARK (Blakely, GA; 6 mi. N. of Blakely off US 27; Phone 912/723-5296) is a multicomponent mound complex. The primary occupation took place between about A.D. 100–500. Excavations have disclosed an elaborate mortuary complex which suggests a chiefdom-level society. The 1,293-acre park contains seven Indian mounds. A museum at the west entrance depicts the area's Indian cultures from 5000 B.C. to the 13th century. One exhibit shows the interior of a mound as the excavating archaeologists left it.

OCMULGEE NATIONAL MONUMENT (Macon, GA; US 80 E. from I-16 exit 4; Phone 912/752-8257) is a spectacular display of several Southeast Native American cultures over the course of 10,000 years. It includes a Mississippian village and ceremonial center, mounds, and museum. (See pages 170–72.)

IDAHO

IDAHO MUSEUM OF NATURAL HISTORY (Pocatello, ID; exit 69 from I-15, on the Idaho State University campus; Phone 208/236-3168 or 208/236-3317) has numerous exhibits dealing with the archaeology of the northern Great Basin and Plateau areas. Many of the items were recovered as part of the Museum's long-standing research program.

OLD MISSION STATE PARK (Kellogg, ID; 11 mi. W. of Kellogg off I-90 exit 39; FAX 208/682-3814) contains the oldest remaining building in Idaho and the restored Old Sacred Heart Mission built in the 1850s by Coeur d'Alene Indians under the guidance of Jesuit priest Father Antonio Ravalli.

ILLINOIS

CAHOKIA MOUNDS STATE HISTORIC SITE (East St. Louis, IL; 6 mi. E. off I-55/70 to SR 111 to Collinsville Rd.; Phone 618/346-5160) was the site of the largest city in native North America, established about 700 A.D. This late Mississippian complex includes the important Monks Mound and Wood-henge celestial observatory (See pages 152–58.)

DICKSON MOUNDS MUSEUM (Springfield, IL; 60 mi. NW of Springfield, SR 97 and 78; Phone 309/547-3721), a branch of the Illinois State Museum, is one of the few on-site archaeological museums in the Midwest. For fifty years, archaeologists have explored the Dickson site. A thousand years ago, the people living here, on the high ground near the present museum, placed their burial ground at the edge of a bluff, the site of Dickson Mounds proper. Starting about A.D. 1100, Mississippian culture dominated this area. By 1250, there stood here a large Mississippian community of villages, camps, and work stations extending several miles upriver. The area was abandoned by A.D. 1350.

FIELD MUSEUM OF NATURAL HISTORY (Chicago, IL; in Grant Park on Lake Shore Dr.; Phone 312/922-9410) is one of the world's preeminent museums of natural sciences. Established in 1893, the 1 million square feet of exhibit, research, and storage space contain highly significant Native American archaeological collections, based in large measure on its excellent program of first-hand, systematic research. The Field Museum is changing so rapidly that it's difficult to write much that will not change before this book appears; the Field Museum has tremendous potential. The North West Coast Indians Hall has recently been refurbished, and it presents an enormous slice of the outstanding collection, many of the objects initially collected for the 1893 exposition. The new Webber Resource Center provides a broad range of hands-on materials, for researchers and for kids. On several cases, signs hang explaining that certain culturally sensitive artifacts have been removed from display at the request of tribal elders. The Field Museum is to be applauded for working so closely and so perceptively with Native American people.

ILLINOIS STATE MUSEUM (Springfield, IL; Spring and Edwards sts., on the SW corner of the Capitol Complex; Phone 217/782-7386) has several archaeological exhibits dealing with the Native American past. The major gallery features a lifesize diorama entitled *Peoples of the Past*, illustrating lifeways from the Late Archaic, Middle Woodland, and Mississippian periods, as well as the historic Kickapoo people.

INDIANA

ANGEL MOUNDS STATE HISTORIC SITE (Evansville, IN; 7 mi. E. at 8215 Pollock Ave.; Phone 812/853-3956) is one of the best preserved Mississippian sites in North America, dating from between about A.D. 900–1600, including reconstructed houses and temple. (See pages 172–74.)

WYANDOTTE CAVE (Leavenworth, IN; on SR 62; Phone 812/738-2782) was an important source of Wyandotte chert, a blue-gray, high-quality aragonite important during Hopewell times. There is clear evidence of prehistoric quarrying of aragonite at the "Pillar of the Constitution," a formation about 4,000 feet from the cave's entrance. Aragonite was particularly important for constructing platform pipes and reel-shaped gorgets, found in major Hopewell centers from Iowa, through the Ohio Valley, into south-central Tennessee.

IOWA

EFFIGY MOUNDS NATIONAL MONUMENT (Marquette, IA; 3½ mi. N. of Marquette on SR 76; Phone 319/873-2356). This spectacular site includes more than 200 mounds dating to the past 2,500 years, including 26 animal effigies and the "marching bears." An adjacent museum recounts information about the Effigy Mound Culture and excavations. (See pages 143–46.)

Museum of Natural History (Iowa City, IA; in Macbride Hall at Jefferson and Capitol sts.; Phone 319/335-0480), a facility of University of Iowa, displays, in the Marquette-Joliet diorama, the earliest European–Native American contact in the upper Mississippi River area. A Mesquakie winter lodge has been reconstructed as part of a larger presentation dealing with the native cultures of Iowa.

Putnam Museum of History and Natural Science (Davenport, IA; 1717 W. 12th St.; Phone 319/324-1933), previously known as the Davenport Museum, has exhibits explaining the past of the Quad Cities region. The "River, Prairie, and People" exhibit contains artifacts from local Hopewell and Mississippian cultures. The exhibit also details the life of the Blackhawk and provides information about the Sac and Mesquaki people.

Sanford Museum and Planetarium (Cherokee, IA; ½ blk. E. of US 59 at 117 E. Willow St.; Phone 712/225-3922) presents archaeological and historical exhibits relating to northwestern Iowa and the Great Plains.

KANSAS

Coronado-Quivira Museum (Lyons, KS; 105 W. Lyon St.; Phone 316/257-3941) displays artifacts from sixteenth-century Native American culture, including artifacts from European contact (such as chain mail).

Indian Center Museum (Wichita, KS; 650 N. Seneca St.; Phone 316/262-5221) features the Mid-America All-Indian Center, dedicated to the preservation of Native American heritage, culture, and traditions. The arrowhead-shaped building contains exhibits on the art of the Southern Plains, Native American basketry, and "The Wichita: A Proud Tradition."

Iowa, Sac and Fox Indian Mission State Historic Site (Highland, KS; 2 mi. E. on US 36, then ¼ mi. N. on SR 136; Phone 913/442-3304) contains the remaining portion of the Presbyterian mission building erected in 1846 to replace the original one-story log structure. Visitors can see Native American artifacts and a restored chapel.

Kansas Museum of History (Topeka, KS; 6425 S.W. 6th St.; Phone 913/272-8681) exhibits archaeological artifacts from all time periods. A Wichita (or Quiviran) grass lodge has been reconstructed and a Cheyenne buffalo hide tipi is displayed. The Pottawatomie Baptist Indian Mission State Historic Site adjacent to it was built in 1848. The exterior of the mission has been restored.

Museum of Anthropology (University of Kansas, Lawrence, KS; Spooner Hall at 14th St. and Jayhawk Blvd.; Phone 913/864-4245) displays ethnographic and archaeological materials from the western Plains.

PAWNEE INDIAN VILLAGE STATE HISTORIC SITE (Courtland, KS; 8 mi. N. of US 36 on SR 266; Phone 913/361-2255) contains a post-contact Pawnee village site occupied about 1818–30. The site has been carefully excavated and the Kansas Historical Society has erected a structure over the exposed floor of an earth lodge, with artifacts left in place. Exhibits and dioramas depict Pawnee life.

SANTA FE TRAIL CENTER MUSEUM AND CULTURAL CENTER (Larned, KS; 2½ mi. W. on SR 156; Phone 316/285-2054) includes displays from a Wichita Indian hunting lodge and Jesuit religious items.

STERNBERG MEMORIAL MUSEUM (Hays, KS; on the campus of Fort Hays State University; Phone 913/628-4286), self-described as "the best kept secret in Kansas," features exhibits on the Indian people of Kansas and elsewhere on the Great Plains, including projectile points, beads, tools, baskets, and pottery. Some Southwestern materials are also on display.

KENTUCKY

MAMMOTH CAVE NATIONAL PARK (Cave City, KY; about 10 mi. W. of Cave City and 8 mi. NW of Park City via I-65; Phone 502/758-2251) has been scientifically investigated a number of times. Mammoth Cave contains more than 300 miles of underground passages, one of the longest cave systems known, and still partially unexplored. People apparently first ventured inside four thousand years ago, lighting their way with cane reed torches. Woven sandals and other artifacts have been recovered, in a remarkable state of preservation owing to the cave's cool temperature and stable humidity.

WICKLIFFE MOUNDS (Wickliffe, KY; ½ mi. NW on US 51/60/62; Phone 502/335-3681) Mississippian village, occupied between approximately A.D. 1000 and 1300. Excavations have taken place in the residential area, and also on the burial and platform mounds. Interpretive exhibits in the three open excavation areas illustrate Mississippian lifeways and archaeological methods.

LABRADOR

RED BAY (Red Bay, LB; No phone) bills itself as the "World Whaling Capital, A.D. 1550–1600." It was the scene of a seasonal Basque whaling industry that had a major impact on both the sea mammal and Native American population here.

LOUISIANA

POVERTY POINT STATE COMMEMORATIVE AREA (Epps, LA; 4¼ mi. E. on SR 134 and 1 mi. N. on SR 577; Phone 318/926-5492) preserves an extensive 400-acre Archaic earthenworks. Excavations may be in progress. (See pages 79–84.)

MAINE

MAINE STATE MUSEUM (Augusta, ME; in the Library-Museum-Archives Building in the Statehouse Complex; Phone 207/287-2301) contains numerous exhibits, which range from the late ice age to the nineteenth century, depicting Maine's cultural heritage, including one entitled "12,000 Years in Maine." Featured are the Museum's excavations in the shellmounds of the Penobscot Bay (3000–1000 B.C.).

MANITOBA

ESKIMO MUSEUM (Churchill, MB; on La Verendrye St. near the mission; Phone 204/675-2030) contains artifacts and exhibits featuring contemporary and historic Inuit (Eskimo) culture. There are kayaks from the pre-Dorset period dating back to 2000 B.C. and a collection of Native American and Inuit artwork is also displayed.

MANITOBA MUSEUM OF MAN AND NATURE (Winnipeg, MB; Main St. and Rupert Ave., part of the Centennial Centre; Phone 204/956-2830 or 204/943-3139) has extensive exhibits on the ancient ecology and culture history of the area.

MASSACHUSETTS

PEABODY MUSEUM OF ARCHAEOLOGY AND ETHNOLOGY (Harvard University Campus, Cambridge, MA; 11 Divinity Ave.; Phone 617/495-2248), established in 1866, houses an excellent New World collection. The recently renovated Hall of the North American Indian has been critically acclaimed.

R. S. PEABODY MUSEUM OF ARCHAEOLOGY (Andover, MA; at Phillips and Main sts.; Phone 508/749-4490) displays its important collection (containing more than 700,000 objects) in a series of permanent and changing exhibits on North American, prehistoric, Southwestern, and Mexican archaeology. One diorama shows life in a Woodland fishing village in an A.D. 1400 Woodland village on the banks of the Merrimack River (in what is now Andover). Other exhibits address the Boylston Street Fishweir (Boston), the Bull Brook Paleoindian site (Ipswich), and numerous "Red Paint" mortuary sites from Maine.

PLIMOTH PLANTATION (Plymouth, MA; 20 minutes N. of Cape Cod on SR 3 and take Plimoth Plantation Highway exit; Phone 508/746-1622) is a living history museum, divided into the *1627 Pilgrim Village, Hobbamock's Homesite,* the *Carriage House Crafts Center,* and the *Mayflower II.* (See pages 192, 196–98.)

MASHPEE-WAMPANOAG MUSEUM (Mashpee, MA; SR 30; Phone 508/477-1536) has a collection focusing on the Mashpee-Wampanoag people. The *Mashpee Tribal Meetinghouse* can also be visited, but permission must be obtained from the tribal office; Phone 508/477-0208. (See pages 197–98.)

MICHIGAN

CRANBROOK INSTITUTE OF SCIENCE (Cranbook, MI; W. of Woodward Ave. at 500 Lone Pine Rd.; Phone 313/645-3200) is a natural history museum. The Anthropology Hall explores human cultures, with an emphasis on the archaeology of North America, as told through artifacts and dioramas.

EARLY MISSIONARY BARK CHAPEL (Mackinac Island, MI; in Marquette Park; Phone 906/847-3328) reconstructs the early Jesuit missions of the area, dating from the late seventeenth century.

MARQUETTE MISSION PARK AND MUSEUM OF OJIBWA CULTURE (St. Ignace, MI; 500 N. State St.; Phone 906/643-9161), a city-owned museum, the presumed site of Father Marquette's grave, has yielded important archaeological evidence about the late seventeenth century Huron, Ottawa, and French settlements.

MINNESOTA

GRAND MOUND INTERPRETIVE CENTER (International Falls, MN; 17 mi. W. on SR 11; Phone 218/285-3332) contains the largest burial mound in this part of the Upper Midwest, constructed between about 200 B.C. to A.D. 800. The interpretive center contains numerous exhibits on this material, and an audiovisual program.

INDIAN MOUNDS PARK (St. Paul, MN; E. of the business district overlooking the Mississippi River; Phone 612/296-6157) contains several burial mounds.

MILLE LACS INDIAN MUSEUM (Onamia, MN; 10 mi. NW on US 169; Phone 612/532-3632) contains an outstanding collection of Ojibwa (Chippewa)-made items. Life-size dioramas showing typical scenes for each season: hunting and trapping in the winter, processing maple sugar in the spring, gardening in the summer, and harvesting wild rice in the fall. This is also the site of an important village of the Dakota who, in the 1740s, were forced westward by armed Chippewa.

MISSION CREEK 1894 THEME PARK (just E. of Hinckley, MN, 1/3 mi. S. of jct. I-35 and SR 48; Phone 612/384-7444) includes replicas of a town and an Indian village of the 1890s.

MUSEUM OF NATURAL HISTORY AND INDIAN ARTS AND CRAFTS (Walker, MN; 3 blks. E. on SR 200/371 in the Leech Lake Area Chamber of Commerce building; Phone 218/547-3300, ext. 251) displays many Ojibwa artifacts.

PIPESTONE NATIONAL MONUMENT (Pipestone, MN; one mi. N. on US 75, then one-half mi. W. at the north edge of town; Phone 507/825-5464) contains nearly three hundred acres of quarries where for centuries, Native Americans mined the red stone from which ceremonial pipes were made. The *catlinite* deposits are now protected, and use is restricted to Native Americans, who continue to make pipes from this stone.

PIPESTONE COUNTY MUSEUM (Pipestone, MN; 113 Hiawatha Ave. in the former Pipestone City Hall; Phone 507/825-2563) interprets local Native American clothing, weapons, quillwork, and beadwork. Hands-on displays, a library and interpretive programs are featured.

MISSISSIPPI

CHICKASAW VILLAGE SITE (Natchez Trace Parkway, MS; NW of Tupelo, MS, between US 78 and SR 6 at milepost 261.8; Phone 601/680-4025) was once a fortified Chickasaw settlement. An exhibit shelter and audio station tell the story of these Indians; a nature trail identifies some of the plants they used for food and medicine.

CHOCTAW MUSEUM OF THE SOUTHERN INDIAN (Philadelphia, MS; 30 mi. N. of I-20 via SR 15; Phone 601/565-5251) is an Indian-operated institution on the lands of the Mississippi Band of Choctaw people.

GRAND VILLAGE OF THE NATCHEZ INDIANS (Natchez, MS; off US 61S at 400 Jefferson Davis Blvd.; Phone 601/446-6502) was the ceremonial mound center and chief settlement of the Natchez Indians. After the tribe attacked a French fort in 1729, the French retaliated and destroyed the village. A museum displays excavated artifacts; renovated mounds, a reconstructed hut and other interpretive exhibits illustrate daily life.

NANIH WAIYA HISTORICAL SITE (Noxapater, MS; on SR 397; Phone 601/773-7988) is one of the latest of the surviving Mississippian cultures, dating from about A.D. 400, and is thought to be the ancestral home of the Choctaw people. (See pages 179–81.)

WINTERVILLE MOUNDS STATE PARK AND MUSEUM (Greenville, MS; 5 mi. N. on SR 1; Phone 601/334-4684) contains a reconstruction of a large Mississippian ceremonial center built here about A.D. 1000. The museum contains numerous Mississippian artifacts, jewelry, pottery, utensils, and art objects. Several unexcavated mounds can be seen in the area.

MISSOURI

MASTODON STATE PARK (Imperial, MO; 1551 Seckman Rd., 20 mi. S. of St. Louis off I-55 at Imperial Exit, follow signs; Phone 314/464-2976) exhibits materials found at the nearby Kimmswick Paleoindian site. Here, in 1979, a Clovis point was found associated with mammoth bones. The Kimmswick

Bone Bed is preserved here, where more than 60 mastodon skeletons have been recovered. The visitor center details the history of excavations and displays several artifacts recovered.

MUSEUM OF MAN, ART, AND ARCHAEOLOGY (University of Missouri, Columbia, MO) contains several dioramas addressing Native American culture from the Midwest. Exhibits range from Paleoindian through contemporary times, with an emphasis on the archaeology of Missouri and the Midwest.

MONTANA

NORTHERN CHEYENNE TRIBAL MUSEUM (Lame Deer, MT; 110 mi. SE of Billings and 75 mi. N. of Sheridan, US 212 crosses the reservation from east to west; Phone 406/477-8283), an Indian-operated institution, presents the history and culture of the Cheyenne people.

HISTORICAL MUSEUM OF FORT MISSOULA (Missoula, MT; S. on Reserve St. to South Ave., then 1 mi. W., following signs; Phone 406/728-3476) is built in center of former Fort Missoula, established in 1877 during the conflict with the Nez Perce under Chief Joseph.

LITTLE BIGHORN BATTLEFIELD NATIONAL MONUMENT (Hardin, MT; main entrance is 15 mi. SE via exit 510 off I-90, then a half mi. E. via US 212; Phone 406/638-2621) commemorates the dramatic Indian victory of June 1876, and also houses national cemetery established in 1879. Just inside the entrance is a visitor center and museum. (See pages 221–29.)

MADISON BUFFALO JUMP STATE HISTORIC SITE (Three Forks, MT; 7 mi. S. of Logan off I-90; Phone 406/994-4042) is a hunting area used over the past two thousand years. At the top is a large grazing area from which buffalo were lured or driven into drive lanes—two long rows of rocks mark the walls of a "funnel" through which the buffalo were driven toward the rim of the jump. Below, on the slope at the bottom of the cliff, crippled animals were killed and carcasses were skinned and butchered.

MONTANA HISTORICAL SOCIETY MUSEUM (Helena, MT; 225 N. Roberts St.; Phone 406/444-2694) houses an outstanding collection of artifacts from the Anzick cache, a Paleoindian find. (See pages 24, 28–29.)

MUSEUM OF THE PLAINS INDIAN (Browning, MT; US 2 crosses the Blackfeet Reservation E. to W. and US 89 angles across from N. to SE; Phone 406/338-2230), an Indian-operated institution, exhibits creative achievements of Native American artists, with an emphasis on Northern Plains tribal people. Next to the Museum is "In the Footsteps of the Blackfeet," a reconstruction of an 1850-era Blackfeet encampment.

MUSEUM OF THE ROCKIES (Bozeman, MT; S. of the Montana State University campus at S. 7th Ave. and Kagy Blvd. opposite the football stadium; Phone 406/994-3466 or 406/994-2251) interprets the history of the northern Rockies, particularly through materials excavated by Montana State University. An important display shows the remains of a mammoth killed and butchered in central Montana.

MUSEUM OF THE YELLOWSTONE (West Yellowstone, MT; 124 Yellowstone Ave.; Phone 406/646-7814), in a Union Pacific Road depot, tells of Plains Indians in the area.

NEBRASKA

UNIVERSITY OF NEBRASKA STATE MUSEUM (Lincoln, NE; in Morrill Hall at 14th and U sts.; Phone 402/472-2642) presents an orderly display of archaeological materials, including a block lift of deposits from the Lipscomb site, a Folsom site in Texas. The museum also houses an outstanding collection of modern and fossil elephants, including a gigantic mammoth. The Nomads of the Plains gallery depicts the history of the Sioux Indians on the Great Plains. Highlights are Atlatl Rock and Mouse Tank with a short trail with prehistoric petroglyphs.

NEVADA

CHURCHILL COUNTY MUSEUM AND ARCHIVES (Fallon, NV; 1050 S. Maine St.; Phone 702/423-3677) features a small but comprehensive exhibition dealing with local Native American culture, particularly artifacts of the Paiute tribe and a display presenting the archaeology of Hidden Cave.

HIDDEN CAVE (Fallon, NV; 12 mi. E. on US 50; Phone 702/423-3677) was the site of an amazing find of well-preserved Archaic artifacts left thousands of years ago. (See pages 51–56.)

LOST CITY MUSEUM OF ARCHAEOLOGY (Overton, NV; on SR 169, near Lake Mead; Phone 702/397-2193), on a restored part of Pueblo Grande de Nevada, displays artifacts recovered during the excavation of the Lost City pueblos and other sites in the area. Several Pueblo-type houses of wattle and daub have been reconstructed on original foundations.

NEVADA STATE MUSEUM (Carson City, NV; in the old Mint Building; Phone 702/687-4810) contains several displays dealing with the archaeology and ethnography of the Great Basin, including an exhibit on the celebrated Washoe basketmaker Dot-So-La-Lee.

STEWART INDIAN MUSEUM (Carson City, NV; 5366 Snyder Ave.; Phone 702/882-1808), an Indian-operated institution, exhibits Native American artifacts, basketry, pottery, and Edward Curtis photogravures. A museum trading post offers handicrafts and original art.

VALLEY OF FIRE STATE PARK (Overton, NV; 14 mi. SW on SR 169; Phone 702/397-2088) contains numerous exposures of pre-contact rock art cut into the eroded red sandstone walls.

NEWFOUNDLAND

L'ANSE AUX MEADOWS NATIONAL HISTORIC PARK (St. Anthony, NF; from Corner Brook, take the Viking Trail 250 mi. N., then highway 430 N. to highway 436, follow it 19 mi. to the park; Phone 709/623-2608 or 709/623-2601) displays various artifacts recovered here. (See pages 185–88.)

NEWFOUNDLAND MUSEUM (St. John's, NF; 285 Duckworth St.; Phone 709/729-2460) explores 9,000 years of Newfoundland's and Labrador's ancient past, including both archaeological and ethnographic artifacts.

NEW JERSEY

NEW JERSEY STATE MUSEUM (Trenton, NJ; 205 W. State St.; Phone 609/292-6464 or 609/292-6308) has numerous exhibits dealing with local Native American archaeology and ethnology.

NEWARK MUSEUM (Newark, NJ; 49 Washington St.; Phone 201/596-6550) includes a gallery of Native American materials from both precontact and historic periods.

NEW MEXICO

ACOMA (Sky City, NM; about 3 mi. NE of Acoma along SR 23; Phone 505/252-1139) is North America's oldest continuously inhabited site (since A.D. 1150). Enchanted Mesa, towering 430 feet above the surrounding plain, contains *San Esteban de Acoma Mission*, largest of the early seventeenth-century Southwestern missions. The visitor center contains a small museum, where visitors must register. A guided tour of Sky City includes the mission and leaves from the visitor center; non-Indians are not allowed on the mesa top unless accompanied by a member of the tribe.

APACHE CULTURAL CENTER (Mescalero, NM; 30 mi. NE of Alamagordo on US 70; Phone 505/671-4494), an Indian-operated institution, presents tribal history and several crafts displays. The Cultural Center is part of the impressive recreational facilities constructed here, including the storied Inn of the Mountain Gods.

AZTEC RUINS NATIONAL MONUMENT (Aztec, NM; just north of Aztec via a spur off US 550; Phone 505/334-6174) is one of the largest and best preserved

Anasazi ruins. The misnomer, "Aztec" was applied by American settlers who incorrectly assumed the builders' identity. The greatest of these sandstone pueblos was built about A.D. 1100; it contained nearly 500 rooms, some of which remain intact. A giant ceremonial building, the Great Kiva, is the only restoration of its kind in North America. The visitor center museum exhibits objects found during a number of excavations.

BANDELIER NATIONAL MONUMENT (Santa Fe, NM; 46 mi. NW, can be reached via US 285 to Pojoaque, then W. on SR 502 and S. on SR 4; Phone 505/672-3861) lies in the rugged canyon and mesa country of northern New Mexico. The Monument contains a number of pueblo and cliff dwellings. Particularly notable are the cave rooms hewn out of the soft tuff rock, houses built on the talus slopes, and a circular community village. The visitor's center has an introductory slide program and displays of materials recovered here.

BLACKWATER DRAW, LOCALITY 1 (Clovis, NM; 5 mi. from south gate of Cannon Air Force Base on SR 467; Phone 505/356-5235) serves as a "living laboratory" of Paleoindian culture. (See pages 13, 16, 20–21.)

BLACKWATER DRAW MUSEUM (Clovis, NM; 12 mi. S. of Clovis on SR 70: Phone 505/562-2202) is the best facility devoted to Paleoindian archaeology and paleontology in native North America. (See page 21.)

CHACO CULTURE NATIONAL HISTORICAL PARK (northwestern NM; from Thoreau take SR 57 about 60 mi. N.; 26 mi. S. of Nageezi Trading Post and 29 mi. S. of Blanco Trading Post via SR 44; Phone 505/988-6727 or 505/988-6716) is an extensive Anasazi complex dating from about 900 A.D. Its important structures include Pueblo Bonito, Pueblo Del Arroyo, and Casa Rinconada. (See pages 100–109.)

DEMING LUNA MIMBRES MUSEUM (Deming, NM; 301 S. Silver St.; Phone 505/546-2382) includes a Mimbres exhibit with pottery and baskets. A 53-foot mural depicting the many-faceted history of the county dominates the exhibit room.

EL MORRO NATIONAL MONUMENT (Grants, NM; 43 mi. SW via SR 53, or 56 mi. SE of Gallup via SRs 602 and 53; Phone 505/783-4226) features the 200-foot-high Inscription Rock and nearby water hole that has attracted visitors for centuries. Carved into the soft rock are numerous pre-contact and historic period petroglyphs, including the inscription left in 1605 by Don Juan de Oñate, governor and colonizer of New Mexico. Two Anasazi villages once thrived atop this mesa. A visitor center and museum are at the head of Inscription Trail.

GILA CLIFF DWELLINGS NATIONAL MONUMENT (45 mi. N. of Silver City, NM, via SR 15; Phone 505/536-9461) includes Mogollon ruins dating from after 1275 A.D.

INDIAN PUEBLO CULTURAL CENTER (Albuquerque, NM; 2401 12th St., N.W.; Phone 505/843-7270), is an Indian-operated institution that depicts the history and culture of the Pueblo Indians.

JICARILLA APACHE CENTER (Dulce, NM; US 64, just south of the CO State line; Phone 505/759-3515), an Indian-operated institution, is the center of an impressive tribal recreational industry. Jicarilla means "little baskets" and several examples of this basketry are displayed.

MAXWELL MUSEUM OF ANTHROPOLOGY (Albuquerque, NM; University of New Mexico campus at University and Ash NE; Phone 505/277-4404) is one of the best museums specializing in the American Southwest and the collection contains enormous quantities of artifacts recovered from University excavations. The *People of the Southwest* exhibit is first-rate, including a reconstruction of excavations at nearby Tijeras Canyon, showing how archaeologists plan and execute problem-oriented excavations. A new permanent hall also introduces the principles and specifics of human evolution.

MUSEUM OF INDIAN ARTS AND CULTURE (Santa Fe, NM; 710 Camino Lejo, on the eastern approach to the city; Phone 505/827-8941), a branch of the Museum of New Mexico, displays extensive collections of Pueblo and Navajo basketry, jewelry, and textiles, plus one of the world's best Southwestern pottery collection.

MUSEUM OF NEW MEXICO (Santa Fe, NM) consists of four separate museums and five monuments. Together, they present a comprehensive picture of the various phases and archaeological sites of the American Southwest. The research museum (The Laboratory of Anthropology) is open to scholars and researchers. Of particular interest is *The Palace of the Governors* (on the N. side of the Plaza on Palace Ave.) erected in 1610; it served variously as the seat of government under Spanish, American Indian, Mexican, and U.S. territorial rule until 1909. Exhibits reflect the history of New Mexico and its varied cultures. The *portal* (porch) is a famous gathering place for Indian artisans. Phone (505) 827-6451.

NUESTRA SEÑORA DE LA ASUNCIÓN DE ZIA (Zia Pueblo, NM; 20 mi. NW of Bernalillo; Phone 505/867-3304) was begun about 1614 and has been rebuilt several times. The bell tower suggests the form of the traditional Anasazi cloud motif.

NUESTRA SEÑORA DE GUADALUPE DE ZUNI (Zuni Pueblo, NM; 40 mi. SW of Gallup; Phone 505/782-5581) was partially excavated and restored by the National Park Service and Zuni Pueblo. Particularly impressive are the life-sized figures of Zuni dancers along the north and south wall of the nave. They were painted by Zuni artist Alex Seowtewa to signify the unity of the modern Zuni people and the old mission.

MISSION DE NUESTRA SEÑORA DE LOS ANGELES DE PORCIUNCULA (Pecos National Historical Park, NM; 25 mi. E. of Santa Fe, I-25; Phone 505/757-6414) was established in 1618, later expanded into a massive adobe church. The ruins have been excavated and stabilized. An on-site museum interprets local mission history.

O'KE OWEENGE (San Juan Pueblo, NM; N. of Santa Fe, off SR 68, E. of Rio Grande River; Phone 505/852-2372) is a cooperative founded by the crafts people of San Juan Pueblo to encourage traditional handmade Indian crafts.

PUEBLO OF ACOMA TOURIST AND VISITATION CENTER (Pueblo of Acoma, NM; intersection of SR 23 and 38; Phone 505/552-6606), is an Indian-operated institution which houses a permanent exhibit entitled "One Thousand Years of Clay: Pottery, Environment, and History." Visitors to the Sky City and San Esteban del Rey must register at the Center.

PUYE CLIFF DWELLINGS (Española, NM; 11 mi. W. via SRs 30 and 5; Phone 505/753-7326) are evidence of the extensive Anasazi occupation in this part of the Pajarito Plateau late in the twelfth century; the area was finally abandoned around 1580 because of severe drought conditions. Caves hollowed out of the soft stone rise from one to three stories.

RED ROCK STATE PARK (Red Rock, NM; 8 mi. E. of Gallup off I-40; 505/722-3839) is home to the Inter-Tribal Ceremonial, the best-known such event in native North America. The ceremonial lasts four days. A museum has permanent exhibits of Navajo, Zuni, and Hopi culture.

SALINAS PUEBLO MISSIONS NATIONAL MONUMENT (center of the town of Mountainair, NM; Phone 505/847-2585) contains three separate but historically related pueblos and seventeenth-century Spanish Franciscan missions. This area was abandoned by both native and Hispanic people in the late seventeenth century. A visitor center is located on US 60 a block west of SR 55 in Mountainair. *Gran Quivira* (25 mi. S. of Mountainair on SR 14). *San Gregorio de Abó* (7 mi. W. of Mountainair on US 60). *Nuestra Señora de la Purísima Concepción de Quarai* (5 mi. N. of Mountainair, on SR 14), begun roughly 1628, embodies heavily buttressed stone architecture, which has been recently stabilized by the National Park Service.

SALMON RUIN (Bloomfield, NM; 2.5 mi. W. of Bloomfield on US 64; Phone 505/632-2013), affiliated with the San Juan Museum Association, displays the results of the extensive excavations conducted here between 1972 and 1978 by Eastern New Mexico University. Salmon Ruin itself was an important Chaco outlier, built in A.D. 1088. An excellent museum presents artifacts from these excavations and also overall exhibits dealing with Southwestern people.

SAN AGUSTÍN DE LA ISLETA (NM; 13 mi. S. of Albuquerque, NM; off I-25; Phone 505/869-3111 or 869-6333) was established in 1613, but partially destroyed in 1680. The mission was restored after the reconquest and has been in constant use ever since. Stained glass has been added, illuminating the 200-year-old paintings inside. Isleta and Acoma compete for the honor of being New Mexico's oldest churches.

SAN BUENAVENTURA DE COCHITI (Cochiti Pueblo, NM; 24 mi. NW of Bernalillo, off I-25; Phone 505/867-3211 or 505/465-2244) was built in 1628 and despite the extensive remodeling, some original portions remain.

SAN ILDEFONSO CHURCH (San Ildefonso Pueblo, NM; NW of Santa Fe, off US 84/285, W. on SR 501; Phone 505/455-2273) dates to the 1700s and has been fully restored. Can be viewed from outside only.

SAN FELIPE (San Felipe Pueblo, NM; 35 mi. SW of Santa Fe; Phone 505/867-3381) was begun in 1736 and has very few alterations.

SAN GERONIMO (Taos Pueblo, NM; 2 mi. N. of Taos off SR 68; Phone 505/758-8626) is still in use. The ruin of the earlier church, blown apart by U.S. cannons in 1847, now functions as a cemetery for the people of Taos.

SAN JOSÉ DE JEMEZ (Pueblo of Jemez, in the Jemez State Monument, NM; 55 mi. from Albuquerque via I-25 to SR 44 and Rte. 4; Phone 505/829-3530), which dates to around 1620, has been stabilized.

SAN JOSÉ DE LAGUNA (Laguna Pueblo, NM; 45 mi. W of Albuqerque, off I-40; Phone 505/552-9330) was begun in the early eighteenth century. The original decorations on the outside walls have been obliterated by whitewash.

SAN LORENZO DE PECURÍS (Pecurís Pueblo, NM; 20 mi. S. of Taos; Phone 505/587-2519) dates to 1776; a museum displays pottery, beadwork, and other local artwork.

SANDIA CAVE (outside Albuquerque, NM; From the east, take I-40 from Albuquerque, exit at the Tijeras exit, take the northern part of the Y exit and follow signs onto North SR 14 to Cedar Crest, follow to National Scenic Highway 536, then turn W. on 536 past the ski area to SR 165 to Placitas; continue on this good dirt road 6 mi. to the cave, which is about 6 mi. in on the right. From the west: Go N. on I-25 from Albuquerque to the Bernalillo exit, turn right onto SR 165 E. to Palcitas; after entering US Forest land, cave is 3 mi. on the left) it is managed by the Sandia Ranger District Station of the Cibola National Forest. Originally thought to pre-date Clovis, the finds in Sandia Cave now seem to be only Clovis in age. Self-guided tours of the cave are available daily. Group guided tours can be arranged through the Ranger District by calling 505/281-3304.

WHEELWRIGHT MUSEUM OF THE AMERICAN INDIAN (Santa Fe, NM; 704 Camino Lejo, on the southeastern approach to the city; Phone 505/982-4636) was begun as a museum of Navajo ceremonial art, and its architecture reflects a hogan style. The Museum has since expanded its collection to include other Native American peoples of the Southwest.

NEW YORK

AMERICAN MUSEUM OF NATURAL HISTORY (New York City, NY; Central Park West at 79th St.; Phone 212/769-5100) has a century-long history of sponsoring archaeological and ethnographic expeditions throughout the Americas, and the vast collection reflects this lengthy interest in Native America. The *Hall of Northwest Coast Indians* contains materials specifically collected for this hall at the turn of the century. The *Hall of Eastern Woodland Indians* and the *Hall of Plains Indians* deal with Native North American culture, mostly during the contact period.

BROOKLYN MUSEUM (Brooklyn, NY; 200 Eastern Pkwy.; Phone 718/638-5000) is particularly well-known for its Precolumbian materials, but a considerable North American collection is also displayed, including South-western ceramics.

BUFFALO MUSEUM OF SCIENCE (Buffalo, NY; Humboldt Pkwy. at North-ampton St.; Best St. exit from SR 33; Phone 716/896-5200) is particularly acclaimed for its exhibits dealing with Iroquois culture, but also addresses several other topics in New World prehistory.

GARVIES POINT MUSEUM AND PRESERVE (Glen Cove, NY; Glen Cove Rd. to fire station and follow signs to Barry Dr.; Phone 516/571-8010), in Hempstead Harbor, displays the development of New World culture, from initial migra-tion from Asia. Dioramas show Native American lifeways on Long Island and trace the path of first European contact.

IROQUOIS INDIAN MUSEUM (Howes Cave, NY; 40 mi. SW of Albany off IS 88, exit 22, right on Rt. 7 to Caverns Rd., left, 1 mi.; Phone 518/296-8949) concentrates on Iroquoisian material. Exhibit cases present 10,000-year-old archaeological sequence, precontact Mohawk, post-contact Oneida and Schoharie Mohawk. The museum building itself connotes a longhouse.

NATIONAL MUSEUM OF THE AMERICAN INDIAN (New York, NY; 3753 Broad-way at 155th St.; Phone 212/283-2420) will soon close as the new Gustav Heye facility, a branch of the Smithsonian Institution, is slated to open in the Custom House in Manhattan's Battery Park area.

NATIONAL SHRINE OF NORTH AMERICAN MARTYRS (Auriesville, NY; E. on SR 5S between exits 27 and 28; Phone 518/853-3033) commemorates the site of the Mohawk Indian village of Ossernenon, the birthplace of the Blessed Kateri Tekakwitha. (See pages 200–202.)

THE NATIONAL SHRINE OF BLESSED KATERI TEKAKWITHA AND NATIVE AMERICAN EXHIBIT (Fonda, NY; ½ mi. W. on SR5; Phone 518/853-3646), 4 miles from the National Shrine of North American Martyrs, commemorates the place where the Mohawk girl lived almost half her life. This is also the site of the Caughnawaga Mohawk village (occupied between 1666 and 1693), an Iroquois village. (See pages 200–202.)

NEW YORK STATE MUSEUM (Albany, NY; Gov. Nelson A. Rockefeller Empire State Plaza; Phone 518/474-5877) has an accurate and realistic reconstruction of life at one of the northeast American Ice Age sites. Changing exhibits and an orientation film are presented; special programs encourage participation in activities related to art, history, science, and technology.

ROCHESTER MUSEUM & SCIENCE CENTER (Rochester, NY; 657 East Ave.; Phone 716/271-1880), longtime leader in the study of Iroquoian culture, has a permanent exhibit in the Elaine Wilson Hall entitled "At The Western Door," which interprets native American–colonial European relations via more than 2,000 Seneca Indian artifacts, a 1790s furnished Seneca cabin, six life-size figure dioramas.

SENECA-IROQUOIS NATIONAL MUSEUM (Salamanca, NY; off US 17 exit 20; Phone 716/945-1738) an Indian-operated institution, illustrates the life and culture of the Seneca people, known as the Keepers of the Western Door of the Iroquois Confederacy. Treaties, wampum belts, costumes, games, modern art, and information on the Seneca social organization are among the displays.

THE TURTLE: NATIVE AMERICAN CENTER FOR THE LIVING ARTS (Niagara Falls, NY; 25 Rainbow Blvd. Mall; Phone 716/284-2427), an Indian-operated institution, presents Native American heritage, culture, symbols, and art, with a special emphasis on the Iroquois Confederacy. The nickname "The Turtle" derives from the Center's distinctive turtle shape, reflecting this animal's importance as a figure in creation stories of many native cultures.

YAGER MUSEUM (Oneonta, NY; on the Hartwick College campus, fourth and fifth floors of Yager Hall; Phone 607/431-4480) has an extensive collection of archaeological materials from the Upper Susquehanna River drainage.

NORTH CAROLINA

MUSEUM OF THE CHEROKEE INDIAN (Cherokee, NC; near the southern entrance of Great Smoky Mountains National Park and the Blue Ridge Parkway; Phone 704/497-3481), an Indian-operated institution, is the 56,000-acre Qualla Boundary Cherokee Indian Reservation, occupied by 8,500 members of the Eastern Band of Cherokees.

SCHIELE MUSEUM OF NATURAL HISTORY AND PLANETARIUM (Gastonia, NC; 1500 E. Garrison Blvd.; Phone 704/866-6900) features a series exhibits and activities exploring the Native American Heritage of the Lower Catawba

River Valley. In the reconstructed Catawba Indian Village, visitors participate in a walk-through history lesson in the Catawba lifeway. They see a thatched roof Town House, place of central government in this early eighteenth-century town. The Bark House and log houses show the early days of European contact. Each year, thousands of students use the village to learn the native history of the area.

TOWN CREEK INDIAN MOUND STATE HISTORIC SITE (Mount Gilead, NC; 5 mi. SE between SR 731 and 73; Phone 910/439-6802) is a 53-acre archaeology area containing two reconstructed temples, a mortuary, and palisade wall. Town Creek was an important cultural, religious, and political center, thought to have been developed during the sixteenth century by a Creek-related people. The visitor center offers interpretive exhibits, a film, and a slide show.

NORTH DAKOTA

FOUR BEARS MUSEUM (New Town, ND; tribal headquarters SE of Minot on SR 23; Phone 701/627-4781), an Indian-operated institution, serves as the tribal museum for the Three Affiliated Tribes (Arikara, Mandan, and Hidatsa).

KNIFE RIVER INDIAN VILLAGES NATIONAL HISTORIC SITE (Stanton, ND; 3 mi. N. on CR 37; Phone 701/745-3309) includes the remains of three Hidatsa Plains Indian villages and a visitor center. (See pages 147–49.)

NORTHWEST TERRITORIES

THE PRINCE OF WALES NORTHERN HERITAGE CENTRE (Yellowknife, NWT; Box 1320, X1A 2L8; Phone 403/873-7551) exhibits artifacts ranging from Paleoindian through contemporary Dene and Inuit (Eskimo) peoples.

NOVA SCOTIA

MIC MAC MUSEUM (Pictou, NS; Phone 902/485-4723) is an Indian-operated institution.

NOVA SCOTIA MUSEUM (Halifax, NS; off Bell Rd. at 1747 Summer St.; Phone 902/429-4610) exhibits artifacts to tell the story of ancient Nova Scotian social history.

PORT AUX CHOIX NATIONAL HISTORIC PARK (Port Au Choix, NS; 15 km. W. of the Port Saunders–Port au Choix turnoff off Hwy. 430; Phone 709/623-2608 or 709/623-2601) interprets on-site archaeological excavations. The visitor center displays artifacts recovered from the Maritime Archaic Indian culture and from the Dorset and Groswater Eskimos, who also populated the area. An excellent movie is also available.

OHIO

CLEVELAND MUSEUM OF NATURAL HISTORY (Cleveland, OH; Wade Oval in University Circle; Phone 216/231-4600) contains important Native American materials, with excellent exhibits on Paleoindian and Hopewell traditions. Two outdoors areas contain examples of plant and animal life indigenous to Ohio; these areas include a bog, prairie, and various woodland settings.

FLINT RIDGE STATE MEMORIAL AND MUSEUM (Brownsville, OH; 3 mi. N. of US 40 on SR 668; Phone 614/787-2476) is the site of an important quarry from Hopewell times. The Ohio pipestone was a widely traded commodity. (See pages 138–39.)

FORT ANCIENT (Lebanon, OH; 7 mi. SE off Middleboro Rd. on SR 350; Phone 513/932-4421) is a Hopewell settlement atop the bluff overlooking the Little Miami River. Protected by a defensive wall, Fort Ancient encompasses about 100 acres containing circular mounds and the remains of village sites.

INDIAN MUSEUM OF LAKE COUNTY (Painesville, OH; in the Kilcawley Center at Lake Erie College; Phone 216/352-3361, ext. 203) emphasizes local archaeological manifestations, particularly the Hopewell and Adena cultures.

MIAMISBURG MOUND STATE MEMORIAL (Miamisburg, OH; 1 mi. SE on I-75 [exit 44] and SR 725; Phone 614/297-2300) has a huge, conical Adena Mound—standing 68 feet high and covering 1½ acres—the largest known in Ohio.

MOUND CEMETERY (Marietta, OH; located on Fifth St.; No phone) contains a 30-foot-high aboriginal mound, originally part of an extensive complex of earthworks. This was one of the first Native American earthworks described in European writings, and has been the subject of considerable speculation. Although Hopewell artifacts have been found nearby, the cultural affiliation of the mound cannot be conclusively established.

HOPEWELL CULTURE NATIONAL HISTORIC PARK (Chillicothe, OH; 4 mi. N. of Chillicothe; Phone 614/774-1125) contains one of the most important Hopewell sites, consisting of a 13 acre area with 23 interpreted mounds. (See pages 129, 132–36).

NEWARK EARTHWORKS (Newark, OH; 1 mi. SW of SR 16 on SR 79; Phone 614/344-1920) includes the Mound Builders State Memorial, which features one very large earthwork and numerous smaller mounds. (See pages 139–41.)

OHIO HISTORICAL CENTER (Columbus, OH; jct. I-71 and 17th Ave.; Phone 614/297-2300) houses the Ohio Historical Society's administrative offices, a historical research library and the state archives. The museum contains arguably the best collection of pre-contact American Indian objects from eastern

North America. Exhibits contain spectacular Native American artifacts, including several "classic" Adena and Hopewell pieces.

SEIP MOUND STATE MEMORIAL (Bainbridge, OH; 3 mi. E. of Bainbridge on US 50; Phone 614/297-2300) contains a great central Hopewell mound earthwork and a related exhibit. (See page 137.)

SERPENT MOUND (Locust Grove, OH; 4 mi. NW of Locust Grove on SR 73; Phone 513/587-2796) is a spectacular and enigmatic ancient mound site dating from perhaps 800 B.C. Includes a museum. (See pages 130–32.)

SUNWATCH ARCHAEOLOGICAL PARK (Dayton, OH; located S. on U-75 to exit 51, W. 1 mi. on Edward C. Moses Blvd., then S. 1 mi. on West River Rd.; Phone 513/268-8199) represents a twelfth-century Fort Ancient tradition Mississippian culture. The reconstructed village includes a woodhenge calendar. (See pages 174–77.)

OKLAHOMA

ATALOA LODGE MUSEUM (Muskogee, OK; on the Bacone College campus; Phone 918/683-4581, ext. 283) displays Indian artifacts collected from tribes throughout the country.

CHEROKEE HERITAGE CENTER (Tahlequah, OK; 3 mi. S. of Tahlequah on SR 62; Phone 918/456-6007), an Indian-operated institution, contains four separate attractions, operated by the Cherokee National Historical Society. *Adams Corner Rural Village* is a reconstruction of this small crossroads community (1875 to 1890) showing the late stages of the Old Cherokee Nation. *Cherokee National Museum* uses state-of-the-art technology, multimedia exhibits and displays to tell the story of the Cherokee people, from the time of European arrival in North America to the present. *"Trail of Tears" Drama* is an outdoor performance depicting the rebuilding of the Cherokee Nation after the forced march in 1838–39 from Georgia and North Carolina to Oklahoma. *"Trail of Tears" Drama* is an outdoor performance depicting the rebuilding of the Cherokee Nation after the forced march in 1838–1839 from Georgia and North Carolina to Oklahoma. *Tsa-La Gi Ancient Village* re-creates a seventeenth-century Cherokee settlement, with regular demonstrations of basketweaving, flintknapping, and pottery-making.

CHICKASAW COUNCIL HOUSE MUSEUM (Tishomingo, OK; on Court House Sq.; Phone 405/371-3351) contains the restored first council house of the Chickasaw Nation, and a display depicting the history of the Chickasaw tribe since their migration from Mississippi and Alabama to Oklahoma in 1838–40.

CREEK COUNCIL HOUSE MUSEUM (Okmulgee, OK; 106 W. 6th St.; Phone 918/756-2324), an Indian-operated institution, was built of local stone in 1878. It was the pride of the Muscogee Creek Tribe. Today, it contains Indian craftwork, weapons, clothes, and early documents, and stands as a reminder of the determination of this tribal nation.

THE FIVE CIVILIZED TRIBES MUSEUM (Muskogee, OK; Phone 918/683-1701), an Indian-operated institution, depicts the history and culture of the Cherokee, Chickasaw, Choctaw, Creek, and Seminole Indians.

FORT SILL APACHE TRIBAL HEADQUARTERS (Apache, OK; 15 mi. S. of Anadarko via US 62/281; Phone 405/588-2314), an Indian-operated institution, displays artwork by its famous tribal member, Allan Houser.

INDIAN CITY USA (Anadarko, OK; 2½ mi. S. on SR 8; Phone 405/247-5661) re-creates a broad range of authentic Plains Indian habitations, including tipis, grass houses, earth lodges, and wattle-and-daub structures from the Kiowa, Caddo, Comanche, Wichita, Pawnee, Navajo, Pueblo, and Apache tribes. A museum displays items of the Southern Plains Indians.

MUSEUM OF ART (Norman, OK; University of Oklahoma Campus, 410 W. Boyd St., Phone 405/325-3272) features rotating exhibits of contemporary art, including native American pieces.

MUSEUM OF THE CHEROKEE STRIP (Enid, OK; 507 S. Fourth St.; Phone 405/237-1907) exhibits Native American and pioneer artifacts depicting the European colonization of the area from 1820 to the present.

MUSEUM OF THE GREAT PLAINS (Lawton, OK; Elmer Thomas Park; Phone 405/353-5675) exhibits materials from the Domebo mammoth kill, excavated in nearby Caddo county in 1962. A diorama presents Paleoindian hunters killing an Imperial mammoth, in a canyon east of Stecker, Oklahoma. Radiocarbon dating places the age of the site at about 10,100 years old. A reconstructed excavation unit is also shown, containing a variety of mammoth rib fragments, mammoth teeth, and Clovis points that are part of the assemblage from this site.

MUSEUM OF THE WESTERN PRAIRIE (Altus, OK; 1100 N. Hightower St.; Phone 405/482-1044) depicts the lifestyles from Oklahoma's western prairie country, including native American materials.

NO MAN'S LAND HISTORICAL MUSEUM (Goodwell, OK; Sewell St. on the campus of Panhandle State University; Phone 405/349-2670) contains pioneer and American Indian artifacts depicting the development of Oklahoma's so-called No Man's Land.

OKLAHOMA MUSEUM OF NATURAL HISTORY (University of Oklahoma, Norman, OK; 1335 Asp Ave.; Phone 405/325-4712) exhibits a variety of archaeological and ethnographic materials, including an excellent collection of Spiro Mound artifacts.

OSAGE TRIBAL MUSEUM (Pawhuska, OK; 600 N. Grandview Ave. Phone 918/287-2495, ext. 280), an Indian-operated institution, contains permanent exhibits of Osage history, art, government, and religion. Changing exhibits show contemporary Osage art; classes are offered in Osage culture and language.

PLAINS INDIANS AND PIONEERS MUSEUM (Woodward, OK; 2009 Williams Ave.; Phone 405/256-6136) contains ethnographic materials from northwestern Oklahoma.

SAC AND FOX TRIBAL MUSEUM (Stroud, OK; 6 mi. S. of Stroud; Phone 918/968-3526 or 405/275-4270), an Indian-operated institution, displays Sac and Fox history, including features on well-known tribal members, including Black Hawk and Jim Thorpe.

SEMINOLE NATION MUSEUM (Wewoka, OK; 1 mi. SE of junction of US 270 and SR 56; Phone 405/257-5580), an Indian-operated institution, contains dioramas, artifacts, crafts, paintings, and other exhibits depicting the history and culture of the Seminole people.

SOUTHERN PLAINS INDIAN MUSEUM AND CRAFTS CENTER (Anadarko, OK; ½ mi. E. on SR 8 and US 62; Phone 405/247-6221), operated by the Indian Arts and Crafts Board of the U.S. Department of the Interior, has permanent displays of Southern Plains Indian history and culture.

SPIRO MOUNDS ARCHAEOLOGICAL PARK (Spiro, OK; 2½ mi. E. on SR 9; then 4¼ mi. N.; Phone 918/596-2700) includes remains of Craig Mound and other complexes linked to the Southern cult in Mississippian times. (See pages 168–70.)

THOMAS GILCREASE MUSEUM (Tulsa, OK; off US 64/SR 51; Phone 918/596-2700) possesses the finest and most comprehensive collection of art of the American West, augmented by relevant documents and artifacts. These 350,000 pieces tell the tale of the human settlement of North America, from the first American to the present.

ONTARIO

CANADIAN MUSEUM OF CIVILIZATION (Ottawa, ON; 1 blk. S. of Hull side of Alexandra Bridge at 100 Laurier St. in Hull; Phone 819/776-7000) is a world-class museum, exhibiting Canada's early history. Highlights include life-size reconstructions of a West Coast Indian village and other historic sites present a dramatic interpretation of the country's past.

CHAMPLAIN TRAIL MUSEUM (Pembroke, ON; 2.5 km E. via old Hwy. 7 at 1032 Pembroke St. E.; Phone 613/735-0517) displays Algonguin artifacts and other materials from the early history of the Ottawa Valley.

KINGSTON ARCHAEOLOGICAL CENTER (Kingston, ON; 370 King St., W. in the J. K. Tett Creativity Complex; Phone 613/542-3483) displays photographs and artifacts interpreting the history of the area.

HURONIA MUSEUM (Midland, ON; at the King St. entrance to Little Lake Park; Phone 705/526-2844 or 705/526-8757) displays various Huron artifacts. A sixteenth-century Huron village has been reconstructed here, based on extensive archaeological evidence and historical documentation. Features include a tobacco patch, loghouse, and wigwam, sweat lodge, and lookout tower.

LAKE OF THE WOODS OJIBWA CULTURAL CENTER (Kenora, ON; Main St. S. in Memorial Park; Phone 807/468-8865 or 548-5744) displays Native American and other memorabilia of this area.

LONDON MUSEUM OF ARCHAEOLOGY (London, ON; 2 blks. S. of Hwy. 22 at 1600 Attawandaron Rd.; Phone 519/473-1360) is both an active research facility and an interpretive resource. The permanent galley presents 11,000 years of Native American survival in southwestern Ontario. *The Lawson Prehistoric Village*, adjacent to the museum, is Canada's only ongoing excavation and reconstruction of a precontact village, retracing the Neutral Indian lifeway of five centuries ago.

MUSEUM OF NORTHERN HISTORY (Kirkland Lake, ON; at Sir Harry Oakes Chateau, 2 Chateau Dr., off Hwy. 66 at the W. end of Kirkland Lake; Phone 705/568-8800) contains Native American artifacts from the northeastern Ontario area.

NORTH AMERICAN INDIAN TRAVEL COLLEGE (Cornwall Island, ON; The Living Museum; Phone 613/932-9452), an Indian-operated institution, presents traditional dwellings of the Cree, Ojibway, and Iroquois Nations during the early eighteenth century. The Visitor Center contains numerous ethnographic materials.

OLD FORT WILLIAM (Thunder Bay, ON; 4 km S. of the jct. of hwys. 11B, 17B and 61 via Hwy. 61. then 4 km SW on Broadway Ave.; Phone 807/577-8461) reconstructions this early nineteenth-century inland headquarters of the North West Co. and includes an American Indian encampment and a site where large cargo birchbark canoes are made.

ROYAL ONTARIO MUSEUM (Toronto, ON; 100 Queen's Park Crescent W., just N. of Queen's Park; Phone 416/586-5551) is a place, they say, "to spend a few hours with all the time in the world." Canada's largest museum combines art, archaeology, and science into three major buildings. The ROM, as everybody calls it, is a major research institute, with active research scientists working throughout the hemisphere. Several massive totem poles are displayed; its very important collections and the Ontario Prehistory Gallery relate the story from Paleoindians to the Iroquoian culture of four centuries ago. One favorite diorama shows the first Americans butchering a woolly mammoth. Around the exit of the gallery, on a granite wall, are red ocher paintings based on two actual pictograph sites in Ontario.

SKA-NAH-DOHT INDIAN VILLAGE (London, ON; in the Longwoods Road Conservation Area on Hwy. 2, 5 km W. of Hwy. 402 exit 86; Phone 519/264-2420) is a reconstructed Iroquois village depicting life in southwestern Ontario about a thousand years ago. A visitor center presents a slide show and exhibits Native American artifacts. Artifacts from several nearby archaeological excavations are housed in the Longwoods Road Conservation Area.

WOODLAND INDIAN CULTURAL EDUCATION CENTRE (Brantford, ON; 184 Mohawk St.; Phone 519/759-2650), an Indian-operated institution, presents exhibits dealing with Native Americans of the Eastern Woodland area.

OREGON

HIGH DESERT MUSEUM (Bend, OR; 6 mi. S. on US 97; Phone 503/382-4754) is an outstanding, relatively new museum devoted to the natural and cultural heritage of the arid Intermountain West. Exhibits stress the relationship of the rugged terrain to those who lived there, including Native Americans. There are self-guiding nature trails through the 20-acre park, and a bookshop.

MUSEUM OF NATURAL HISTORY, UNIVERSITY OF OREGON (Eugene, OR; 1680 E. 15th St.; Phone 503/346-3024). Among other items exhibited are the famous 10,000-year-old sagebrush sandals, discovered at Fort Rock Cave by Luther Cressman, distinguished archaeologist and first director of the museum.

PORTLAND ART MUSEUM (Portland, OR; 1219 SW Park at Jefferson; Phone 503/226-2811), founded in 1892, has an excellent collection of Native American artworks.

PENNSYLVANIA

THE CARNEGIE MUSEUM OF NATURAL HISTORY (Pittsburgh, PA; 4400 Forbes Ave.; Phone 412/662-3172 or 665-2602) is known for its displays dealing with the natural and cultural history of the area.

INDIAN STEPS MUSEUM (Airville, PA; 4½ mi. NE on SR 425, then ¾ mi. SE on Indian Steps Rd.; Phone 717/862-3948) has ample displays dealing with American Indian occupations in this area over the past 3,500 years. This museum is constructed on the site where the Susquehannock once lived during the historic period.

POCONO INDIAN MUSEUM (Bushkill, PA; 3 mi. S. on US 209; Phone 717/588-9338) depicts the lifeway of the Delaware Indians; many of the artifacts were recovered from the nearby Delaware Water Gap area.

THE UNIVERSITY MUSEUM OF ARCHAEOLOGY AND ANTHROPOLOGY (Philadelphia, PA; University of Pennsylvania; 33rd and Spruce Sts.; Phone 215/898-DIGS) contains more than thirty galleries, including considerable native North American artifacts from its extraordinary archaeological collections.

PRINCE EDWARD ISLAND

ALBERTON MUSEUM (Alberton, PEI; on Hwy. 12 [Church St.]; Phone 902/853-2794) displays Native American artifacts from the area.

MICMAC INDIAN VILLAGE (Rocky Point, PEI; W. from Charlottetown on Rt. 1 to Cornwall, then follow Route 19; Phone 902/675-3800) is a reconstructed sixteenth-century Micmac village. Some local archaeological materials are also displayed.

QUEBEC

ABENAKIS MUSEUM (Odanak, PQ; on Rte. 226, reached from Hwy. 132 at the N. end of the Pierreville Bridge [follow signs] or from Hwy. 20 [exits 175–185]; Phone 514/568-2600) presents the history of the Abenaki people in this area.

McCORD MUSEUM OF CANADIAN HISTORY (Montreal, PQ; 690 Sherbrooke Street West; Phone 514/398-7100), now under reconstruction, plans extensive treatment of First Nations archaeological and ethnographic materials.

MUSEUM OF THE SAGUENAY-LAC ST-JEAN (Chicoutimi, PQ; 534 rue Jacques-Cartier Est; Phone 418/545-9400) displays collections of regional Native American and Inuit (Eskimo) artifacts.

SAINT FRANCIS XAVIER MISSION AND SHRINE OF KATERI TEKAKWITHA (Kahnawake, PQ; at the center of the reservation; Phone 514/632-6030) is the burial spot of Kateri Tekakwitha. (See pages 200–202.)

RHODE ISLAND

TOMAQUAG INDIAN MEMORIAL MUSEUM (Arcadia, RI; 325 Summit Road; Phone 401/539-7213) displays Native American archaeology from the local area and elsewhere.

SASKATCHEWAN

SASKATCHEWAN MUSEUM OF NATURAL HISTORY (Regina, SK; College Ave. and Albert St. in Wascana Centre; Phone 306/787-2815) uses a thematic approach in its new First Nations Gallery to present the long-term history of their aboriginal people. Beginning with a depiction of the Cree origin tale, the visitor passes through a stunningly visual sequence of pictograph-making from southern Saskatchewan, tribal elders telling traditional stories in many languages, and a guide to subsistence and survival activities of the area.

SOUTH CAROLINA

SANTA ELENA (Parris Island, SC; ask for directions at the entrance to the Marine base; Parris Island Museum has a section on the dig: Phone 803/525-2951), the early Spanish settlement dating from 1565 has been discovered beneath the U. S. Marine Corps golf course. Excavations continue at this important site, and arrangements can be made for visitation.

SOUTH DAKOTA

H. V. JOHNSTON CULTURAL CENTER (Eagle Butte, SD; Phone 605/964-2542), on the Cheyenne River Sioux Reservation, is a tribally operated museum depicting the history of the reservation, providing information on prominent tribal members, and offering native artwork.

THE MAMMOTH SITE (Hot Springs, SD; 1½ mi. SW of Hot Springs on the US 18 bypass; Phone 605/745-6017) has one of the larger concentrations of mammoth bones found in the Western Hemisphere. The approximately 26,000-year-old site is believed to have been a sinkhole fed by springs; it is the only *in-situ* (left as found) site for mammoth bones in America. Mammoths, giant short-faced bears, and other animals entered the pond, became trapped in the slippery, quicksand-like banks, and died of starvation.

MITCHELL PREHISTORIC INDIAN VILLAGE (Mitchell, SD; 1 mi. N. of Corn Palace on Indian Village Rd.; Phone 605/996-5473) contains an eleventh-century fortified Indian village on Lake Mitchell. The site includes the Boehnen Memorial Museum and Visitors Center, the Patton Gallery Exhibit of Prehistoric Farmers/Hunters of the James River Basin, and a walk-through scale model of a reconstructed lodge.

SIOUX INDIAN MUSEUM (Rapid City, SD; on West Blvd. near Main St., just off entrance to I-190; Phone 605/348-0557) exhibits perhaps the best available collection of historical and contemporary artifacts pertaining to the Sioux Nation.

W. H. OLIVER STATE MUSEUM (Vermillion, SD; SR 50 at Ratingen St.; Phone 605/677-5228) contains considerable Sioux artifacts and historical photographs.

WOUNDED KNEE BATTLEFIELD (Wounded Knee, SD; 8 mi. E. of Pine Ridge, north of US 18 on Reservation Road; No phone) is no battlefield at all. It is where in 1890, members of the Seventh Cavalry, still seeking revenge for their humiliation at the Little Bighorn, gunned down more than 300 native people, including many women and children. A small monument marks the mass grave of the victims. Congress has yet to recognize Wounded Knee as a National Historical Landmark.

TENNESSEE

CHUCALISSA INDIAN MUSEUM (Memphis, TN; 5 mi. S. of Memphis on US 61, then 4½ mi. W. on Mitchell Rd., next to Fuller State Park; Phone 901/785-3160) is a site excavated by the Department of Anthropology at Memphis State University. The site was occupied between about A.D. 900–1600. The paramount chief's house and a temple structure stood atop the low platform mound.

FRANK H. MCCLUNG MUSEUM (Knoxville, TN; in Circle Park on the University of Tennessee campus; Phone 615/974-2144) is a showcase of Tennessee's ancient past. The McClung Museum houses some of the finest specimens of native American artifacts recovered from the southeastern United States.

OLD STONE FORT STATE ARCHAEOLOGICAL AREA (Manchester, TN; 4½ mi. N. on US 41 from jct. I-24, exit 114; Phone 615/723-5073) is a 2,000-year-old ceremonial site, a mystical place for Indian people even before they began building here. Mounds and walls were combined with cliffs and rivers to form an enclosure measuring 1¼ miles around.

PINSON MOUNDS STATE ARCHAEOLOGICAL AREA (Pinson, TN; off US 45 at 460 Ozier Rd.; Phone 901/988-5614) contains one of the largest Hopewell mound groups in North America. The archaeological area contains a dozen burial mounds and crematory areas. The visitor's center houses a replica of the burial mounds, other exhibits, an archaeological library, and a theater.

SEQUOYAH BIRTHPLACE MUSEUM (Vonore, TN; 1 mi. E. on SR 360 from jct. with US 411; Phone 615/884-6246), an Indian-operated institution, honors the Cherokee statesman and soldier, Sequoyah (1776–1843). He is best known for creating the Cherokee alphabet, which took him a dozen years.

SHILOH NATIONAL MILITARY PARK (Savannah, TN; 10 mi. SW of Savannah; Phone 901/689-5275) contains more than 30 mounds, believed to have been built between A.D. 1100 and 1300; several of these are flat-topped Mississippian mounds, and a large burial mound is also present, as was a central plaza.

TEXAS

ALIBATES FLINT QUARRIES NATIONAL MONUMENT (Amarillo, TX; 34 mi. NE of Amarillo off SR 136; Phone 806/857-3151) provides a firsthand look at a Paleoindian quarry. (See page 22.)

CADDOAN MOUNDS STATE HISTORIC SITE (Alto, TX; 6 mi. SW Alto on SH 21; Phone 409/858-3218) contains two mounds and a village area dating approximately A.D. 800–1300. An early Caddo house is re-created here, and the visitor center has exhibits and an audio-visual presentation on the Caddoan people who lived here.

MUSEUM OF THE SOUTHWEST (Midland, TX; 1½ mi. W., 1 blk. S. of US 80 business route, at 1705 W. Missouri; Phone 915/683-2882) houses art and archaeological collections in a 1934 mansion.

SAN ANTONIO MISSIONS NATIONAL HISTORICAL PARK (San Antonio, TX) includes four eighteenth-century Spanish missions. A "Mission Trail" driving map is available from the San Antonio Visitor Information Center, in Alamo Park.

Mission Nuestra Señora la Purísima Concepción de Acuña (3 mi. SW of downtown San Antonio, TX; Mission Road near Mitchell St.; Phone 512/229-5732) was built in 1739. Traces of original frescoes remain.

Mission San Francisco de la Espada (6½ mi S. on US 281 to Bergs Mill, then W. on Mission Rd. and S. on Espada following signs; Phone 512/627-2021), originally founded in 1690, moved to the San Antonio area in 1731. Museum here.

Mission San Juan Capistrano (San Antonio, TX; 6½ mi S. on US 181, then W. on Bergs Mill and ¼ mi. S. by county road; Phone 512/229-5734) was established in 1731. The convent now houses offices and a museum.

San Jose y San Miguel de Aguayo Mission (6539 San Jose Dr., 6¼ mi. S. of San Antonio on US 281; Phone 512/229-5701) was founded in 1720. Impressive restorations and the soldiers' barracks, granary, and many of the Indian quarters appear as they did during the mission period.

EL PASO CENTENNIAL MUSEUM (El Paso, TX; on the UTEP campus at University Ave. and Wiggins Rd.; Phone 915/747-5565). The museum has exhibits dealing with the archaeology and ethnology of the American Southwest and northern Mexico.

EL PASO MISSIONS TOUR (El Paso, TX; tour of the lower valley sites begins at the Ysleta Mission, 14 mi. E. of El Paso on I-10; Phone 915/534-0696). This self-guiding tour includes communities and buildings dating from the early 1680s.

HUECO TANKS STATE HISTORICAL PARK (El Paso, TX; 30 mi. E. of El Paso on US 180/62, then 8 mi. N. on FM 2775; Phone 915/857-1135) contains one of the area's few natural watering places. Since Paleoindian times, these rock basins or *huecos* collected rainwater and attracted both humans and animals. A huge collection of five thousand rock art elements is silent testimony from the succeeding cultures that once lived here.

LUBBOCK LAKE STATE AND NATIONAL LANDMARK (Lubbock, TX; on NE edge of Lubbock near intersection of 289 and US 84; Phone 806/741-0306) is an important Paleoindian locality, and investigators from Texas Tech University continue to excavate there. (See pages 32–34, 38.)

MISSION ESPIRITU SANTO DE ZUNIGA (SE of San Antonio, TX; Goliad State Historical Park; Phone 512/645-3405) was established in 1749. The church and adjacent *Presidio La Bahio* complexes have been extensively reconstructed, and a museum presents the mission history.

MUSEUM OF TEXAS TECH UNIVERSITY (Lubbock, TX; 4th St. and Indiana Ave.; Phone 806/742-2490) Exhibits deal with the environment, history, and cultures of this area, with special emphasis on the Paleoindian excavations at nearby Lubbock Lake and elsewhere in Texas.

SEMINOLE CANYON STATE HISTORICAL PARK (Comstock, TX; from Del Rio, drive 40 mi. NW on US 90 to directional signs; Phone 915/292-4464) has several spectacular limestone rock shelters in which are preserved several noteworthy pictograph murals. The visitor center explains the Archaic adaptations of the people who utilized these shelters.

TIGUA INDIAN RESERVATION AND PUEBLO (El Paso, TX; Phone 915/858-1033 or 859-3916), an Indian-operated institution, displays the history of this Pueblo tribe, who relocated from New Mexico during the revolt in 1680. In 1682, under Spanish direction, they built the Ysleta mission, one of the oldest in North America. The present structure incorporates the original foundations and some of the original adobe walls.

UTAH

ANASAZI INDIAN VILLAGE STATE PARK (Boulder, UT; on SR 12; Phone 801/335-7308) has a visitor center introducing an Anasazi site previously excavated by the University of Utah. A life-size, six-room replica of an Anasazi dwelling has been built, to give visitors an idea of what Anasazi life was like eight centuries ago.

BRYCE CANYON NATIONAL PARK (Panguitch, UT; 26 mi. SE via US 89, SR 12 and SR 63; Phone 801/834-5322) has a visitor center that contains exhibits pertaining to the geology, biology, archaeology, and history of the region. But be forewarned: the sites in this park are not readily seen, being both inaccessible and often invisible to the untrained eye.

CAPITOL REEF NATIONAL PARK (Torrey, UT; 5 mi. E. of Torrey on SR 24; Phone 801/425-3791) has several pre-contact rock art panels that can be seen on the surrounding canyon walls. The visitor center presents the cultural history of the area.

COLLEGE OF EASTERN UTAH PREHISTORIC MUSEUM (Price, UT; in the municipal building; Phone 801/637-5060) has exhibits of Fremont and Anasazi cultures.

EDGE OF THE CEDARS STATE PARK (Blanding, UT; just off US 191 at 660 W. 400 North St.; Phone 801/678-2238 or 801/678-3392) presents an Anasazi village site and an adjoining museum facility. Exhibits present materials from Anasazi through historic period Ute and Navajo. Video presentations are also available.

FREMONT INDIAN STATE PARK (Richfield, UT; 24 mi. SW at the jct. of I-70 and SR 89; Phone 801/527-4631) exhibits archaeological materials of the Fremont culture from nearby Five Fingers Hill.

HOVENWEEP NATIONAL MONUMENT (straddling the Utah/Colorado boundary from Cortez, CO, drive N. 18 mi. on US 666 to Pleasant View; turn west at the sign and follow graded road 27 mi.; Phone 303/529-4461) is not easy to get to, and all approach roads are graded dirt; they can easily become muddy and sometimes impassable; inquire locally for directions and road conditions.

Hovenweep, a Ute word meaning "deserted valley," is an unreconstructed slice of Anasazi life. The visitor can walk among the remains of many-roomed pueblos, small cliff dwellings and towers. Scattered refuse over canyon slopes tells the story of the sizable population that once lived in this now-desolate country.

MUSEUM OF PEOPLES AND CULTURE (Provo, UT; Brigham Young University; 710 N. 100 East; Phone 801/378-6112) contains exhibits emphasizing the archaeological and paleontological history of eastern Utah.

NEWSPAPER ROCK STATE PARK (Monticello, UT; at Indian Creek Canyon, 15 mi. N., then 12 mi. W. off US 163/191 on the paved highway to Canyonlands National Park; Phone 801/587-2141) is a massive cliff mural consisting of ancient rock art, probably drawn during the Fremont and historic periods.

UTAH MUSEUM OF NATURAL HISTORY (Salt Lake City, UT; University of Utah campus; Phone 801/581-6927), provides an excellent introduction to the anthropology of the eastern Great Basin and Colorado Plateau.

UTE TRIBAL MUSEUM (Ft. Duchesne, UT; located 23 mi. from airport in Vernal; Phone 801/722-4992), on the Uintah and Ouray Reservation, is part of the opulent Bottle Hollow Inn and Conference Center. The facility includes a library and audio-visual center.

VIRGINIA

JAMESTOWN ISLAND (Colonial National Historical Park, Virginia; on the western end of the Colonial Parkway; Phone 804/229-1607) commemorates the first permanent English colony founded in 1607 on the land destined to become the United States. *Indian Village* (Jamestown Settlement) presents the lifestyle of the seventeenth-century Powhatan Indians as it was encountered by the English settlers in 1607. The village, based on archaeological evidence, eyewitness drawings and accounts of the period, consists of several lodges.

Incised vessels and human effigies recovered from the Menard Site (Arkansas), a seventeenth-century French-Indian trading center. (Courtesy of the American Museum of Natural History.)

PAMUNKEY INDIAN MUSEUM (King William, VA; Rt. 1, Box 2050; Phone 804/843-4792), an Indian-operated institution features numerous artifacts and exhibits portraying the history of the Pamunkey Indians, once members of the powerful Powhatan confederacy.

VIRGINIA MUSEUM OF NATURAL HISTORY (Martinsville, VA; 1001 Douglas Ave.; Phone 703/666-8600) contains several Native American exhibits, including *The Dan River People*, a 16-foot traveling diorama showing the relationship of Native Americans to their environment.

WEST VIRGINIA

GRAVE CREEK MOUND (Moundsville, WV; 801 Jefferson St.; Phone 304/843-1410). Also known as Mammoth Mound, the 70-foot-tall structure is the largest Adena mound yet discovered, housing two burial chambers. The adjacent *Delf Norona Museum* recounts its excavation in the nineteenth century. (See pages 128–29.)

WASHINGTON

BURKE MUSEUM (Seattle, WA; University of Washington campus, 17th Ave., N.E. entrance; Phone 206/543-5590) holds extensive collections and features exhibits relating to the natural and cultural heritage of the Pacific rim. Although this research-oriented museum has a relatively small proportion of its archaeological holdings on display, there is a computer touch screen in the public gallery that allows access to 14,000 catalogued pieces of Northwest coast art and artifacts.

CHELAN COUNTY HISTORICAL MUSEUM AND PIONEER VILLAGE (Cashmere, WA; at the eastern entrance to town; Phone 509/782-3230) displays the pre-Columbian heritage of the Columbia River basin. Some rank this collection of native American Indian artifacts among the best in the Northwest.

CHENEY COWLES MEMORIAL MUSEUM (Spokane, WA; 2316 First Ave.; Phone 509/456-3931) exhibits the cultural history of the Inland Empire. Also displayed are numerous pieces from the Museum's extensive collection of native American material culture.

COLVILLE MUSEUM AND GALLERY (Coulee Dam, WA; 516 Birch St.; Phone 509/633-0751), an Indian-operated institution, features murals (painted by tribal members in 1989) showing how the Kettle Falls fishing grounds might have looked 150 years ago. Life-size dioramas depict fishing, gambling, the sweat-lodge, and a tule-reed tipi. From a tribal point of view, perhaps the most important part of the collection, is the large series of tribal photographs dating back to the 1870s.

ILWACO HERITAGE MUSEUM (Ilwaco, WA; 1 blk. E. of US 101 at 115 SE Lake St.; Phone 206/642-3446) has displays of Native American artifacts, with a gallery of American Indian art.

MAKAH CULTURAL AND RESEARCH CENTER (Neah Bay, WA; on SR 112; Phone 206/645-2711) an Indian-operated institution, includes recreations from the spectacularly preserved Ozette village. (See pages 63–65, 71.)

THE MUSEUM OF ANTHROPOLOGY, WASHINGTON STATE UNIVERSITY (Pullman, WA; College Hall; Phone 509/355-3441) contains exhibits highlighting Inuit cultural ecology, early settlement of the Pacific Northwest, and the transformation of western U.S. basketry during the historic period.

MUSEUM AND ARTS CENTER (Sequim, WA; 175 W. Cedar Street; Phone 206/683-8110) contains displays about the Manis Mastodon excavations, discovered in 1977. For nine field seasons, archaeologists worked here, uncovering evidence of four mastodons, several bison, and artifacts made of stone and preserved wood; the find dates to about 12,000 years ago.

MUSEUM OF NATIVE AMERICAN CULTURES (Spokane, WA; E. 200 Cataldo St.; Phone 509/326-4550) exhibits Native American material culture from throughout the Western Hemisphere, including an extensive collection of trade beads.

SACAJAWEA STATE PARK MUSEUM AND INTERPRETIVE CENTER (Pasco, WA; 3 mi. SE on US 12 and 395 at the confluence of the Snake and Columbia rivers; Phone 509/545-2361) recapitulates the story of explorers Lewis and Clark, who passed through here in October 1805. Displays emphasize the positive role played by Sacajawea.

STEILACOOM TRIBAL CULTURAL CENTER AND MUSEUM (Steilacoom, WA; 1515 Lafayette Street; Phone 206/584-6308), an Indian-operated institution, presents the history of the Steilacoom tribe. On the lower level is a simulated archaeological dig, where children are encouraged to dig for "artifacts."

ST. FRANCIS XAVIER MISSION (Toledo, WA; 2 mi. NE of Toledo on Jackson Hwy., then ¼ mi. S. on Spenser Rd.; No phone) was founded in 1838, the first Catholic church in the state and one of the oldest missions in the Northwest.

ST. PAUL'S MISSION (Colville, WA; 12 mi. NW of Colville where US 395 meets the Columbia River; Phone 509/738-6266) is part of the Coulee Dam National Recreation Area. Begun as a small chapel to missionize local Indians in 1845, it operated until the 1870s. The log church has been restored to its 1847 appearance.

SUQUAMISH MUSEUM (Suquamish, WA; 2 mi. S. of Suquamish on SR 305 at the W. end of Agate Pass Bridge; Phone 206/598-3311) interprets the lifestyles of Native Americans, particularly the Salish people, in the Puget Sound area, before and after European and Asian contact. The grave of Chief Sealth is nearby, at St. Peter's Catholic Mission Church.

YAKIMA NATION MUSEUM AND CULTURAL HERITAGE CENTER (Toppenish, WA; just off I-82, US 97 runs through the reservation; Phone 509/865-2800), an Indian-operated institution, suggests a traditional tule-mat house. The nucleus of this collection are 10,000 books and artifacts that belonged to Nipo Strongheart, once a performer in Buffalo Bill's Wild West Show and a successful Hollywood actor.

WISCONSIN

AZTALAN STATE PARK AND MUSEUM (Lake Mills, WI; 4 acres 3 mi. E. on County B next to Aztalan State Park; Phone 414/648-8845) contains important late Woodland and Middle Mississippian sites. First excavated in the 1930s, it consists of truncated pyramidal mounds, domestic area, high status burials, and a palisade with bastions.

LIZARD MOUND COUNTY PARK (West Bend, WI; 4 mi. N. on SR 144, then ¼ mi. E. on County A; Phone 414/335-4445) features numerous animal effigy mounds in the shape of lizards, birds, and other creatures. (See pages 142–43.)

LOGAN MUSEUM OF ANTHROPOLOGY (Beloit, WI; Bushnell St. on the Beloit College campus; Phone 608/363-2677) is a teaching museum that has recently renovated its displays of ethnological and archaeological materials, spanning the last 10,000 years.

ONEIDA NATION MUSEUM (Oneida, WI; 7 mi. W. of Green Bay on SR 54, 886 Double E Rd.; Phone 414/869-2768), an Indian-operated institution, relates the history and culture of the Iroquois, with an emphasis on the Oneida Indian Nation as it moved from New York to Wisconsin. A stockaded village has been built, with a full-scale replica of an Oneida long house.

SHEBOYGAN MOUND PARK (Sheboygan, WI; E. of S. 12th St. off Panther Ave.) contains 33 effigy mounds shaped like panthers and deer. Probably constructed between A.D. 500–1000, it is one of the few mound groups still intact.

WYOMING

ANTHROPOLOGY MUSEUM (Laramie, WY; University of Wyoming; in the Anthropology [Old Law] Building; Phone 307/766-5136) contains about forty displays on Plains archaeology and world ethnography.

BUFFALO BILL HISTORICAL CENTER (Cody, WY; on US 14/16/20 at 720 Sheridan Ave.; Phone 307/587-4771) is an impressive complex of four museums dedicated to the history of the American West. The Plains Indian Museum contains an extensive collection of artifacts, ceremonial items and beadwork, dress and weaponry of the Sioux, Blackfeet, Cheyenne, Shoshone, Crow, and Arapaho tribes.

MEDICINE WHEEL (Bighorn National Forest, WY; at 10,000-foot level of Medicine Mountain, off US 14A; Phone 307/672-0751) is a massive stone circle, nearly 90 feet in diameter. Steeped in antiquity, the exact meaning and age of the Medicine Wheel is uncertain. Visitors should be aware that this remains a sacred place to several Native American tribes; please respect their religious practices if you choose to visit. (See pages 236–41, 244).

NOTES

p. xiii   The quote beginning "After five centuries . . ." is from *The Native Americans: An Illustrated History*, by David Hurst Thomas, et al. (Atlanta: Turner Publications, 1993), p. 19.

p. xiv   The quote beginning "vast and virgin continent . . ." is from James Axtell's "Europeans, Indians, and the Age of Discovery in American textbooks." *American Historical Review* 92:624, 1987.

p. xiv   The quote "People without history" is taken from *Europe and the People without History*, by Eric R. Wolf (Berkeley: University of California Press, 1982).

p. 6   The quote in the sidebar beginning "excavating ancient fire-places . . ." is from "Afterword" by Vine Deloria, Jr. In *America in 1492*, edited by Alvin M. Josephy, Jr. (New York: Alfred A. Knopf, 1992), p. 433.

pp. 6–7   The story beginning "A Diegueno Case History . . ." are from *The Encyclopedia of Native American Religions*, by Arlene Hirschfelder and Paulette Molin (New York: Facts On File, Inc., 1992), pp. 58–60.

p. 13   The quote beginning "at least fifteen . . ." is from Alfred V. Kidder's article "Early Man in America." *The Masterkey* 1-5:5-13, 1927.

p. 14   The sidebar "What's in a Name?" by Suzan Shown Harjo has been modified by the author from her "Forward" to *North American Indian Landmarks: A Traveler's Guide* (Detroit: Visible Ink Press, 1993).

p. 15   The illustration is based on figure 3 in "Bone foreshafts from a Clovis burial in southwest Montana," by Larry Lahren and Robson B. Bonnichsen. *Science* 186:147–150 (1974).

p. 17   The illustration is based on figure 3 of "Clovis-Folsom Geochronology and Climatic Change," by C. Vance Haynes, Jr. In *From Kostenki to Clovis: Upper Paleolithic-Paleo-Indian Adaptations*, edited by Olga Soffer and N. D. Praslov (New York: Plenum Publishing Corporation, 1993), pp. 219–238.

p. 26   The illustration is based on figure 3 in *Radiocarbon Dating: An Archaeological Perspective*, by R. E. Taylor (Orlando: Academic Press, 1987).

p. 29   The quote beginning "The Clovis projectile point . . ." is from "North American High Plains Paleo-Indian Hunting Strategies and

Weaponry Assemblages," by George Frison. In *From Kostenki to Clovis: Upper Paleolithic-Paleo-Indian Adaptations*, edited by Olga Soffer and N. D. Praslov (New York: Plenum Publishing Corporation), p. 241.

p. 36   The quote beginning "They take a stick . . ." by Juan de Torquemada, appeared in the article "Mesoamerican polyhedral cores and prismatic blades" by Don Crabtree. *American Antiquity* 33–4:449 (1968).

pp. 41–42   The sidebar "Ancient Worlds," by Roger C. Echo-Hawk has been modified by the author from his article by the same name in the *Bulletin of the Society for American Archaeology* 11–4:5–6 (September 1993). It is reprinted here with the permission of the author and the Society for American Archaeology.

p. 42   The quote beginning "It is an historical fact . . ." is from Thomas R. Hester, Robert F. Heizer, and John A. Graham in *Field Methods in Archaeology*, Sixth Edition (Palo Alto, CA: Mayfield Publishing, 1975), p. 116.

p. 45   The quote beginning "We believe we have established . . ." is from Louis Leakey in *Pleistocene Man at Calico*, edited by Walter C. Schuiling (Bloomington, CA: San Bernardino County Museum Association, 1972), p. 75.

p. 45   The quote beginning "Calico is indeed . . ." is from "An Introduction to the Calico Early Man Site Lithic Assemblage," by Ruth DeEtte Simpson. *San Bernardino County Museum Association Quarterly* 36(3):87.

pp. 46–47   The *minimum requirements* for establishing the presence of people have been taken from the seminal article "The Earliest Americans," by C. Vance Haynes. *Science* 166: 709–715 (1969).

p. 59   The illustration is based on figure 1 in "Adoption of the Bow in Prehistoric North America," by John H. Blitz. *American Archaeologist* 9–2:123–146 (1988).

p. 79   The illustration is based on figure 1 in *Poverty Point: A Culture of the Lower Mississippi Valley*, by Jon L. Gibson (Louisiana Archaeological Survey and Antiquities Commission, Anthropological Study 7, 1983).

p. 106   The illustration is based on artwork in *Roads to Center Place: A Cultural Atlas of Chaco Canyon and the Anasazi*, by Kathryn Gabriel (Boulder, CO: Johnson Books, 1991), p. 4.

p. 112   The illustration is based on figure 9.2 in "The Quest for Subsistence Sufficiency and Civilization in the Sonoran Desert," by Bruce Masse. In *Chaco and Hohokam: Prehistoric Regional Systems in the American Southwest*, edited by Patricia L. Crown and W. James Judge (Santa Fe, NM: School of American Research Press, 1991), pp. 195–224.

p. 117   The illustration is based on figure 10.1 in "Hohokam Exchange and

Interaction" by David E. Doyel. In *Chaco and Hohokam: Prehistoric Regional Systems in the American Southwest*, edited by Patricia L. Crown and W. James Judge (Santa Fe, NM: School of American Research Press, 1991), pps. 225–252.

p. 119 The illustration is based on artwork in *Native American Architecture*, by Peter Nabokov and Robert Easton (New York: Oxford University Press, Inc., 1989), p. 357.

p. 156 The illustration is based on figure 27 in "The American Woodhenge" by Warren L. Wittry. In *Explorations into Cahokia Archaeology*, edited by Melvin L. Fowler (Bulletin 7, Illinois Archaeological Survey, 1973), pp. 43–48.

p. 176 The quote beginning "The first three days . . ." and others from Turnbow appeared in the *Cleveland New Dealer* Feb. 4, 1992, p. B1.

pp. 180–81 The quote beginning "Let us call this place . . ." is from Gideon Lincecum's "Choctaw Traditions about their Settlement in Mississippi and the Origin of their Mounds," *Publications of the Mississippi Historical Society* 8:521–542 (1904).

p. 193 The expression "An American Holocaust" derives from "The Consequences of Contact: Toward an Interdisciplinary Theory of Native Responses to Biological and Cultural Invasion," by David E. Stannard. In *Columbian Consequences, Volume 3: The Spanish Borderlands in Pan-American Perspective*, edited by David Hurst Thomas (Washington D.C.: Smithsonian Institution Press, 1991), pp. 519–540.

p. 213 The quote beginning "At the fair that brought America . . ." is from "The Spanish Influence: Architecture in America," by Aaron Betsky. *Horizon* 28(10):53–68, 1985.

p. 217 The quote beginning "Mission Revival version . . ." is from *The Guide to Architecture in San Francisco and Northern California*, by David Gebhard, Eric Sandweiss, and Robert Winter, rev. ed. (Salt Lake City, Utah: Peregrine Smith Books, 1985), p. 394.

p. 220 The quote beginning "Concocting a moral basis for the American appropriation . . ." is from "The Little Bighorn" by Andrew Ward (*American Heritage*, April 1992), p. 86.

p. 224 The quote beginning "The people of this tribe . . ." is from *The Crow*, by Frederick E. Hoxie (New York: Chelsea House Publishers, 1989), p. 27.

p. 225 The quote beginning "a century earlier . . ." is from *The Crow*, by Frederick E. Hoxie (New York: Chelsea House Publishers, 1989), p. 59.

p. 226 The quote beginning "unencumbered by American Victorian standards . . ." is taken from *Archaeological Perspectives on the Battle of the Little Bighorn*, by Douglas Scott, et al. (Norman: University of Oklahoma Press, 1989), p. 11.

p. 228 The quote beginning "What the archaeology and the Indian accounts told me . . ." by Richard Fox appears in *American Heritage* (April 1992), p. 85.

p. 228   The quote beginning "It looked like . . ." is from Barbara Booher in "General Custer Loses at Little Bighorn," by W. Plummer and B. Shaw. *People* 33(6):92–96 (1990).

p. 231   The quote beginning "Not long ago . . ." by W. Richard West, Jr., appeared in a promotional appeal produced by the National Campaign Office for the National Museum of the American Indian (Nov. 1, 1992).

p. 234   The quote beginning "To our children . . ." appears over the entryway to the Museum at Warm Springs, on the Warm Springs Reservation in central Oregon.

p. 236   The quote beginning "From time immemorial . . ." by Vine Deloria, Jr., appeared in "Sacred Lands," *Winds of Change* 8 (4): 31, 33 (1993).

pp. 238–39   The quote beginning "Red Plume, a famous Crow chief . . ." is taken from "Sheridan's historic settings" by D. W. Greenburg. *The Midwest Review* 7(10):66 (1926).

p. 241   The quote beginning "A well-known archaeological structure . . ." is from "Astronomical alignment of the Bighorn medicine wheel," by John A. Eddy. *Science* 184(4141):1035–1043.

pp. 242–43   The poem entitled "Sacred Ground," by Suzan Shown Harjo first appeared in the *Native American Rights Fund Legal Review* 18(2):9, and is reproduced here with permission of the author.

FOR FURTHER READING

SOME GENERAL BOOKS ON HOW ARCHAEOLOGISTS WORK

Anderson, Joan. *From Map to Museum: Uncovering Mysteries of the Past*. New York: Morrow Junior Books, 1988.

Hayden, Brian. *Archaeology: The Science of Once and Future Things*. New York: W. H. Freeman and Co, 1993.

Renfrew, Colin, and Paul Bahn. *Archaeology: Theory, Methods, and Practice*. New York: Thames and Hudson, 1991.

Thomas, David Hurst. *Archaeology*, second edition. Fort Worth: Harcourt Brace, 1989.

——. *Archaeology: Down to Earth*. Fort Worth: Holt, Rinehart, and Winston, Inc., 1991.

Webster, David L., Susan Toby Evans, and William T. Sanders. *Out of the Past: An Introduction to Archaeology*. Mountain View, CA: Mayfield Publishing Co., 1993.

SOME GENERAL BOOKS ON NATIVE AMERICAN ARCHAEOLOGY

Coe, Michael, Dean Snow, and Elizabeth Benson. *Atlas of Ancient America*. New York: Facts on File, 1986.

Folsom, Franklin, and Mary Elting Folsom. *America's Ancient Treasures*, fourth edition. Albuquerque: University of New Mexico Press, 1993.

Grant, Campbell. *Rock Art of the American Indian*. New York: Thomas Y. Crowell Company, 1967.

Jelks, Edward B., and Juliet C. Jelks (eds.). *Historical Dictionary of North American Archaeology*. New York: Greenwood Press, 1988.

Justice, Noel D. *Stone Age Spear and Arrow Points of the Midcontinental and Eastern United States*. Bloomington: Indiana University Press, 1987.

Kopper, Philip. *The Smithsonian Book of North American Indians: Before the Coming of Europeans*. Washington D. C.: Smithsonian Institution Press, 1986.

Nabokov, Peter, and Robert Easton. *Native American Architecture*. New York: Oxford University Press, 1989.

Willey, Gordon R., and Jeremy A. Sabloff. *A History of American Archaeology*, third edition. New York: W. H. Freeman and Company, 1993.

THE GLOBAL PROLOGUE

Burenhult, Göran (ed.). *The Illustrated History of Humankind, Vol. 1: The First Humans*. San Francisco: HarperSanFrancisco, 1993.

Johanson, Donald C., and Kevin O'Farrell. *Journey from the Dawn: Life with the World's First Family*. New York: Villard Books, 1990.

Leakey, Richard, and Roger Lewin. *Origins Reconsidered: In Search of What Makes Us Human*. New York: Doubleday & Co., 1992.

Tattersall, Ian. *The Human Odyssey: Four Million Years of Human Evolution*. New York: Prentice Hall, 1993.

Tattersall, Ian, Eric Delson, and John Van Couvering. *Encyclopedia of Human Evolution and Prehistory*. New York: Garland Publishing, 1988.

THE FIRST AMERICANS

FOR THE GENERAL READER

Between November, 1986, and January, 1988, *Natural History* magazine ran a special series of articles exploring archaeological sites and other lines of evidence bearing on the peopling of the New World; these are highly recommended.

Fagan, Brian M. *The Great Journey*. London and New York: Thames and Hudson, 1987.

MORE SPECIALIZED SOURCES

Bonnichsen, Robson, and Karen L. Turmire. *Clovis: Origins and Adaptations*. Corvallis: Center for the Study of the First Americans, Oregon State University, 1991.

Bryan, Alan L. (ed.). *New Evidence for the Pleistocene Peopling of the Americas*. Orono, ME: Center for the Study of Early Man, 1986.

Carlisle, R. (ed.). *Americans before Columbus: Ice Age Origins*. Pittsburgh: Department of Anthropology, University of Pittsburgh, 1988.

Dillehay, Tom D.. and David J. Meltzer (eds.). *The First Americans: Search and Research*. Boca Raton: CRS Press, 1991.

Johnson, Eileen (ed.). *Lubbock Lake: Late Quaternary Studies on the Southern High Plains*. College Station: Texas A&M University Press, 1987.

Laughlin, William S., and Albert B. Harper. *The First Americans: Origins, Affinities, and Adaptations*. New York: Gustav Fisher, 1979.

Soffer, Olga, and N. D. Praslov (eds.). *From Kostenki to Clovis: Upper Paleolithic-Paleo-Indian Adaptations*. New York: Plenum Press, 1993.

Stanford, Dennis J., and Jane S. Day (eds.). *Ice Age Hunters of the Rockies*. Boulder: University of Colorado Press, 1992.

SPREADING OUT ACROSS AMERICA

FOR THE GENERAL READER

Grayson, Donald K. *The Desert's Past: A Natural Prehistory of the Great Basin*. Washington D. C.: Smithsonian Institution Press, 1993.

Keyser, James D. *Indian Rock Art of the Columbia Plateau*. Seattle: University of Washington Press, 1992.

Kirk, Ruth, with Richard D. Daugherty. *Hunters of the Whale: An Adventure in Northwest Coast Archaeology*. New York: William Morrow and Company, 1974.

Madsen, David B. *Exploring the Fremont*. Salt Lake City: University of Utah Press, 1989.

Moratto, Michael J. *California Archaeology*. New York: Academic Press, 1984.

MORE SPECIALIZED SOURCES

Bamforth, Douglas. *Ecology and Human Organization on the Great Plains*. New York: Plenum Press, 1989.

Damas, David (ed.). "Arctic," *Handbook of North American Indians, volume 5*. Washington D. C.: Smithsonian Institution Press, 1984.

D'Azevedo, Warren L. (ed.). "Great Basin," *Handbook of North American Indians, volume 11*. Washington D. C.: Smithsonian Institution Press, 1986.

Frison, George C. *Prehistoric Hunters of the High Plains*, second edition. San Diego: Academic Press, Inc., 1991.

Gibson, Jon L. *Poverty Point: A Culture of the Lower Mississippi Valley*. Louisiana Archaeological Survey and Antiquities Commission, Anthropological Study 7, 1983.

Heizer, Robert F. (ed.). "California," *Handbook of North American Indians, volume 8*. Washington D. C.: Smithsonian Institution Press, 1978.

Helm, June (ed.). "Subarctic," *Handbook of North American Indians, volume 6*. Washington D. C.: Smithsonian Institution Press, 1981.

Speth, John. *Bison Kills and Bone Counts*. Chicago: University of Chicago Press, 1983.

Suttles, Wayne (ed.). "Northwest Coast," *Handbook of North American Indians, volume 7*. Washington D. C.: Smithsonian Institution Press, 1990.

Thomas, David Hurst (ed.). The Archaeology of Hidden Cave, Nevada. *Anthropological Papers of the American Museum of Natural History* 61(1):1–430, 1985.

AGRICULTURAL IMPERATIVES IN THE AMERICAN SOUTHWEST

FOR THE GENERAL READER

Ambler, J. Richard. *The Anasazi*. Flagstaff: Museum of Northern Arizona Press, 1989.

Brody, J. J. *The Anasazi*. New York: Rizzoli, 1990.

———. *Anasazi and Anasazi Painting*. Albuquerque: University of New Mexico Press, 1991.

Brody, J. J., Catherine J. Scott, and Steven A. LeBlanc. *Mimbres Pottery*. New York: Hudson Hills Press, 1983.

Cordell, Linda S. *Prehistory of the Southwest*. Orlando: Academic Press, Inc., 1984.

Ferguson, William M., and Arthur H. Rohn. *Anasazi Ruins of the Southwest in Color*. Albuquerque: University of New Mexico Press, 1990.

Frazer, Kendrick. *People of Chaco: A Canyon and Its Cultures*. New York: W. W. Norton, 1986.

Gabriel, Kathryn. *Roads to Center Place: A Cultural Atlas of Chaco Canyon and the Anasazi*. Boulder: Johnson Books, 1991.

Gumerman, George J. *A View from Black Mesa*. Tucson: University of Arizona Press, 1984.

Noble, David Grant. *Ancient Ruins of the Southwest: An Archaeological Guide*, revised edition. Flagstaff: Northland Publishing, 1991.

Patterson, Alex. *A Field Guide to Rock Art Symbols of the Greater Southwest*. Boulder: Johnson Books, 1992.

Schaafsma, Polly. *Indian Rock Art of the Southwest*. Santa Fe: School of American Research Press, 1990.

MORE SPECIALIZED SOURCES

Cordell, Linda S., and George J. Gumerman. *Dynamics of Southwest Prehistory*. Washington D. C.: Smithsonian Institution Press, 1989.

Crown, Patricia, and W. James Judge. *Chaco and Hohokam: Prehistoric Regional Systems in the American Southwest*. Santa Fe: School of American Research Press, 1991.

Gumerman, George J. *Exploring the Hohokam*. Albuquerque: University of New Mexico Press, 1991.

Haury, Emil. *The Hohokam, Desert Farmers and Craftsmen: Excavations at Snaketown, 1964–1965*. Tucson: University of Arizona Press, 1976.

Lekson, Stephen H. *Great Pueblo Architecture of Chaco Canyon*. Albuquerque: University of New Mexico Press, 1989.

Lister, Robert H., and Florence C. Lister. *Archaeology and Archaeologists: Chaco Canyon*. Albuquerque: University of New Mexico Press, 1981.

Noble, David Grant (ed.). *New Light on Chaco Canyon*. Santa Fe: School of American Research Press, 1984.

Ortiz, Alfonso (ed.). "Southwest," *Handbook of North American Indians, volume 9*. Washington D. C.: Smithsonian Institution Press, 1979.

————. "Southwest," *Handbook of North American Indians, volume 10*. Washington D. C.: Smithsonian Institution Press, 1983.

Schaafsma, Polly. *Rock Art in New Mexico*. Albuquerque: University of New Mexico Press, 1992.

Wills, S. H. *Early Prehistoric Agriculture in the American Southwest*. Santa Fe: School of American Research Press, 1989.

HARVESTING THE EASTERN WOODLANDS

FOR THE GENERAL READER

Brose, David S., James A. Brown, and David W. Penny. *Ancient Art of the American Woodland Indians*. New York: Harry N. Abrams, 1985.

Chapman, Jefferson. *Tellico Archaeology*. Knoxville: University of Tennessee Press, 1985.

Struever, Stuart, and Felicia Antonelli Holton. *Koster: Americans in Search of Their Prehistoric Past*. New York: Doubleday, 1979.

Silverberg, Robert. *Mound Builders of Ancient America*. Greenwich, CT: New York Graphic Society, 1968.

MORE SPECIALIZED SOURCES

Ford, Richard I. (ed.). *Prehistoric Food Production in North America*. Ann Arbor: University Museum of Anthropology, University of Michigan, 1985.

Keegan, William F. (ed). *Emergent Horticultural Economies of the Eastern Woodlands*. Carbondale, IL: Center for Archaeological Investigations, 1987.

Rindos, David. *The Origins of Agriculture: An Evolutionary Perspective*. New York: Academic Press, 1984.

Trigger, Bruce G. (ed.). "Northeast," *Handbook of North American Indians, volume 15*. Washington D. C.: Smithsonian Institution Press, 1978.

MISSISSIPPIAN TRANSFORMATIONS

Cohen, Mark N., and George Armelagos (eds.). *Paleopathology at the Origins of Agriculture*. Orlando: Academic Press. 1984.

Cowan, C. Wesley, and Patty Jo Watson. *The Origins of Agriculture: An International Perspective*. Washington D. C.: Smithsonian Institution Press, 1992.

Emerson, Thomas E., and R. Barry Lewis. *Cahokia and the Hinterlands: Middle Mississippian Cultures of the Midwest*. Urbana: University of Illinois Press, 1991.

Galloway, Patricia. *The Southeastern Ceremonial Complex: Artifacts and Analysis*. Lincoln: University of Nebraska Press, 1989.

Smith, Bruce D. (ed.). *Mississippian Settlement Patterns*. New York: Academic Press, 1978.

———. *The Mississippian Emergence*. Washington D. C.: Smithsonian Institution Press, 1990.

Smith, Bruce D. *Rivers of Change: Essays on Early Agriculture in Eastern North America*. Washington D. C.: Smithsonian Institution Press, 1992.

COLLIDING WORLDS: OLD AND NEW?

FOR THE GENERAL READER

Dor-Ner, Zvi. *Columbus and the Age of Discovery*. New York: William Morrow and Company, Inc., 1991.

Kessell, John L. *Kiva, Cross, and Crown: The Pecos Indians and New Mexico, 1540–1840*. National Park Service, 1979.

Thomas, David Hurst. *St. Catherines: An Island in Time*. Athens: University of Georgia Press, 1988.

Utley, Robert M. *The Lance and the Shield: The Life and Times of Sitting Bull*. New York: Henry Holt and Company, 1993.

Viola, Herman J., and Carolyn Margolis. *Seeds of Change: Five Hundred Years Since Columbus*. Washington D. C.: Smithsonian Institution Press, 1991.

Weatherford, Jack. *Native Roots: How the Indians Enriched America*. New York: Crown Publishers, Inc., 1991.

MORE SPECIALIZED SOURCES

Fitzhugh, William W. (ed.). *Cultures in Contact: The European Impact on Native Cultural Institutions in Eastern North America, A.D. 1000–1800*. Washington D. C.: Smithsonian Institution Press, 1985.

Fitzhugh, William W., and Jacqueline S. Olin. *Archaeology of the Frobisher Voyages*. Washington D. C.: Smithsonian Institution Press, 1993.

Hudson, Charles. *The Southeastern Indians*. Knoxville: University of Tennessee Press, 1976.

Josephy, Alvin M., Jr. (ed.). *America in 1492: The World of Indian Peoples Before the Arrival of Columbus*. New York: Alfred A. Knopf, 1992.

McEwan, Bonnie (ed.). *The Missions of La Florida*. Gainesville: University of Florida Press, 1993.

Milanich, Jerald T., and Charles Hudson. *Hernando de Soto and the Indians of Florida*. Gainesville: University of Florida Press, 1993.

Milanich, Jerald T., and Susan Milbrath (eds.). *First Encounters: Spanish Explorations in the Caribbean and the United States, 1492–1570*. Gainesville: University of Florida Press, 1989.

Peterson, Jacqueline. *Sacred Encounters: Father De Smet and the Indians of the Rocky Mountain West*. Norman: University of Oklahoma Press, 1993.

Reff, Daniel T. *Disease, Depopulation, and Culture Change in Northwestern New Spain, 1518–1764*. Salt Lake City: University of Utah Press, 1991.

Rogers, J. Daniel, and Samuel M. Wilson (eds.). *Ethnohistory and Archaeology: Approaches to Postcontact Change in the Americas*. New York: Plenum Press, 1993.

Scott, Douglas D., Richard A. Fox, Jr., Melissa A. Connor, and Dick Harmon. *Archaeological Perspectives on the Battle of the Little Bighorn*. Norman, OK: University of Oklahoma Press, 1989.

Thomas, David Hurst (ed.). *Columbian Consequences, Volume 1: Archaeological and Historical Perspectives on the Spanish Borderlands West*. Washington D. C.: Smithsonian Institution Press, 1989.

———. *Columbian Consequences, Volume 2: Archaeological and Historical Perspectives on the Spanish Borderlands East*. Washington D. C.: Smithsonian Institution Press, 1990.

———. *Columbian Consequences, Volume 3: The Spanish Borderlands in Pan-American Perspective*. Washington D. C.: Smithsonian Institution Press, 1991.

Thomas, David Hurst, Jay Miller, Richard White, Peter Nabokov, and Philip J. Deloria. *The Native Americans: An Illustrated History*. Atlanta: Turner Publishing, Inc., 1993.

Verano, John W., and Douglas H. Ubelaker. *Disease and Demography in the Americas*. Washington D. C.: Smithsonian Institution Press, 1992.

EPILOGUE

FOR THE GENERAL READER

Cantor, George. *North American Indian Landmarks: A Traveler's Guide*. Detroit: Visible Ink Press, 1993.

Christensen, Thomas, and Carol Christensen (eds.). *The Discovery of America & Other Myths: A New World Reader*. San Francisco: Chronicle Books, 1992.

Eagle/Walking Turtle. *Indian America: A Traveler's Companion*, second edition. Santa Fe: John Muir Publications, 1991.

Gattuso, John (ed.). *Native America*. Hong Kong: APA Publications, Ltd., 1992.

Tiller, Veronica E. (ed.). *Discover Indian Reservations USA: A Visitor's Welcome Guide*. Denver: Council Publications, 1992.

Viola, Herman J. *After Columbus: The Smithsonian Chronicle of the North American Indians*. Washington D. C.: Smithsonian Books, 1990.

MORE SPECIALIZED SOURCES

Deloria, Vine, Jr. "Sacred Lands," *Winds of Change* 8(4):31–35, 1993.

Washburn, Wilcomb E. (ed.). "History of Indian-White Relations," *Handbook of North American Indians*, *volume 4*. Washington D. C.: Smithsonian Institution Press, 1988.

Wilson, Michael, Kathie L. Road, and Kenneth J. Hardy. *Megaliths to Medicine Wheels: Boulder Structures in Archaeology*. Alberta: University of Calgary, Proceedings of the Eleventh Annual Chacmool Conference, 1981.

INDEX

Figures are indicated in boldface.